Nigeria

PALL MALL LIBRARY OF AFRICAN AFFAIRS

The Pall Mall Library of African Affairs is intended to provide clear, authoritative, and objective information about the historical, political, cultural, and economic background of modern Africa. Individual countries and groupings of countries will be dealt with as will general themes affecting the whole continent and its relations with the rest of the world. The library appears under the general editorship of Colin Legum, with Philippe Decraene as consultant editor. Each volume is written by an acknowledged expert on its subject.

Already Published

Nigeria

WALTER SCHWARZ

PALL MALL PRESS · LONDON

Published by the Pall Mall Press Ltd.
5 Cromwell Place, London, S.W.7

© 1968 WALTER SCHWARZ

First published 1968

SBN 269.16158.9

DT
515.5
.S3

Printed in Great Britain by
The Garden City Press Limited, Letchworth, Hertfordshire

Contents

v

Maps and Illustrations

The illustrations are reproduced by courtesy of the Federal Government of Nigeria (Ia, Ib, Ic, Id, IIa, IIb, IIc, IVa); the *Guardian* (IId); the *Daily Mirror* (IIIa, IIIb); and *West Africa Magazine* (IVb).

For Wole

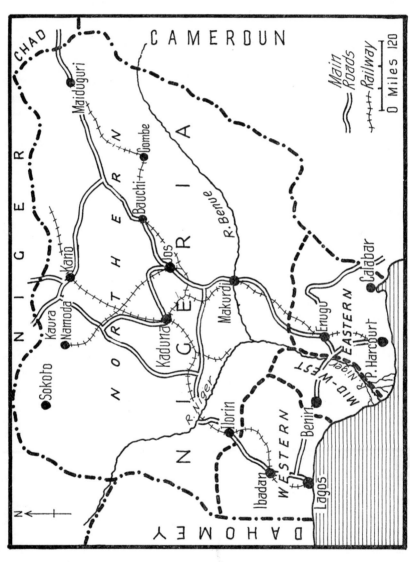

1. The Regions, to 1967

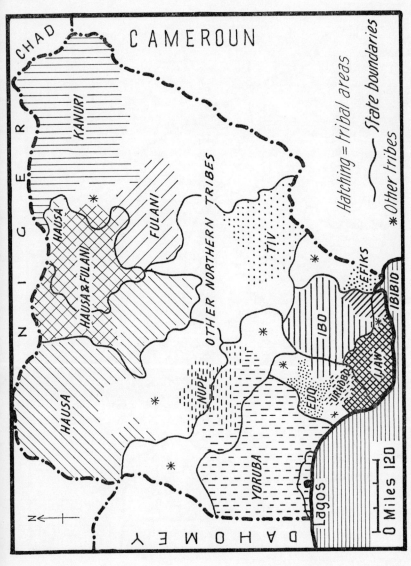

2. Main Tribal Groups

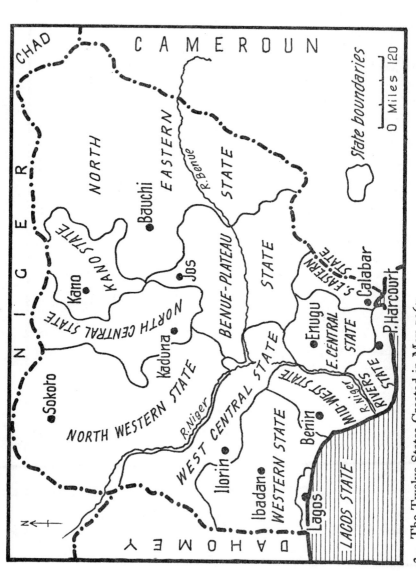

3. The Twelve States Created in May 1967

Introduction

A WRITER on present-day Nigeria is in a difficult position, especially if his book goes to press during a civil war from which it is not at all clear what kind of Nigeria will emerge. The secession of the former Eastern Region as the Republic of Biafra, in May 1967, and the civil war which followed were the culmination of a series of political traumas that have changed some of the old assumptions. The military coups of January and July 1966 had added an element of violent change to the already complicated power struggles of the previous decade. The massacre, in September 1966, of Ibo and other Easterners living in the Northern Region had been a second shock which had led most of the Ibo towards rejection of a federal state that could no longer protect them. In May 1967, the Federal Military government, under Lieutenant-Colonel Gowon, had decreed that twelve new States should replace the existing four Regions.

This was the profoundest revolution of all, amounting to a third coup. It promised to break up the old power blocs—the Hausa-Fulani of the North, the Yoruba of the West and the Ibo of the East—whose rivalry had dominated federal politics. The new Nigeria was to belong, like Colonel Gowon himself and most of the soldiers who had placed him in power, to the minorities. It was to be a Nigeria of the Kanuri, Tiv, Birom, Idoma, Edo, Itsekiri, Ijaw, Ibibio, Efik, Ogoja and scores of others. But for the Ibo, embattled in a homeland swollen with refugees, bereaved by the thousand, the revolution seemed to have come too late. The splitting of their Eastern Region into three seemed to the Ibo less like a reform than a crude attempt to dismember their potential new country even before they had launched it. They seceded, and war was then inevitable.

At that point the narrative in this book comes to a stop. Yet the war itself promises to be the most traumatic event of all. Optimists felt it could be the making of Nigeria, a second independence, the creation of a new nationhood forged in the discipline and sacrifice of war. But this spirit of rebirth informed not only the militant federalists, fighting to 'keep Nigeria one', but also the Ibo, who were seeking a self-determination of their own. Less sanguine prophets would expect these rival nationalisms—and perhaps others—to continue to clash for a long time. If Nigeria remains one political unit, the struggle may still go on, simmering under the surface. The outright pessimists see the possibility of complete disintegration, as happened in the Congo in 1960.

At first glance, it seems an all-or-nothing struggle for Nigeria. A Federal government victory over the secessionists could lead to a new era, with a strong federal centre surrounded by small states, combining the strength of unitary government with the balances and safeguards of a federal system. The successful secession of Biafra, on the other hand, could lead to further disintegration, and perhaps fresh wars.

However, the real outcome promises to be less drastic; it will be somewhere in between. If the Federation is preserved, there will still be strife within it; if it is not, the resultant units might yet attain a new equilibrium. Whatever happens, then, there will be a measure of continuity in Nigeria. Superficially, Nigeria's problems may qualify it to rank with the defunct federations of Mali, Central Africa, South Arabia and Malaysia. But, unlike any of these, it has been in existence for half a century under linked, if not wholly unified, administrations. Whatever constitutional links emerge among its component parts, the economic, cultural and, above all, human links that remain will preserve it as an entity. To a degree, it must inevitably remain an economic unit. And even a tribal war cannot alter the fact that Nigeria remains, in a profound sense, one society.

Seen from outside Africa, Nigeria has been a disappointment. After independence in 1960, its carefully balanced federal structure had seemed a model of compromise, a proof that British-style parliaments could work in Africa. Under Sir Abubakar Tafawa Balewa it seemed also to have wise leadership and sound commercial sense. The breakdown of the Balewa regime, and the disasters which followed, have been a factor in the progressive disillusionment with Africa—a process which had started with the Congo's failure in 1960 and was carried a stage further by the degeneration into tyranny of Nkrumah's rule in Ghana. Now that Africans seemed less promising, they made less news. Nigerians on both sides of the war have been pained at the lack of interest and the apparent shallowness of sympathies shown by the European and American press, which seemed to lean towards one side or the other according to whichever was winning.

This disillusionment reveals a superficial view of Africa, for the departure of colonial governors was only the first, and easiest, stage of independence. It left almost everything still to be done and to be decided. The right leadership had to emerge, with qualities different from those needed for nationalist agitation; the right type of government had to be chosen or evolved, the right economic philosophy to be selected and applied. Even nations had still to be fashioned. The so-called 'nationalists' had protested against colonial rule ('struggled' would, for the most part, be too strong a term), but what nations did they represent? Was there an African nation, or a Negro nation? Was only the tribe the nation? Or could nations be forged out of the artificial units left over from colonialism, the result of historical accidents, with unnatural boundaries drawn by European powers in their scramble for land? Africa was clearly too big, the tribes were too small. In Nigeria the early nationalists thought of themselves as West Africans—as did those in Ghana and the French-speaking colonies. Later they became Nigerians, but almost at once internal rivalries identified each leader with one of the major tribes. Nigeria's unique problem lay not in the scores of small tribes but in the three principal groups, each large enough to be a nation. Their triangular rivalry makes up much of the political narrative in this book. Two conflicts coincided: the struggles for power common to all states, especially new ones, and the peculiar strains of a plural society.

That such struggles are so bitter cannot be attributed only to African lack of sophistication. Politics in developing countries is concerned with sharing out a pitifully small national cake. The government is the only substantial employer, and the output of school-leavers continually outstrips the number of new jobs available. This makes politics ruthless. Office means a livelihood not only for a politician but for his 'extended' family and, beyond that, his village, town and tribe. In office, politicians will do almost all they can to stay there; out of office, they will do almost anything to get in. This ruthlessness creates a vicious circle between oppression and subversion. And revolution, as the examples of Nigeria and other countries have shown, may lead merely to a new oppression, leading in turn to a new revolt.

A nation is a unit that can hold together: it does not have to be homogeneous. The profoundest aim of the Federal leaders has been to tide Nigeria over its 'growing pains', so that a new generation, freed from the excesses of earlier rivalries, might inherit a potentially great country. For the Biafrans, this was at best a pipedream, at worst a sinister cloak for the ambitions of the populous North to continue to use its numbers to dominate the South. For them, Gowon's creation of twelve new States, imposed arbitrarily and in circumstances that made it look like an anti-Ibo move, was only a blind. Would not the Northerners, into however many States they were divided, continue to think, and vote, alike? The Biafrans, too, claimed to be a nation. This also had its complications. After their secession, the Biafrans were not all Ibo. The role of the Ibibio, Efik, Ijaw and Ogoja in the Republic of Biafra became the most controversial issue of the war. The Biafrans claimed to speak for them all, while the Federal government argued that whatever the Ibo did they had no right to take with them others who had not expressed their views. In the last resort the Biafrans could claim to be in control, which was more than the Federal government had been at the time the Ibo were being massacred in the North. The Ibo plus the Eastern minorities (under whose soil most of the oil wealth happened to lie) constituted a potentially viable unit. A nation must either place its minorities, collectively, in the saddle—as the Federal government under Gowon has tried to do—or it must keep the minorities at least as contented, or as repressed, or as resigned, as the Scots and the Welsh.

Rival nationalisms cannot always be decided by negotiation, in the twentieth century any more than in the tenth. A traveller in Nigeria and Biafra just before the outbreak of war in July 1967 could not avoid the feeling that only a fight could decide the issue. Each side was so profoundly convinced the other could not fight. The Northerners, especially, thought of the Ibo as clerks and traders, who would run away, just as they had done during the massacres of the previous year. When he finally launched the war as a short, sharp 'police action', Gowon called the Ibo 'an army of penpushers'. The Ibo were equally contemptuous of the Northerners, with their known shortages of technical and organisational skills. 'No power in Black Africa can subdue us', boasted Colonel Ojukwu, the Biafran leader. Only war could decide who was correct. Its outcome will be remembered by the generations to come.

'If Nigeria breaks up, it will be the end of Africa', federal spokesmen were arguing in support of the war effort. This is another level of conflict—a struggle to keep African nations large and strong enough to play an effective part in world politics. No African state is homogeneous, and most have potential secessionists. With this in mind, the Organisation of African Unity, with a unanimity perhaps more apparent than real, sided with Lagos when it first considered the issue in August 1967. On this level, Biafra's aim was to convince Africa that its case was special —that it sought not merely secession but self-determination.

Not the least profound effect of the civil war is in Nigeria's foreign relations. The British, who have been the dominant cultural and commercial influence, have lost ground, perhaps irretrievably.

They had no special attachment to one tribe or another, though they felt a loyalty which went beyond legalities to the Federation they had fathered. Commercial interest was also hard to evaluate as the oil, the biggest single investment, was in Biafra while the overwhelming preponderance of other investments were on the federal side. After some hesitation, and an abortive effort to stay neutral, Britain decided to support Lagos, though only in a luke-warm manner. The British now appear to have lost almost as much goodwill and prestige on the federal side as on the Biafran. The Russians, who had for years been kept at arm's length by politicians brought up with British attitudes (the Sandhurst-trained army officers proved even more conservative), now seized the opportunity offered by British hesitations and sent jet aeroplanes to Lagos. After a major setback in Ghana in 1966, the Russians clearly saw this as a chance of obtaining a secure foothold in the biggest and potentially the richest state in Africa. They will now seek to consolidate this position. The other European countries and the Americans were able to stay on the sidelines for longer. They are therefore in a better position to come back as friends after the war, whatever its outcome.

1. Tribes and a Nation

By whichever way the new arrival comes in, he is likely to get a somewhat jaundiced view. He will probably be met by leaden skies, drenching rain and steamy heat, or by a burning sun and swarms of flies, but he will admit that everywhere is much greener than he expected.—*Colonial Office Handbook*, 1953.

> Where is our school of ballroom dancing?
> Who here can throw a cocktail party?
> We must be modern with the rest
> Or live forgotten by the world;
> We must reject the palm wine habit
> And take tea, with milk and sugar.
>   Wole Soyinka, *The Lion and the Jewel*, 1963.

NIGERIA may be 'greener than expected', but it is not the green of English lawns. It is the intensity of the light and, despite the 'leaden skies', the sheer strength of colour that first strikes a visitor from Europe. It is the bold blue dresses of Yoruba women, and their top-heavy headgear; the brash philosophy painted on the tailboards of 'mammy waggons' (AFTER THIS MERCEDES, SEA NEVER DRY); the competitive clamour of business signs (CHAIRS FOR RENT, CITY GIRL POOLS, SHOW CUTS—LONDON-TRAINED DRESSMAKER). As striking as the colour is the animation. A brilliantly robed horseman canters by the side of a Northern road; commuters in and out of Lagos hang from the train doors or overflow from buses; a corpulent, pin-striped lawyer reclines in his chauffeur-driven Peugeot; and an endless procession of women carry bundles on their heads.

In the town, in the village, or along the road, almost everything can be done in the open: trading, gossiping, washing clothes, washing bodies, sleeping. But especially trading. The village, the pavement or the street is a market and every female, from the age of six to sixty, seems to take part. Small, wise-looking girls sit by their trays, lit eerily at night by candles or home-made oil-lamps, selling matches, cigarettes (singly), oranges (four a penny in season), red pepper, white cassava flour, green leaves, stockfish, snuff, kola nuts, pineapples.

Despite the muggy, soporific climate of the South, Nigeria is an exacting and exhilarating country, for its own people as well as for visitors. No one can know much of it intimately. Its society ranges from the shy, naked pagans of the Jos Plateau to the sophistication of the Permanent Secretary, with a First at Cambridge, who may have seen more of life and power at thirty-five than his European counterpart at fifty. Yet, despite its vast range, it is a society without the awful contrasts of India or Egypt. No one starves and the beggars are few and unobtrusive. Everywhere, in town and village, new buildings are going up.

Even before the upheavals of 1966–68, each of Nigeria's four Regions was sufficiently large and sufficiently distinct in character to be counted a country in its own right. In area as in population, the Northern Region had an over-all majority: 282,000 square miles and almost 25 million people, against the Western Region's 30,000 square miles and 7 million people, the Eastern Region's 29,000 square miles and 12 million people, the Mid-West's 19,000 square miles and 2 million people, and the Federal Territory of Lagos's 27 square miles and 0·7 million people (see chapter 7, pp. 157–64). Two of the Regions had distinct minority groups so large and so cohesive that they, too, were potential states on their own: the Middle Belt in the North and the so-called 'Rivers' area of the Niger Delta in the East. According to other criteria, the potential number of regions in Nigeria is infinitely variable. Chief Awolowo, for example, has proposed eighteen, on a linguistic and ethnic basis.[1] In 1967, General Gowon created twelve.

PHYSICAL CONTRASTS

The deepest divergence is between North and South. The arid, predominantly Moslem North and the tropical, predominantly Christian South are different countries. The South shares its long sand beach with Nigeria's western neighbours: Dahomey, Togo, Ghana and the Ivory Coast. This palm-lined beach, buffeted by formidable Atlantic breakers which impede stevedoring and swimming alike, is no more than a narrow bar, stretching from Lagos westwards to Dahomey and separated from the mainland by a complex of lagoons and creeks. Hot, humid, monotonous and unspoiled, the beach is backed by mangrove swamps and lagoons and endless palm trees. Towards the east the bar peters out into the Niger Delta, with its ancient fishing and trading stations, and the mangrove swamp yields gradually to the oil palms.

Behind the beach and behind the creeks and lagoons, the belt of swamp is rarely less than ten miles wide. From an aircraft it looks like a watery maze, without firm distinction between islands and mainland. For people in Lagos and other coastal towns, the limitless creeks offer a pleasant compensation for the humidity, the mosquitoes and the sandflies. One can swim or fish, while the creeks and lagoons are a paradise for canoes or outboard motors.

To the north of the swamp belt lies the majestic rain forest—'virgin' forest to the unpractised eye but in reality mostly bush that has been cut down at some stage, cultivated and allowed its freedom again. The rain forest belt, a hundred miles wide, yields in its turn, further north, to a wider belt of open woodland and grass savannah. North of that, bare, sandy scrub denotes the approaches of the Sahara. From the air the transition from dense forest to open woodland comes with remarkable suddenness just north of Ibadan, while the further transition to scrub and, finally, desert is almost imperceptible. The traveller by road feels with relief the progressive lessening of humidity.

Sharp physical contrasts are not confined to the North-South axis. The Cameroon-Adamawa mountain range, with peaks over

5,000 feet, straddles the eastern border. Sufferers from the coastal dampness can take refuge in the cattle ranch, admirably organised for tourists, at Obudu, 5,000 feet above sea level. In the North the Jos Plateau, another climatic refuge, reaches a similar altitude, rising abruptly from a 2,000 feet high plain.

Just as the forest-to-savannah transition separates North from South, so the river Niger divides West from East. Flowing into Nigeria from the republics of Mali and Niger, it continues south-east to the heart of Nigeria at Lokoja. Here it is joined by the Benue (which has come westwards from the Cameroon mountains) and descends due south to the Delta. The fast, wide and long-uncharted Niger has played a decisive part in Nigerian history. For four centuries the European traders on the coast could not penetrate the interior to get at the primary market because of the unhealthy forest and its warlike inhabitants; the traders had to be content with doing business with the African middlemen on the coast. The only north-bound highway was the Niger and its secrets were not unravelled until the nineteenth century.

As the Europeans finally overcame the obstacle and sailed up the Niger, so the Nigerians have long ceased to let the river be an ethnic barrier. Ibo have for centuries lived both on the west bank, in the Asaba region, and on the east at Onitsha. The subjugation of this natural barrier seemed complete in 1965, with the opening of the Niger motor bridge between Asaba and Onitsha. Just as in the nineteenth century the Niger formed a highway for European traders and missionaries from the South, so it promised in the twentieth century to link Northern and Southern commerce. The Niger dam project was designed to make the river navigable along most of its length.

The climate accentuates the North-South contrast. The South is very wet half the year and hot and very humid all the time. Between May and July and again in September and October it has between 100 and 140 inches of rain a year, while humidity ranges between 80 and 98 per cent. The North is hot and dry. Annual rainfall ranges between 20 and 40 inches, while humidity as low as 10 per cent is not uncommon in the afternoons. The North has the typical desert characteristics of hot dry days and cool or cold nights. Maximum temperatures increase from the coast northwards, while minimum temperatures rise from the North southwards. During the hottest months in the South (March and April), mean maximum temperatures range between 90 and 95 degrees, while in the North, where it is hottest during April, the mean monthly figure rises to 105 degrees. Mean minimum temperatures are 70 degrees in the South and are lowest at 55 degrees in the North. The *harmattan*, a hot desert wind, raising sand and dust, makes life trying in the North but cooler in the South for several months of the year.

THE PEOPLES

Nigerians themselves are as varied as their environment, though their tribal groups are divided more by language, culture and history than by race. Some scores of languages are spoken. Of the three predominant tribal groups, Hausa-Fulani is the language of some 28 per cent of the population, Ibo of some 18 per cent and Yoruba of some 16 per cent. The 'forest Negro' is the dominant racial group in the South, but it has been observed that 'the frequency of relatively finely cut features and fair complexions among many of the Southern people, such as the Yoruba and Jekri, suggests a considerable measure of hybridisation in the past with non-Negro groups of problematic origin'.[2] In the Northern plains the 'savannah Negro' type predominates, while the wavy-haired, light-skinned, nomadic Fulani, whose affinities seem to be with the Mediterranean basin, are a distinct group. These are known as 'cattle Fulani' to distinguish them from the 'town Fulani', who have largely lost their tribal identity by intermarriage with the Hausa majority around them.

For their national dress, Nigerians have adopted the traditional costume of two of their major groups, the Yoruba and the Hausa. The *agbada* consists of baggy trousers and a loose shirt worn under a voluminous robe, with a distinctive cap in cloth or velvet. The *agbada* is equally effective in dazzling white or gorgeously patterned

5

cloth; when it is hand-embroidered it can cost as much as a Savile Row suit. Until the 1950s, the symbol of dignity was the suit, collar and tie—as it still is in ex-French countries. Then the men of the North were seen in Lagos in their impressive robes, usually of sombre colours, and robes became fashionable as a symbol of nationalism. In the West and North, the *agbada* is now in general and everyday use. The Easterners, traditionally a lightly-clad people, prefer either a simple wrapper, worn by men and women as a kind of sarong, or European clothes. Suits and ties are still the rule among businessmen and senior officials—an unsuitable and uncomfortable outfit for the tropics, even for people with air-conditioned offices.

Nigerian women have adapted traditional styles with considerable ingenuity. Most distinctive are the Yoruba, whose rich robes, often hand-dyed in indigo and finely patterned, and tall head-ties make a group of them look like birds of paradise. Popular in all Regions is a blouse with a cotton wrapper—cool, comfortable and modest. More fashionable is the 'up and down'—a straight skirt or wrapper and matching top in traditional or modern patterns, an outfit susceptible to infinite variation. In the 'bush' away from Moslem areas girls still go bare-breasted to the well or the river, to bring back water in jars on their heads. The shrivelled breasts of older women are often of unequal size because they have given suck on one side rather than the other.

Lagos: The Federal Capital

Perhaps 4 million of the 50 million Nigerians live in towns. The population of Lagos, officially (and, in this instance, plausibly) estimated at 700,000 in the 1963 census, had more than doubled in the previous decade. The townward drift, so familiar a pattern in developing countries, has been less marked among the Yoruba of the West because they have, for more than a century, been an urbanised people. Of eleven Nigerian towns with more than 200,000 inhabitants, eight are Yoruba towns.

Lagos has always been commercial and cosmopolitan. It was first heard of in the fifteenth century as a slaving outpost of the great Benin empire. The Portuguese gave Lagos its name (it means 'lagoon') in 1472. Sir Richard Burton in 1861 found it 'detestable... unfortunately there is no better within many a league. . . . The first aspect is as if a hole had been hollowed out of the original mangrove forest. . . .' Burton found its sticky climate deadly, and the brave British consulate struck him as 'a corrugated iron coffin or plank-lined morgue, containing a dead consul once a year'.[3]

On Lagos island the heavy buildings of complacent colonial days blend felicitously with the stark simplicity of a modern capital. The elegant new parliament buildings and the supreme court flank the old racecourse, sharing this spacious and leisurely site with King's College, the oldest and most exclusive boys' 'public' school, which itself hides away an astonishing amount of land for its playing fields. Dominating its own corner of the racecourse is the government office skyscraper. Little is left of the 'thin line of European buildings that occupy the best site fronting the water' seen in 1861,[4] but the Marina remains a distinguished street by the standards of any city. From it, looking across the lagoon to the Apapa quays, one can see every ship in port. The elegant part of the island almost touches the neighbouring island of Ikoyi, formerly the European residential preserve. Ikoyi's solid but unpretentious villas, behind their lawns and flowers and hedgerows, are now occupied largely by Nigerian civil servants, but they still retain their cool, colonial look.

Lagos is elegant only on its south-east side. On the northern and western parts of the island live the Lagosians—88,000 to the square mile—in a slum that fails to keep them dry when it rains and, in many a dry season, has them queueing up for water. The whole complex of islands, including Ikoyi island and Victoria island—the new luxurious, diplomatic quarter being developed—is being stifled by sprawling slum-suburbia on the mainland. Yaba, an old main-land suburb, and Suru-lere, a new, planned estate, contain reserves of middle-class Nigerians. For the rest, unplanned and still largely unserviced settlements of immigrants from the States reach out in

7

long strings far to the north, until they almost touch the Western State town of Ikeja fourteen miles away. Real Lagosians constitute only a tiny minority. Lagos is a city, especially in its mainland sprawl, of immigrants and strangers from the States. There are almost exclusively Ibo communities around Yaba (seriously depleted during the 1966 upheavals) and the Ibo also possess vast hinterlands along the Ikorodu and Agege truck roads, while Ebute Metta is a stronghold of the Yoruba.

The expatriate Europeans, comprising few civil servants but a growing diplomatic corps and commercial staff from a dozen countries, ceased long before independence to dominate the social scene. Only in their remaining clubs—the Ikoyi Club, the Polo Club, the Apapa Club and the Ikeja Country Club: open to all, of course, but too European in spirit to attract many Nigerians—and in a few of the pricier nightclubs are they anything but a pale, almost apologetic, minority among a people who, with money or without, are more highly skilled in the art of enjoying life.

OTHER TOWNS

Ninety miles to the north of Lagos is an even bigger city. Ibadan's 1·3 million people make it the largest African town south of the Sahara.[5] There is nothing cosmopolitan about Ibadan except its university, Nigeria's oldest. It is a Yoruba town, owing its size not so much to the drift from the land as to the fact that over a century of constant warfare has made the Yoruba an intensely urban people. Indeed Ibadan is only the first of eight Yoruba towns—Ogbomosho, Oshogbo, Ife, Iwo, Abeokuta, Oyo and Ilesha—each of which has over 100,000 inhabitants, the first three with over 200,000.

Ibadan began as a war camp in 1829 and later became a haven for refugees. Today it is the Western state capital—a noisy, crowded town of narrow streets and big and small markets. Like Jerusalem, it is built on several gentle hills and their contours lend charm to an undulating sea of corrugated aluminium roofs.

In spite of its handsome public buildings with wide approach roads, its elegant modern housing estates, its luxury hotel and its multi-storey office block, it is an obdurately unmodern town. Thousands of tiny shops and ramshackle factories (there must be a thousand bookshops and several hundred small printing works) are strung together along winding streets, giving an unusually warm and cosy character to so large a city. It is the Yoruba themselves who really characterise Ibadan—unruly, individualistic, politically unpredictable, brilliant traders not renowned for hard work, always good-humoured and ready to jest about their adversities in their loud, nasal, sing-song language.

Seven hundred miles further north, Kano, the north's biggest city, is a complete contrast. In the twelfth century Kano was famous as a market town; in the fourteenth it was converted to Islam. Until it was overtaken by Katsina in the eighteenth century, it was the paramount trading town of Hausaland, dominating the trans-Sahara trade route, exchanging gold, slaves and kola nuts for salt, textiles and household manufactures. The city walls of thick mud, as well as much of Kano city's administrative arrangements, still speak of the past, while a visitor to the emir's palace glimpses a feudalistic world only just beginning to yield to real change. Modern Kano has declined, as the new Northern capital of Kaduna attracted the pick of new industry.

Kano is the centre of the groundnut industry. The smell of nuts being crushed in oil factories pervades the atmosphere, and near the railheads are gigantic, fifty-foot pyramids of nuts stacked in bags. Kano's four hundred-year-old market, still supplied and patronised by a far-flung desert population, is as absorbing as it appeared to the German traveller Barth in the nineteenth century.[6] Kano, a trader's city, has long had a mixed population. A few hundred yards of dusty no-man's-land separated two ways of life. On one side is the old, walled city, with its narrow streets, donkeys and mud houses, peopled by the Hausa. On the other side is the *sabon gari* (new town), the 'strangers' quarter', built by Ibo and Yoruba merchants. Just how separate the two communities

9

Nigeria

were was tragically shown in the riots of 1953, and again in the two much more extensive massacres of 1966. On each occasion, the Hausa killer-bands advanced across the no-man's-land to slaughter the Ibo living in the *sabon gari*. After the pogrom of October 1966 the 'strangers' quarter' looked like a ghost town.

Benin is the capital of the oldest of Nigeria's kingdoms, and of the newest of its regional states: the Mid-West. The sprawling, down-at-heel city has few obvious remnants of history outside the oba's palace and the tiny museum, but there is something intangibly different—a certain wild, inscrutable pride. One visitor got the same impression from the city as he did from the famous Benin bronze sculptures and reliefs he had found in the museum: 'Hooded, costumed and withdrawn, the Obas, Queen Mothers and other dignitaries look out from their masks with no sign of emotion; their vitality and strength lie in their quiet watchfulness and elusiveness. Benin is haunted as much by its present as by its past.'[7]

In Benin at the turn of the present century the inhabitants were still sacrificing scores of the relatives of a newly-dead oba. Today the prevalence of shrines and *ju-jus* has been dramatically attested in the Owegbe Cult Inquiry of 1965 (see chapter 11, pp. 280-1). The new role of state capital is slowly transforming Benin. A new council hall serves for the time being as its parliament building and the makeshift, ramshackle office blocks which provisionally house its ministries are beginning to be rebuilt.

Kaduna and Enugu, which were capitals of the Northern and Eastern Regions respectively, are both artificial creations, owing their existence to Lord Lugard's planning in 1900. The one was chosen as the headquarters of the North because of its central and salubrious position; the other resulted from the accidental discovery of coal and became the administrative capital of the Southern provinces. Both are spaciously laid out, quiet administrative capitals, with less than 150,000 people in each.[8] Both, however, have ambitions to become important industrial centres. The East has no town bigger than Onitsha (160,000) and Port

Harcourt (180,000).[9] The vigorous trading community of Onitsha has been called 'the realm of the merchant princesses' because of the wealth of its women traders. It is famous for its market, perhaps the biggest and the most modern in West Africa, with its three thousand stalls. Enclosed in a vast structure which cost half a million pounds,* the market serves as the entrepôt for trade for the Delta ports and the trading centres up the Niger and Benue rivers. The wealth of Onitsha is unfortunately not reflected in the quality of such civic services as refuse disposal, drainage and street cleaning. The trouble seems to be that most Onitsha people—and most of its town council—come from elsewhere in Iboland and go home at weekends after business is over. Port Harcourt is the East's thriving, newly oil-rich industrial centre and port. Further east along the coast lies Calabar, where the missionaries first established schools in Nigeria. It still wears its look of remote, if decaying, respectability.

A businessman or official may proceed 'on tour'—which is the colonial expression, reminiscent of the itinerant District Officer, still used to denote a trip out of town. Emerging from damp, claustrophobic Lagos, over the traffic-jammed, thirty-year-old Carter bridge that connects it to the mainland, he can drive for days to the north or east. Or, if he drives westwards, he can be over the Dahomey border in two hours. He will be driving on passable, paved roads and he will encounter drivers so unpredictable that his own driving will become more prudent for the rest of his life. He can set off after breakfast, take lunch in Ibadan and put up at the Catering Rest House at Ilorin, the frontier of North and South, a Yoruba town with the desert in its air. The following evening he can be in Kaduna or Kano and then swing eastwards through the cotton and groundnut country to Jos, Bauchi and Maiduguri. He will have passed through three societies—Yoruba, Hausa and Bornu. Taking a different route from Lagos, he can drive eastwards along the new forest road to Benin, a fast road when none of the bridges is flooded. Beyond Benin he can cross the new bridge to

* The market building was destroyed in the 1967–68 civil war.

Onitsha, the gateway to the East. Wherever he travels, he may put up at a new luxury hotel in the regional capital. More often, he is likely to spend the night in a chalet at the Catering Rest House—indifferently appointed but unfailing with the tap at the door at 6.30 A.M., announcing the early morning tea.

After warning new arrivals about the flies and the heat, the old Colonial Office Handbook went on in more promising vein:

> Throughout Nigeria, even in the monotony of the mangrove swamp, there is scenery to treasure; in the North and on the Plateau there are scenes which are biblical in their setting, in the highlands of the Cameroons there is natural beauty unsurpassed anywhere in the world and in the middle belt there are vast expanses of a comforting and fertile land . . . The West Coast of Africa, despite its climate, has had a reputation for casting a spell upon its guests, and Nigeria has omitted none of the charms from her box of tricks.

NATIONALISM AND TRIBALISM

After all it has been through, is Nigeria still a nation? Was it ever one? Thirteen years before independence the politician Chief Awolowo argued that it was 'a mere geographical expression'—at best an agglomeration of tribal nations. 'There is as much difference between them as there is between Germans, Russians and Turks, for instance.'[10] Yet in 1960 Nigeria was launched as an independent country, with a federal prime minister, cabinet, parliament and civil service. A few years later one of its most senior officials remarked that he would be prepared to take up arms to defend its unity—even if it meant fighting his own tribe.[11] Even as he spoke, tribal rivalries were threatening to capsize the political boat. In January 1966 the boat did capsize and the army took over. For the first time since 1953, all Nigeria was effectively ruled from Lagos. The new Supreme Commander declared that 'rigid adherence to Regionalism was the bane of the last regime and one of the main factors which contributed to its downfall'.[12] In May 1966 he formally abolished the Regions, making Nigeria into a unitary state. But this drastic dose of unity led to the worst tribal explosion of all. The civil servant who had been ready to die for unity a year earlier now saw tens of thousands of his tribesmen killed in a massacre. He himself, with hundreds of his colleagues, fled from Lagos to his own Region, to put his abilities to work on plans to break the country apart after all. Within ten months Nigeria had gone full circle, from disintegration to unity and back to disintegration.

Nigerian nationalism has had only a short history. In colonial days, the early agitators saw themselves as Africans rather than Nigerians. Later, when independence became a real prospect, they became West Africans, dreaming of a West African federation. But that, too, seemed an improbable basis for statehood. In 1897 Flora Shaw, who was to be the wife of Lord Lugard, had coined the word 'Nigeria' in an article for *The Times* (see chapter 3, p. 60). Seventeen years later, for administrative convenience, the British amalgamated the Northern and Southern Provinces of the colony and protectorate. However, the British had few illusions about Nigerian nationhood: in 1920 the Governor, Sir Hugh Clifford, described the very idea as 'farcical'.[13] Though unified in theory, the Northern and Southern Provinces continued to be administered as separate units right up to the end. When self-government came, it came separately, at different times to the North and the South. Independence was possible only because the federal system enabled the various peoples to keep each other at arms length. Above all, the system was intended to provide a guarantee that no one tribe could easily dominate the rest.

For all that, a feeling of Nigerian nationhood did develop with the advent of independence. 'I am a Nigerian', students in London would say when asked what they were, and the more xenophobic among them would refuse to give more details when questioned further. The size, and even the diversity, of the country bred its own pride. It was the largest country in Africa, eight times bigger than the famed Ghana of Nkrumah, three times as populous as the

Congo, the thirteenth most populous state on earth. (See chapter 7 for details of population.) Its federal institutions—the corporations, the foreign service, the armed forces—provided a melting pot of nationalism. However, as easily as Jekyll could become Hyde, the Nigerian could become the Yoruba, the Hausa or the Ibo.

The end of the anti-colonial struggle was the beginning of politics—and what was politics if not tribalism? What else was there to argue about? Tribes were more sharply differentiated than social classes. As an authoritarian, radical regime on Nkrumahist lines would hardly have been practicable in so diverse a country, hardly anyone suggested it. The only real radicalism had been against the British. Now that the British were gone, the main thing to argue about was how to share a severely-limited national cake. There were only so many scholarships and so many jobs. If an Ibo were appointed chairman of the railway corporation, it was automatically assumed that every possible stoker, linesman and railway clerk would be Ibo. A Northern majority in the Federal Parliament was automatically expected to mean that an undue preponderance of industries would be sited in the North, and an unfair proportion of funds for social services spent there. A Yoruba minister of Education, it was assumed, could hardly face his electorate until he had visibly increased the proportion of Yoruba receiving federal scholarships to study abroad. This was the stuff of life. After all, for every job there were a hundred applicants.

Tribalism is naturally a pejorative word, in Nigeria no less than elsewhere. Is it a fair one? It would be more accurate to talk of nationalism. Nigeria has some four hundred linguistic groups. Most of them are small, but it is not the small ones that cause trouble. The real trouble is caused by the rivalry of the few large groups, especially the Hausa-Fulani of the North, the Yoruba of the West and the Ibo of the East. Each of these groups has a common origin, a common history, a common language and a common way of life. They are not only nations but big ones. There are perhaps 20 million Hausa-Fulani in Northern Nigeria alone. There are another million of them in the neighbouring republic of Niger and there are yet others in northern Ghana and northern Cameroon. The Yoruba of the West comprise officially 10 million; they also spill over into Dahomey and into the Northern States. The Ibo accounted for between 60 and 70 per cent of the population of the East, officially 12 million in 1963. They, too, spill over into the Mid-West State and, until the 1966 upheavals, there were almost 2 million in the North and many more in the West and in Lagos.

The rivalries of these nations are as bitter as the struggle between Jews and Arabs in Palestine. While the Palestine argument is largely over land, the Nigerian one is over jobs, contracts, scholarships and the right of traders to establish themselves outside their Region of origin. Behind the main battle between the three main nations—each formerly dominating a particular Region—was the subsidiary battle of the minority tribes in each Region. The Tiv, the Kanuri and the Nupe fought for their rights against the dominant Hausa-Fulani in the North; the Ibibio, the Ijaw and the Efik fought the same battle against the Ibo of the East; and so did the non-Yoruba people of the West, until their own Mid-West Region was created in 1963.

There are thus two nationalisms in Nigeria. There is the modern kind, the kind that makes civil servants, soldiers, politicians, professional men and schoolchildren alike take pride in their country. As yet this does not penetrate very far in society, and it received a catastrophic setback during the upheavals of 1966-68. The other nationalism, the one felt deep down in the bones, is not concerned with Nigeria but with Ibo, Yoruba or Hausa. It is by no means confined to the illiterate. Hence the painful paradox of university professors quarrelling bitterly on the campus over tribal issues. The University of Lagos all but broke asunder in 1965 because a shift in the political balance of power had caused an Ibo Vice-Chancellor to be replaced by a Yoruba.

A similar tragedy beset the army officers—another elite who used to be perhaps the most patriotic of all Nigerians—when they murdered each other on tribal lines in coups and counter-coups. In normal times they could afford to be 'above' tribe, just as they were 'above' politics. The politicians might be deplorable fellows but they did, in their vulgar and clumsy way, look after one's tribal interests. Then the politicians were removed from the scene. After that, if a chap did not look after one's own people (i.e. tribe) who else would? At its deepest level, tribalism had become a struggle for national self-determination. 'For twenty years we Ibos have been second-class citizens in our own country and this will not continue', said Colonel Ojukwu, the East's Military Governor, during the crisis of self-determination in 1967.[14] Whether self-determination could be achieved inside or outside a Nigerian framework was the question then at issue.

One might argue about tribalism and nationalism and their respective roles. But it is hard to deny that by 1966 Nigeria had become a society in its own right, with a vigorous and cohesive way of life. The society functioned before the British came and has survived their departure. In some respects, of course, it is not one but many societies: principally an Ibo, a Yoruba and a Hausa-Fulani society and, on the social rather than the political level, there is also a Kanuri, a Nupe, a Tiv, an Igala, an Ibibio, an Efik, an Idoma, a Jukun, an Itsekiri and an Edo society. But all are linked and all interact. Commercial intercourse long predated the arrival of the British— even where it consisted largely of slave raiding. Inter-regional trade has increased rapidly in recent years and has been estimated at £60 million a year. Inter-tribal migration has also increased—though this trend was reversed sharply in the tragic events of 1966.

Nigeria is not free from the well-known evils of detribalisation, the cultural vacuum that arises when people lose old links and values without acquiring satisfactory substitutes. The frustrations of the civil servant, trying to cope with the social and financial pitfalls of Lagos life, are movingly depicted in Chinua Achebe's novel *No Longer at Ease*. Similar malaise pervades Lagos social life. The 'modern' Lagos wife wonders why, when she gives her husband all that the European wife does, he remains monumentally unfaithful. The 'malaprop' hostess serves wine with her peppery stew, chips with her rice.

SOCIAL LIFE

Most Nigerians are part of social groups which have little relevance to the modern units of family, office, factory or state. Beyond the immediate family circle is the extended family. Even when this is not physically present it is never wholly absent from the mind. Beyond it is the lineage group, clan or sub-tribe, the village or township 'improvement society', or the craft guild. The chief, with his paraphernalia of courts and councils, provides authority more permanent and familiar than that of the politician or state official.

In its assertive African-ness, Nigeria contrasts with its ex-French neighbours, like the Ivory Coast or Dahomey. There the French, with their zeal for exporting French civilisation, left an isolated elite, more French than African, living by French subsidies, largely divorced from a populace scarcely affected by independence. In those countries, much of the administration and most of the big business is still in French hands; hotels, small butchers' shops and even cafes are French-owned and French-run. Nigerian life is African in all departments and at all levels. Literature, both in English and in the Nigerian languages, has flourished here as in no other African country; so has the drama, music and sculpture. Government at the local level, which is the level that matters to people, is shaped by chiefly and traditional conciliar institutions. It is a changing pattern: the power of the chiefs and the emirs is being eroded by the politicians, while the business tycoons are emerging as a new aristocracy. But, even in change, it remains Nigerian. A Yoruba passing a white man in the street or the village calls out the greeting 'oyinbo', meaning simply 'white man'. He says it without hostility and without deference. There is not a trace of the reverence he bestows on 'kabyesi', the greeting he reserves for even a minor chief.

Nigerian societies are still largely polygamous, but this does not mean that women are down-trodden. They are in charge of trade—ranging from village or pavement-level buying and selling to the

17

big business of the Lagos markets. This gives them, at least, a measure of independence and, at most, can make them exceedingly rich. In the village their life has a strongly communal flavour, and most of it is lived in the open air. Village women are perhaps less bored than the suburban housewife. Whatever its church, society remains to a large extent pagan. Even in Lagos a man may shop around for his medicine, passing from the dispensary to the native doctor. The rural society of Yorubaland, at any rate, has been shown statistically to be neither more nor less neurotic than that of Stirling County in north-east America.[15]

The impact of Western ways is happier in some contexts than in others. In Achebe's *Things Fall Apart* the Ibo village hero who revolts against the missionaries ends up as their victim. In Wole Soyinka's Yoruba village tale, the play *The Lion and the Jewel*, the *oyinbo* (white man) appears only in the absurd aspirations of the half-educated schoolmaster who wants to bring the village into the twentieth century. The teacher cannot afford even the bride price for his girl. It is the lecherous *bale*, the village chief, who gets the girl, with every sign of the author's approval.

2. Behind the Elite

The relationship between the new elected government and the traditional forces represented by the Chiefs is one that confronts every government in Nigeria and has a certain superficial resemblance to the problems which in England faced the Tudor kings when they attempted to establish a central monarchy after the chaos of the Wars of the Roses.—Sir Henry Willink, 1958.[1]

As for the remaining masses, they are ignorant and will not be bothered by politics. Their sole preoccupation is to search for food, clothing and shelter of a wretched type. To them, it does not seem to matter who rules the country, so long as in the process they are allowed to live their lives in peace and crude comfort. If they bestir themselves at all, as they do occasionally, it is because they have been unduly oppressed by a tribal chieftain, or outraged by the blunders of an Administrative Officer.

—Chief Awolowo, 1947.[2]

IT IS TEMPTING for a European to see Nigerian society in terms of his own history. This can be resented as patronising but it is at least better than assuming that, because things do not run as smoothly as they do at home, Africans must be inferior. Yet historical parallels are difficult to pin down. Sir Henry Willink's comparison with England after the Wars of the Roses is, as he admits, superficial. Even in the North, where the emirs represent traditional authority in its most powerful Nigerian form, real power has long rested with a government which inherited it directly from the British. In the South as well as the North, chiefs are an indispensable intermediary between government and governed. The most that can be said of them is that politicians need to handle them with care.

One thing Nigeria does have in common with fifteenth-century England is the precarious nature of patriotism. Another is the

19

fragility of power at the centre. A degree of anarchy prevailed in the Western Region in the final months of the Balewa regime, and, in the months that followed the second army coup of 1966, it threatened to cover a much wider area. Happily, most Nigerians do not yet depend as much as Europeans do on the paraphernalia of modern society. These may break down, as the electric power or the running water or the bus service may fail—but life goes on. Another obvious parallel with Western history is the role of corruption. The politician who calculates the outcome of elections in terms of bribes and thugs seems to have come straight from the English rotten boroughs or the era of Reconstruction in the United States. Inequalities of wealth, too, are as spectacular as they were in nineteenth-century Britain—though such battles as those over the Factory Acts are already won (child labour being exploited only in relatively mild forms, in the home, in the fields or in the market place).

Comparisons with the European present are by no means always invidious. Nigerian society has a quality of excitement that our own lost long ago. Reversals of fortune have a Shakespearian flavour. A fabulously rich and powerful minister may be in prison, or dead, or penniless, in a day. A village schoolmaster can become prime minister within a decade. In a society where the state is the biggest employer and where power is constantly disputed between tribal nations, politics really matters. It is everyone's business. Not many British playwrights find themselves in the dock, as Wole Soyinka did after the rigged election in the Western Region in 1965, accused of having held up the radio station with a pistol, confiscated the Premier's taped broadcast and substituted a revolutionary text of his own.* After the second coup of 1966, the poet Christopher Okigbo figured in a drama of gun-running between Brussels and Eastern Nigeria.[3] Nigerian writers, at any rate, cannot yet afford ivory towers.

* He was acquitted for lack of evidence of identity.

RURAL SOCIETY

For all its drama and gusto, Nigerian political life is played out against a backcloth of mud huts, with impoverished peasants as the uncomprehending audience. Almost 80 per cent of Nigerians are farmers. Regional development plans have attached a high priority to modernising the farms with fertilisers, new techniques and social amenities, but these have had only a marginal impact. Modern farming needs much bigger units of production than are available in tiny family holdings; breaking these up to form large units requires a major social revolution. Roads have improved, but most of the added profits from food sales have gone to the transport contractors and middlemen rather than the farmers. At election time the farmer sees his politician, who promises more approach roads, a village dispensary, a school and a post office. But the farmer has learned to expect little. Even where there is a dispensary, its services are not always superior to those provided by the native doctor, who at least offers a good doctor-patient relationship.

Compared to the famine areas of India and China, nature is kind. If malnutrition still keeps infant mortality at about 50 per cent in the villages, this is the result of ignorance rather than lack of good food. It is not easy to starve in Nigeria. The most desperately disappointed job-seeker in the towns can, as a last resort, go back to his village—but it remains a last resort. The over-riding aim of Nigerian planning is to try and stem the flood of job-seekers leaving the villages by making life more attractive on the land. As yet, no real progress has been made. Farm settlements on the pattern of the Israeli *moshav* have been tried, but found too expensive and inappropriate to the social environment. The only solution is to lavish immense patience and expertise on changing the social patterns and consolidating the land holdings. So far, only a few pilot projects are under way (see chapter 10, pp. 264–6). It is still universally accepted that the boy who goes to school (generally one or two out of a large family) is the one destined to leave the land. 'He couldn't stay here anyway: he hasn't the strength', a farmer might say of his schoolboy son, but what will really drive the boy away is that the village has even less to offer than the big city.

Nigeria's staple foods are gari (cassava meal), millet, yam, rice, peppers, palm-oil, groundnut oil and kola. Most farming families can afford, if not meat, a little stockfish with their stew, though not perhaps every day. Rural economy covers a wide range, from sub-sistence farming to modern plantations. In most family holdings, cash crops and food crops are mixed, with most of the cash crops destined for the domestic market. The North sends livestock and guinea corn to the South; yams come from the East and the Middle Belt; palm-oil comes from the East and the Mid-West. Rice, fruit, cassava, sugar and kola nuts are all grown for cash. Export agricul-ture is also largely of the peasant variety. Groundnuts, benniseed, cotton and soya beans come from small Northern fields; cocoa, palm produce and rubber from Southern trees. Plantations of rubber, cocoa and palm, and ranches for cattle, are small but grow-ing industries which were fostered by all regional governments to boost production.

Farmers of the different areas do not differ dramatically in their standards of living. Until its sharp decline in world markets in 1960–65, cocoa made its farmers in the West and Mid-West Regions a rural aristocracy. But the boom was not soundly based. In 1965 the producer price of cocoa had to be halved from £120 to £60 a ton. A farmer who seemed the wealthiest in sight in a village near Gusau, in the North, listed his income from cotton, groundnuts, millet and guinea corn: the total came to about £100 a year, out of which about half was spent in paying labourers. A farmer near Aba, in the East, was found to earn around £50 a year from the sale of yams and cassava. Both the Northern and the Eastern farmer live with several wives in thatched mud huts. Asked about the changes they had experienced in the last ten years, both mentioned[4] that life is more orderly, safer from brigands and from the extortions of chiefs, but hardly more prosperous than it was.

THE UNEMPLOYED

Next to the farmers, the most numerous class in Nigeria is the un-employed. No one has ever counted them. They merge at one end with the farming community (a young man may be in his village on a Monday and job-hunting in the nearest town on Tuesday) and at the other with those at work (he may be taken on to an already swollen staff, for a pittance, at a garage or a bakery owned by a relative). There were well over 3 million primary school pupils in 1964, of whom about 800,000 were in senior grades; another quarter of a million were in secondary schools; in 1965 Nigeria's five universities turned out a thousand graduates, while their student population of 6,700 was increasing at the rate of about a thousand a year. Even before the expensive upheavals of 1966–67, there seemed little prospect of increasing employment opportunities at anything like the same rate as the increase in the number of school and college leavers. Traditional concepts of 'development', with stress on capital-intensive factories, were making virtually no im-pact on the problem. The answer seemed to lie in small, labour-intensive industries and in somehow making life more attractive on the land.

No one can live or travel in Nigeria without coming across the job-seekers. They constitute an industry, paying out large sums every year in petty bribes to works foremen, recruitment officers and other, largely bogus, middlemen. They write flowery letters of application, promising God's eternal favour and the humble appli-cant's infinite gratitude for the favour of an interview. They are known as 'applicants'. Everyone in a job has several applicants in his family, perhaps even in his own house, and loses no opportunity on their behalf. But for most, the quest is hopeless. The alert, well-mannered and well-spoken youth who had tried everything and everyone he knows over the past year and is clearly degenerating in his despair is prominent on Nigeria's human landscape. The 'appli-cants' are not always docile and the growing percentage of graduates among them has begun to make them a political factor to be reckoned

23

with. They have long provided permanent recruiting material for the private armies of thugs retained by politicians. In Port Harcourt during the general strike of 1964 most of the demonstrators and pickets were 'applicants'—a remarkable episode in the history of strikes. More important than the demand for higher wages was general protest against the corruption and the inequalities of the regime and in this the 'applicants' were naturally in the vanguard.

THE WORKING CLASS

After the unemployed comes the almost equally depressed class of workers and small clerks. Their grievances, briefly dramatised in the 1964 general strike, included the relentless fall of real wages, the shortage of cheap housing, archaic conditions of service and wage differentials based on the concepts of colonial days. The Lagos consumer price index rose about 20 per cent in the first six years of independence; the rise was even steeper in Enugu, while the up-heavals of 1966–67 have made food prices in all areas soar beyond all known limits. Union pressure had in 1963 led to the appointment of the Morgan Commission—comprising a judge, a chemist, a lawyer, an economist and a civil servant—to enquire into wages and conditions of service among junior employees. The Commission concluded that for a worker with one wife and two children to live decently in Lagos he would need to earn £16 16s. a month, to be allocated as follows:[5]

	£	s.
Food	7	10
Rent	3	0
Transport	2	0
Clothing	1	0
Fuel and soap	1	0
Mat, blanket, tax, cigarettes, entertainment, etc.	1	10
Savings		16
Total:	£16	16s.

At the time the minimum wage rate for government employees in Lagos was £7 10s. The Morgan Commission recommended that it be raised to £12. The government counter-offered £9 2s. and was eventually compelled to accept £10. The figures were graded for different zones: the Commission found £11 a month reasonable in the rural areas of the North but demanded only £6 10s. The prevailing level was £4 2s.; the government counter-offered £4 15s. and finally accepted £5 10s. In Lagos, even before the award was announced, the market women had raised their food prices by an equivalent amount, thus cancelling its effect.

The Morgan Commission also stressed the absurdity of wage differentials, which constituted an economic wonderland. A university lecturer—expatriate or Nigerian—gets roughly the same salary as his counterpart in Britain and perhaps two-thirds of the salary earned by his American colleague, though Nigeria's per capita income, at around £30, is only a twelfth of Britain's and a twenty-fifth of America's.[6] A Nigerian permanent secretary or a cabinet minister might earn £3,000 a year, plus important perquisites in the form of housing subsidies, car loans, free telephone and other services. In contrast, a labourer or messenger might earn £95 in Lagos or £72 in the North, while an executive officer might be on a salary of £450 to £550. The ratio between the earnings of a messenger and those of a permanent secretary, between 1:30 or 1:40 in Nigeria, is about 1:12 in Britain and about 1:15 in the United States. After tax the disparity is even greater because Nigerian income tax allowances err on the side of generosity. Fringe benefits which further widen the gap include car loans, mileage allowances and the provision of furnished houses at very low rentals. It has been calculated that some £6 millions are annually locked up in motor loans advanced by government;[7] if half of that sum were used to provide an efficient public transport system, most of the car loans would not be needed.

The Morgan Commission also found it 'unjust, unfair and immoral' that large numbers of workers, including many who had seen more than ten years' continuous service, were still employed as daily-paid labour and therefore deprived of security of tenure, notice, leave pay, retiring benefit and sick leave. The Commission also attacked the exploitation of rents; a single room for a whole family often costs £5 a month, eating up more than three-quarters of earnings.

The trade unions have so far achieved little for Nigeria. Their basic handicap is that, although they have about a million nominal members, they represent only about 2 per cent of the population, while the entire wage-earning class is probably not more than 4 per cent. Chronic unemployment further weakens the unions' bargaining strength. The widespread tendency of unions to split into factions, each with its own foreign affiliations, has also hit Nigeria hard. The unity of action displayed in the 1964 general strike was a glorious exception.

The outstanding Nigerian unionist, a household word throughout two decades of labour politics, was Michael Imoudou, the fiery, eloquent railwaymen's leader, who was the hero of the 1964 strike (see chapter 7, pp. 155–6, for his role and career). Leaders of both the 'moderate' and the 'radical' wings of the movement have tended to emerge from within the National Council of Nigerian Citizens (NCNC), Nigeria's first national and radical party. Both Laurence Borha, secretary of the 'moderate' United Labour Congress, and Samuel Bassey, secretary of the 'radical' Nigerian Trade Union Congress, are still NCNC members, though the latter holds views far to the left of the former. Both men began their careers in the army, moving on to the civil service where they became pioneer union organisers before resigning to become full-time unionists. Borha, born a Catholic, was a Marxist in his youth but became disillusioned with it in the 1950s; Bassey, who avoids ideological labels, remains an admirer of the Soviet or Nkrumah-type state, accepting state-run trade unions provided the state is controlled by a 'people's government'.[8]

It is remarkable that so politically vibrant a country as Nigeria should have failed to produce a sharply defined and forceful left wing. Trade unions have, from the beginning, had their Marxist leavening, but it has been as ill-defined as the 'Socialism' in such avowedly Socialist parties as the NCNC. A steady trickle of Nigerian students have found their way to Russia, Eastern Europe and China; a high proportion of them went merely because they failed to find places in the West; of the others, many have returned more firmly anti-Communist than before. In the fervour of the 1964 general strike Imoudou obtained a mandate, by massive acclaim at a public meeting, to launch a Nigerian Labour Party. The party was indeed formed, but Imoudou lacked the educational background to lead it effectively. At the other extreme, its general secretary, Eskor Toyo, a Lagos schoolteacher, was too much of an 'intellectual' to provide forceful leadership. The party rapidly split into opposing ideological factions. It made no visible impact on the electorate in the 1964 general election, when Imoudou stood in a Lagos constituency. A better-known popular symbol of the extreme left during the Balewa regime was a prosperous private doctor, Tunje Otegbye, president of the Nigerian Youth Congress and founder of the Socialist Workers and Farmers Party. He had the advantage, rare among revolutionaries, of an ebullient temperament; but his prosperity counted against him; his rivals quickly exploited the fact that he was a property owner of some substance. He seems to have enjoyed the confidence of the Russians; he was actually in Russia 'on holiday' at the time of the 1964 general strike, an unfortunate absence that detracted from his public image. His party made little impact at the polls.

THE MIDDLE CLASS

Nigerians run their own administration, own and operate much of their own business and require few foreigners in their professions. This provides a growing middle class of civil servants, businessmen and professionals. It has begun to show class solidarity and to become a cohesive factor in politics. However, Nigerian society is still extremely fluid. The house servants in a doctor's home may well be his brothers or his wife's cousins; a senior civil servant's spare room is likely to be permanently occupied by relatives, while the servants' quarters attached to his house may shelter the unemployed relatives of the master or the servant, or both. If a Nigerian builds himself a comfortable house, he may dispense with the old-fashioned servants' quarters, but he will tend to add a guest wing for his relations.

Perhaps the most like the British are the senior civil servants. They have taken over the suburban houses of their British predecessors in Ikoyi and, in the regional capitals, the corresponding residential 'reserves'. In their offices, they have adopted a traditional routine much marked by its Britishness. They tend to play tennis, though they do not go as far as going to the beach or riding or going out in a motor boat on Sundays: they prefer to call on friends and talk politics, or simply to sleep. They are overworked, because of the general incompetence of junior staff. They are well paid, but the extended family and the price one pays to run a car in Nigeria nowadays combine to ensure that they are never free from money worries.

THE TYCOONS

The newly-rich businessmen are naturally more colourful, somehow more Nigerian, and certainly more individualistic. Bank Anthony, the Lagos contracting and importing magnate, has a penthouse on top of the Federal Palace Hotel in Lagos. His grandfather was a slave called Antonio who was repatriated to Nigeria from Brazil in 1869 and settled on land granted by the government. Antonio's son married a daughter of one of the merchant princes of Lagos. Their son Bankole, later named 'Bank' by Europeans who could not pronounce the name, tried various lines on his own as soon as he left school. A scheme for a palm oil pressing industry took him to Germany. The scheme failed but he did not return empty handed: he brought back some patent medicines which sold so well he became known as 'Doc'. He broadened his range to include German watches and clocks, calling his headquarters 'Clock House'. He later switched to fountain pens from Britain, daring to compete with the big British firms: his headquarters then became, and still is, Fountain Pen House. The turning point of his career, which is the classic Nigerian tycoon story, came when he took the risk of selling part of his family land for a speculative business trip. From Italy he brought back the contracting firm of Borini Prono. He became chairman of its new Nigerian branch, which has since built a good proportion of the country's roads and bridges. He also became the agent for the Law, Union and Rock insurance company.

Bank Anthony lives a Westernised life, wears suits rather than *agbadas* and, as well as the pent-house, has an elegant town house. In the entirely different atmosphere of Kano, Alhaji Dantata Sanussi is the oldest-established and richest of the groundnut-buying magnates. He lives the traditional and religious life of a Moslem, speaks only halting English and visits Mecca every year. His father had been the first Nigerian to join the big British and French produce firms in the buying business. When he was four-teen, after only a primary education, he went into 'the bush' with a pair of scales hitched to a donkey, buying from the farmers on his father's behalf. Today the shortage of capital among his competitors keeps him dominant in a vast trade.

Nigerian tycoons number perhaps a score: some are rich from transport, others from manufacturing, yet others from agencies or insurance. Transport is a promising field in an economy spread over so large an area. The Nigerian who made most money out of lorries was Sir Odumegwu Ojukwu, an Ibo whose son, Colonel Ojukwu, became the Eastern Region's Military Governor in 1966. When he was twenty-five Sir Odumegwu had resigned from John Holt's, the British trading firm, and bought a second-hand lorry. From that he built a vast transport fleet and was reputed a millionaire when he died in 1966, having acquired property all over Nigeria. Manu-facturing, in competition with imported products and later with the local industries established by the big foreign companies, was for Nigerians a more uphill enterprise. Among the most successful were Chief T. A. Odutola, with his nation-wide tyre retreading industry, and Joseph Ade Tuyo, who ran a large wholesale bakery in Lagos. Perhaps the richest field of all is contracting, though few did as well in this as the Ghanaian Chief Biney, who came to control the entire dock labour supply in both Lagos and Accra ports.

THE PROFESSIONALS

Professional people provide the nucleus of the middle class; they are largely independent of politicians and therefore an increasingly valuable counterweight to their influence. Among the professionals, lawyers predominate. The rapid pace of social change assures them a plentiful supply of land litigation, chieftancy disputes and business and real estate cases. Law is traditionally the student's favourite degree course, offering the surest income and status. It is also the traditional ladder for a political career, as it proved to be for a high proportion of politicians. The law was the first of the professions to be widely Nigerianised and some of today's established lawyers and judges have been in practice for twenty-five years.

There are perhaps two thousand lawyers, practising without distinction between barrister and solicitor. Among them are star performers who have become household names, like Chief Rotimi Williams, a formidable advocate who also happens to be physically one of Nigeria's largest men. He was Western Region Minister of Justice until the Action Group crisis of 1962, when he survived the political storms of that year by withdrawing from politics. He still occupies the splendid modern house (in Rotimi Williams Avenue, Ibadan) which he had built when he was a minister; now, with remarkable energy as well as brilliance, he travels all over the country in his chauffeur-driven Mercedes, handling the most important and lucrative cases. At the other end of the scale, there is a steady surplus of junior men who nowadays find it hard to scrape a living. In 1965 the Bar Association, of which Chief Williams was President, passed a motion urging the government to hasten the departure of the handful of remaining expatriate solicitors who, it was felt, still had an undue share of the lucrative company business in Lagos and the regional capitals.

Apart from the lawyers, Nigerian professionals are only beginning to become numerous. A 1963 survey showed that among 'high-level' (graduate) manpower there were only about 5,000 Nigerians, working alongside about 2,500 expatriates.[9] This number had probably at least doubled by 1967. The 1963 survey showed there were 600 Nigerian senior engineers, 1,000 accountants and auditors and 425 registered doctors and dentists. Among university professors Nigerians are still only a sprinkling among expatriates. Academicians, at the social apex of the professional class, include several professors who are familiar names to the newspaper-reading public. Professor Kenneth Dike, a distinguished historian, was vice-chancellor of Ibadan University until the tribal tensions of 1966 led him to resign (he was an Ibo in a Yoruba environment). Professor Eni Njoku built up Lagos University with a verve and skill that earned him the loyalty of most of the expatriate staff in the bitter dispute over the vice-chancellorship in 1965. Equally distinguished was his successor, the historian Professor Biobaku. Academicians have not yet played a prominent part in political controversies, though Dr Samuel Aluko, head of the Economics Department at the University of Nigeria, Nsukka, was a persistent critic of the Balewa regime. After the departure of the first generation of politicians, a new civilian order is likely to call for greater academic participation.

THE CHIEFS

Nigeria's upper classes are the chiefs and emirs and, until their eclipse in 1966, the politicians. In a society poised between two cultures, chiefs are still important in social and political life. Under military rule, after the departure of the politicians who had curbed their power, the chiefs came temporarily back into prominence; the first all-Nigeria meeting of chiefs took place in 1966 after the second military coup seemed to threaten law and order. In the North, the military rulers needed to rely on the emirs to maintain order and local government, just as Lord Lugard had done.

Nigerian 'chiefs' cover a wide spectrum, from the emir presiding

31

over the government of millions of Northerners, to the corrupt, anachronistic village chieftain, grovelling to whatever government is in power for the sake of his salary. Nor are all Nigerians who call themselves 'chief' genuine traditional rulers. The Yoruba sometimes annex the title as an honorific. Successful Ibo purchase their titles as a mark of dignity in later life. Chiefs in all Regions, in addition to their functions in local government, gained a constitutional role with the advent of parliamentary government, in the regional Houses of Chiefs. However, these 'upper houses' have in practice fulfilled little useful purpose and are likely to be reformed or eliminated.

'Chiefs' are at their most important in the North, where the emirs ruled large independent kingdoms until the turn of the century, and where the British were careful to preserve as much as possible of the structure of power and politics. More than a hundred Northern chiefs and emirs are only now beginning to lose control of local government; in 1966 they still held courts with the power of life and death, and, in times of crisis, temporarily assumed a measure of real power. Paramount among them is the Sultan of Sokoto, spiritual overlord of some 20 million Moslem Hausa. During the upheavals of 1966 he became a natural spokesman of the North. It has seemed a permanent factor in Nigerian politics that a whisper of 'holy war' from the Sultan would have immediate and dire consequences. The richest of the emirates is that of Kano, whose administration has an annual budget of more than £2 million.

At the other end of the spectrum are the petty chiefs of the East. The Ibo traditionally have few kings; indeed the British had to create some to bring the East's local government into line with the 'indirect rule' practised in the other Regions. More recently, chieftancy has been further encouraged by the political need to fill the House of Chiefs in Enugu. But the chiefs have no great status. In one village visited by the author, the chief was sufficiently important for a drummer to play while he was having his meal, but in a political discussion which ensued he was shouted down by his more vociferous subjects. In the Mid-West, on the other hand, the

Oba of Benin, direct descendant of the rulers of a vast empire, is still an influential natural ruler. His sprawling mud palace, with its priceless collection of Benin carvings and his large harem (where the children of his retainers are distinguished from his own by bronze rings on their ankles) is a reminder of Benin's not so distant imperial greatness. Oba Akenzua II, however, is very much a present-day Nigerian. He played a key political part in the agitation leading to the creation of the Mid-West state in 1963. He is modern in his social habits, and invites British residents to the palace for afternoon billiards. Every evening at dusk he drives round the town in his large car.

The West's pre-eminent chief is the Oni of Ife, whose home town is traditionally regarded as the centre of Yorubaland. He was a natural choice as the first Governor of the Region in 1960, but he became identified with the ruling Action Group and he was replaced when it fell from power in 1962. The exceptional bitterness of politics in the West has made deep inroads into the prestige and independence of Yoruba chiefs. No longer able to live from traditional gifts and tributes, they have become dependent on the government of the day.

The return of chiefs to political importance under military rule was only temporary; indeed, the military regime itself brought a new impetus for radical reform. In the North, the military government progressively annexed the important strongholds of the emirs' power, beginning with the local prisons and the local police and ending with the emirs' own courts. Chiefly power in Nigeria is in inverse proportion to the prevailing strength of political power at the centre.

The Politicians

By January 15, 1966, when independent Nigeria's first generation of politicians went out of business, the political class had been grievously discredited. Its corruption, nepotism, tribalism and inefficiency had become legendary and the new military rulers achieved immediate popularity. The verdict of history will perhaps be kinder, especially as the soldiers who took power effected only marginal improvements and brought about new catastrophes of their own. For all their faults, most of the politicians were at least good at politics—a quality appreciated only when its absence among the ruling soldiers brought the country to the verge of ruin—and many of them were outstanding in patriotism and ability. The final judgement might be that national independence had made them an anachronism. They had risen to power first as visionaries and then as agitators, but independent nationhood demanded very different qualities.

Nnamdi Azikiwe, the 'local Ibo boy made good', returning from America laden with degrees, author, orator, newspaper magnate, pan-Africanist, was a brilliant figure. Yet, for all his vision, in the end he lacked the political common sense to remain a national leader. Chief Awolowo, his early rival, was an equally articulate nationalist, and a forceful lawyer; he seemed born to lead but, after independence, found himself in opposition and became impatient. Sir Abubakar Tafawa Balewa, as Federal Prime Minister, developed a truly Nigerian outlook; he was in many ways a wise and gentle ruler, but he lacked the forcefulness for holding a centrifugal federation together. The Sardauna of Sokoto, the flamboyantly conservative champion of Northern rights, was, on the contrary, too ruthless and never managed to become a Nigerian.

The political class was remarkably large. Members of the federal and the four regional assemblies numbered 750, of whom almost 200 were senior or junior ministers. Hundreds more were politically-appointed chairmen, directors or members of federal or regional corporations. Another twenty-five were politically-appointed Provincial Commissioners. Members of the Federal Senate and of the regional Houses of Chiefs numbered 200 in all. Few Nigerians would claim that these politicians were collectively worth the cost. Yet individually they earned their keep after a fashion—and therein lay their most flagrant shortcomings. The speeches of MPs consisted largely of pleas for more industries or amenities in their home towns.

Their main political preoccupation was the need to feed their extended family, their village and their clan.

These pressures were illustrated in a leaflet issued for the 1964 federal election campaign by Mathew Mbu, who was then Minister of State for the Navy, in his constituency at Ogoja, in the Eastern Region. In it he listed and answered the hostile questions of his opponent.

Q: How many federal services and amenities have you secured for Ogoja?
A: The tarring of the Ogoja-Enugu road, the two new post offices....
Q: Did you or did you not deprive Ogoja farmers of loans by your taking a £4,000 loan from the Eastern Region Development Corporation?
A: There is no iota of truth in this unfounded allegation....
Q: Can you name one whole scholarship you have awarded for Ogoja?
A: He is a simpleton who does not know by now that among the many recipients of Hon. Mbu's full scholarships is a boy from Odaje in Mbube clan....
Q: Is the allegation that you on several occasions refused Ogoja sons seeking jobs in Lagos true or false?
A: There are not less than 40 Ogoja boys serving in the Nigerian Navy....

Politicians lived well, some extravagantly so. It began as a hangover from the colonial past, when both power and money belonged to the white man and the sight of an African in a big car warmed nationalist hearts. But this mentality quickly disappeared with the realisation that Nigerian money belongs to Nigeria. That realisation was one of the main reasons for the January 1966 coup.

That politicians were corrupt became less and less of a secret, until it reached even the necessarily-restrained pages of Lagos newspapers. This happened in the famous Mbadiwe land case in 1965. Kingsley Ozuomba Mbadiwe is a chubby, jovial politician of immense bonhomie and a flair for the bombastically-homely phrase that makes audiences laugh without their quite knowing whether they are laughing with or at the speaker. For all his buffoonery, Mbadiwe was a shrewd businessman and a distinguished nationalist. He was a graduate of Columbia and New York universities and a close companion of Azikiwe in his early years. In the well-worn Nigerian manner he has quarrelled with his party, been expelled, formed his own party and, seeing it led nowhere, returned to the fold. After his student days he founded the Greater Tomorrow Transport Company before entering politics. In 1957 he became Nigeria's first Minister of Commerce and was later Minister of Transport.

In February 1965 a Lagos newspaper columnist described a land deal in which Mbadiwe had leased a plot of Lagos land from the government at a rental of £1,170 a year and later subleased the land for a rent of £3,570 to a football pools company in which the government had shares.[10] In his inimitable language the Minister retorted in a statement that 'the operative key in this case' was that the land had originally been offered to him when he was still a private citizen. He had intended to develop it for a much bigger profit than he was now getting. 'Giving out three acres of land in a premier industrial site to a company for a chicken-feed rental in place of elephantine income is a great sacrifice. . . .'[11] In the end the Prime Minister resisted a press campaign to dismiss Mbadiwe. He ordered that the land be returned and promised steps to ensure that 'such things do not happen again'. Six months later Mbadiwe opened a luxurious mansion, which he characteristically called the Palace of the People, in Arondizuogu, his home village. It was the climax of a career of bombast and ostentation. Among 2,000 guests were the Federal Prime Minister and the Eastern Region's Premier and Governor. There were bands, speeches and, of course, unlimited champagne. One Eastern regional official was appointed director of operations for the occasion, another director of processions, a third director of publicity. In his speech of welcome, Mbadiwe, using another typical phrase, remarked in his own justification: 'It is the known

36

and the unknown that have contributed to what I am today.' A Nigerian reporter commented wryly: 'He can say that again!'¹² This was December 22, twenty-four days before the coup.

Chief Festus Okotie-Eboh, Federal Finance Minister until the January 1966 coup, was already a prosperous Mid-West timber and rubber contractor and a school proprietor when he joined the cabinet in 1957. He never allowed his ministerial duties to interfere with his continually-expanding business interests. He triumphantly survived a storm in the House of Representatives after he had started a shoe factory and then increased the duty on imported shoes. His ever-growing wealth enabled him to play a uniquely independent role in politics, sometimes defying his own party, which he largely financed. When the soldiers struck in January 1966, they singled him out as the only federal minister to share the fate of Balewa.

THE EXPATRIATES

Another part of the elite are the 'expatriates', to use the neutral term reserved for Europeans, just as the 'natives' are now more acceptably known as Nigerians. There are 40,000 Britons and possibly half as many again of other nationalities—French, Germans, Dutch, Italians, Greeks, Lebanese, Swiss and Americans. The expatriates used to be chiefly civil servants; now all the civil services except that of the North have been 'Nigerianised' apart from a few technical and contract officers. The departing civil servants have been replaced by the rapidly-growing commercial and technical aid community, which is international rather than British.

Race relations—if so problematic a term were ever used in Nigeria —are perhaps easier and less inhibited than anywhere else in Africa. Nothing is segregated. In government departments, business houses, factories, schools, clubs, hotels and on beaches, foreigners mingle with their Nigerian social equals. Almost all big expatriate companies have Nigerians on their boards. In big commercial firms, like the United Africa Company, the Nigerian Tobacco Company or John Holt's, at least half the managerial staff is Nigerian. Almost every Lagos evening has its quota of cocktail and dinner parties, where the Nigerians and the foreigners entertain each other.

Yet such intercourse lacks depth. From the Nigerian point of view, the change from administrators to businessmen was a change for the worse. The old colonials, whatever their various personal attitudes, at least tried to understand the country. Today's expatriate tends to be posted more or less willingly to a country he has no interest in. He enjoys the extra money he earns and the leap into the whisky-drinking, boat-owning, party-giving, waited-on class. His cook, his steward and his nanny will call him 'master', a term which in fact means nothing more than 'employer' but which nevertheless sounds comforting. To all this, Nigeria is little more than a back-drop. Expatriates tend to entertain Nigerians only when there is an ulterior motive. Diplomats naturally do so all the time: they are given an allowance for it and presumably submit lists of their guests in justification. Company directors entertain fellow directors or customers or useful government officials. When among themselves, a large part of expatriate conversation centres on the theme: 'aren't they useless?' Women repeat it endlessly about their stewards and nannies, forgetting that at home they had no servants at all, and also that if they themselves had been called upon to perform alien rites in a foreign language with next to no education they would have acquitted themselves no better. The men repeat it endlessly about their subordinates and colleagues at work, forgetting that if the Nigerians were as efficient as they in their own technical field their presence would not have been required in the first place.

For the few who really do try to make friends, the going is uphill. The more sensitive and educated a Nigerian is, the more he is likely to have been marked by the humiliations of lingering colonial attitudes. He tends to be prickly and suspicious, not to turn up for dinner parties, or to come hours late. If there is a hint of racial snobbery in Nigeria it is the notion prevalent among the Nigerian intellectual elite—permanent secretaries, top journalists and university lecturers—that it is not entirely socially acceptable to have too many Europeans for dinner.

NIGERIAN SOCIETY

How well does Nigerian society function? It is at its best at its top and bottom levels. At the top, the senior civil servant can be as efficient and as patriotic, and is perforce very much more hard-working, than his European counterpart. At the humblest level, that of the village co-operative society, the clan union, the local chief mediating in a quarrel, the villagers clubbing together to build themselves a post office, it is an admirably efficient society. In between the two extremes, the picture is less bright.

Local government, which is 'the government' for the ordinary citizen in his everyday needs, is generally corrupt and inefficient. In the North the 'native authorities', as they are still called, were taken over more or less intact from the emirs by the British, in accordance with the philosophy of 'indirect rule'. Efforts to streamline and modernise them, started by the British and carried on energetically by the Northern government after independence, are only beginning to be felt. Here, as well as in the South, local government has been bedevilled by politics and venality. Elected councils, introduced piecemeal, have proved even more corrupt and less efficient than the chiefs and officials they replaced. They have been disbanded in large numbers in all Regions, to be replaced by official rule once more.

How serious is corruption? A visitor may become aware of it from the moment of arrival when the customs official at the port or airport accepts, or even solicits, a bribe. Its flagrancy strikes all Nigerians, who are aware of it almost every day. 'Bribery is no more a secret or privilege for the traffic policeman, but a right', complained a reader of a Lagos paper. 'The fact is that the practice is so well known to travellers that immediately a motor vehicle is stopped for "checking" by these crooked policemen, the passengers shout the driver out of his seat, asking him to give Caesar his due and save their time.'[13] Numerous commissions of inquiry, both before and after independence, have exposed unrestrained corruption in local councils and in government corporations. The finger has pointed at people of all ranks. They include regional premiers, as in the 1956 Foster-Sutton Inquiry which found that Azikiwe's conduct as Premier in the affairs of the government-owned African Continental Bank 'had fallen short of the expectations of honest, reasonable people'.[14] They include party leaders, as when the 1962 Coker Commission found that Chief Awolowo, leader of the Federal Opposition, had been privy to what it called 'reckless and indeed atrocious and criminal mismanagement and diversion of public funds'.[15]

At the other end of the scale, they include councillors, municipal officials and policemen. Reports on local councils present a picture of total cynicism, in which a job is a sinecure that one expects to pay to get, in the expectation of profit, and, having got it, one expects to pay to keep it. A 1955 report on Ibadan Council told of officials who blandly demanded £10 from each of four revenue collectors at the municipal car park as a bribe to avoid dismissal.[16] The same report concerns an official who had been dismissed for embezzlement but was offered reinstatement to a job that did not involve the handling of cash. 'He politely objected to this posting because he had been out of a job for some time and his reinstatement had cost money, and he had been promised he would be sent to Dugbe Market. The Treasurer asked him to put his objection in writing, and sent a letter to the Chairman with a minute asking him to confirm that Mr X should return to his old job. The Chairman endorsed the letter with instructions to the Treasurer to place Mr X in his former job, which was the collection of market tolls.'[17] In Port Harcourt in 1955, one councillor, on his own initiative, engaged a gang of labourers and set them to work. 'A little higher up the social scale, however, it appeared that a labour overseer might have to pay some £15 for his job, and a case is quoted of a cemetery keeper being mulcted of £23 for a £33 a year rise.'[18]

Corruption ranged from the bottom to the top. The political complications that followed its military coups of 1966 prevented Nigeria from probing as deeply as Ghana has done in documenting the notorious '10 per cent' ministerial commission on contracts that had become habitual in West Africa, for the benefit of either personal or party funds. How rife the custom was in Nigeria, how many of the Balewa administration were guilty of it and how many were innocent, is a story not yet told. The first reports published under the military regime—on Lagos Town Council and on the Northern Region Development Board—appeared to run true to form. Balewa himself had the reputation of being uncorrupt, but, no doubt for political reasons, he was astonishingly lenient on the subject.

No non-Nigerian need feel much smugness about corruption. Only a small minority of countries have, for relatively short periods of their history, been relatively uncorrupt. In their study *Corruption in Developing Countries—Including Britain in the 1880s*, Ronald Wraith and Edgar Simpkins advance the thesis that only in conditions where power and wealth are no longer concentrated in the same hands can corruption be eliminated. Such a separation, unknown in developing countries, has been effective in Britain since the sixteenth century. 'The opposition has always had something to offer, so to speak, which the government wanted, so a bargain has been struck.'[19] There are more specific causes of Nigerian corruption. One is a hangover of the colonial mentality, which tends to identify 'public' money with 'white man's' money—which is fair game. After the Foster-Sutton Committee had found against Dr Azikiwe in 1956, he promptly appealed to the electorate—and was returned to power with an increased majority. If anything, he had gained in stature from the incident.

A part is also played by the traditional role of gifts in society. Chiefs lived, and still do live to a degree, by gifts, for there is no more natural way for a subject to show his respect. Bernard Storey commented in his 1953 report on Lagos Town Council: 'It is a custom of West African life (I am informed by those who have spent many years in the country and by Africans themselves) that a person in authority is entitled to expect (and not merely demand) and to receive some form of consideration (formerly a gift in kind but now usually cash) for something done, in the course of exercising his authority, to the benefit of the giver.'[20] This expectation is all too naturally transferred from the chief to anyone else in authority: the traffic policeman, the nurse, the produce inspector, the government clerk or the minister. The Northern Region government once issued a warning to its cattle owners that they need give gifts neither to have their beasts inoculated nor to avoid having them inoculated. The gift habit is further encouraged by the excess of demand over supply in such commodities as hospital beds, jobs and market stalls. All lead to a natural black market.

The extended family system also exerts its influence. Every man in a job partially supports several people with no job. The expenses of a minister, including the presents he is expected to give and the young men and women he is expected to keep at school or university, are out of all proportion to official remuneration. Even when a minister or official builds himself a big house, it is as often as not crammed to the rafters with relatives. However, when there is a large bank account in London or Switzerland, it can be effectively proved that this particular excuse is not enough.

There are many honest officials in Nigeria. There may well have been honest ministers also, though no one who knows Nigeria would find it easy to imagine an honest traffic policeman. Significantly, institutions which have deeper local roots than ministries or hospitals are strikingly uncorrupt. The village self-help groups and clan unions and local co-operative societies have been handling funds for hundreds of years. Today the treasurer of such a group may be a steward in Lagos, whose 'master' would not trust him to do the family shopping.

The 'cure' of corruption will take a long time. In 1964 the Nigerian police, amid much favourable publicity, formed an 'X-Squad' to deal with it. But it seemed to make no difference. An ex-policeman, Solomon Jacob, reported in a Lagos newspaper that 'recently, some X-Squad men arrested some traffic policemen for demanding and receiving money from members of the public; later these same X-Squad men were arrested by other X-Squad men for demanding and receiving money from the traffic policemen whom they had arrested'.[21]

The eradication of corruption was one of the main aims of the 1966 army coup. But the young majors who carried it out did not come to power, and the resultant compromise regime was able to do no more than scratch the surface. The remedy will lie in civic education, and in the emergence of a stronger middle class, providing alternative sources of wealth other than politics to a sufficient number of people. Corruption in elections effectively killed parliamentary democracy under the Balewa regime. 'It is a glaring fact that elections in this country are costing a great deal of money—whether it is a regional election, a federal election or even a local government election', complained an Eastern Region MP in 1965. 'The election candidate is made to spend through the nose before he is duly elected. It is fantastic to think of a candidate spending £5,000 to £10,000 and when such a candidate is elected he tends to lose the sense of mission.'[22] The same member went on to complain about the widespread use of private thugs in elections. 'Doping of thugs with Indian hemp, the burning of cars, the destruction of life and property and the indiscriminate use of curfews are inimical to free and fair elections.'[23] The answer to these and other more sophisticated ways of manipulating elections (see chapter 7, pp. 164–90) might lie in abolishing them altogether. Alternatively reforms might be attempted to reduce the incidence of abuse. Nominations might be made at a central and well-guarded point, instead of in the constituencies, to obviate the notorious disappearance of officials once the government party candidates have filed their papers. The British system of dropping ballot papers into one of several boxes could be changed, to stop massive 'dumping' of papers in a box after the poll. Another aspect of corruption which various inquiries have stressed is that much of the money goes to political parties rather than individuals. If parties are to outlive corruption, a way must be found of financing them.

The quality of service Nigeria provides its citizens is not as high as it would have been if there had been no corruption or if tribal politics had not vitiated public life. However, against the background of limited resources developed in a short time among a vast and

43

complex population, essential social and civic services work tolerably, and sometimes remarkably, well. Courts, except at the lowest level of 'customary' courts, dispense British-style justice. The civil services function, often against odds that would have sent a Whitehall man out of his mind. The railways run, except when rolling stock is out of order through bad maintenance or when political upheavals make it unsafe for crews to pass from one area to another. The airways fly no more unpunctually than elsewhere—and certainly no more so than the French-owned network in French-speaking West Africa. People lucky enough to use electric power and telephones have cause for bad temper, but massive improvements are under way in both departments. Social services, necessarily rudimentary, function as well as they might in a society often too complex, or too poor, or too ignorant to be helped in modern ways. By far the most effective social service is still that of the extended family, a service which was able to absorb almost without visible trace some 1·3 million Ibo refugees from the North in October-December 1966.

JUSTICE

The formidable backlog of cases in high courts, and the inordinate number of lawyers, testify to the love of litigation for which Nigerians are famous. How much justice do they get? At the lowest levels, they get the traditional justice of the Moslem *alkali* courts in the North and the 'customary courts' in the South. This is lay village justice, from which lawyers are excluded. However, it is subject to constant government inspection and improvement and, more important, to appeal up to the highest level. The drawbacks of the system are massive and obvious. In a case of alleged rape heard by the author in December 1965 in the chief *alkali* court of Bauchi in the North, the alleged victim, her sister, her mother and the policeman all gave their evidence in each other's presence. Later the chief *alkali* admitted privately that this was an oversight. The following day, confronted with incriminating medical evidence, the

44

accused still maintained his innocence but refused to swear it on the Koran. The case was again adjourned so that efforts could be made to persuade him either to swear or to confess. The *alkali* said privately that if the man did swear he would acquit him.

The customary courts system has the advantages of simplicity, cheapness and familiarity with local conditions and traditions. Its abuses, particularly the lack of training and of knowledge of the right procedure, were being constantly studied and corrected in all Regions. The most serious complaint against the system, in the South as well as in the North, was that it was open to corruption and political pressure because the judges were appointed by the political authorities. Appeal courts have uncovered innumerable cases in all Regions of customary courts sending people to prison merely for belonging to the wrong party. At least one Nigerian writer had no doubt that customary court judges regularly 'hold sessions about who, in fact, had paid the biggest bribe'.[24]

Magistrates courts and higher courts belong to another world. Judges are appointed from a wide choice of experienced and able barristers. British procedures prevail, including the wigs and the gowns. At this level, too, politics is the main and obvious threat. The famous trial of Chief Awolowo in 1963 was widely regarded by his supporters as ruled by political expediency (see chapter 6, pp. 138–49). In Britain the image of Nigerian justice received a severe jolt when Chief Enahoro's British counsel was refused an entry permit to defend him. In this case, nationalist feelings played a part: the very strength of the Nigerian bar feeds a resentment of British practitioners on Nigerian soil. The integrity of the legal system suffered an apparent setback in 1963 when, as part of the new republican constitution, the Judicial Service Commission which had appointed judges was abolished. The appointment of judges was placed in the hands of regional politicians. A similar step had been taken the same year when appeals to the Judicial Committee of the Privy Council were abolished, making the Lagos Supreme Court the final court of appeal. Both reforms were opposed by the press at the time. Two years later, after further

45

deterioration in the tone of political life, both the Chief Justice and the Bar Association's chairman expressed regret that the Judicial Service Commission had gone—a sentiment which the press decried as being somewhat belated. However there is little evidence that the politicians grossly abused their power to appoint judges. Certainly none was dismissed for a 'bad' judgement, as Sir Arku Korsah was dismissed by Nkrumah in 1964. One guarantee was provided by the strength of the legal profession: it would not lightly see one of its number dismissed or by-passed in promotion.

Political pressures on the judiciary reached a climax in the last years of the Balewa regime. In the West, political murder was rampant; the government party was in office despite an obviously rigged election and the opposition was vociferous. Under such a strain, judges naturally came to be divided into those who resisted the pressure and those who did not. One who had the reputation of firmly resisting was Mr Justice Oyemade, before whom came a case involving the murder of a government party supporter. A local lawyer, known for his sympathies with the government party, drafted an affidavit and had it sworn to by two local men. They swore that they considered the judge biased in this case, and asked for the removal of the case for trial in another area. Mr Justice Oyemade lost his temper. Rejecting the affidavit, he fined the lawyer £25 and sent the two men to prison for six months for contempt of court. He said: 'I will not allow myself to be intimidated into sending innocent persons to jail. Even if this means losing my job, I am still sure of leading a decent life. The only thing we have now in this country is the judiciary. We have seen politicians changing from one policy to another and one party to another. But the only protection the ordinary people have against these inconsistencies is a fearless and upright judiciary.'[25]

EDUCATION

Nigerian politicians have long valued the knowledge that audiences prefer long words to short: they signify education and to most

Nigerians education is synonymous with progress. There is a great national thirst for learning. The typical success story in Southern areas, a characteristic 'folk-myth', retold in novels, songs and poems, is that of the local lad for whom the village clubs together for a scholarship to England or America. On his return he becomes a man of power, preferably a minister, and, even before his physical return to the village, showers his community with special favours. A good deal of the thirst for education has been slaked. In the South the real educational 'explosion' occurred before independence. By the end of the Second World War illiteracy was still almost total: there were no institutions which taught to university level and only a handful of schools. In 1955 the Western Region became the first African government to introduce universal free primary education. By independence there were three million children in 17,000 schools. At that time the Northern Region, which had over half the population of Nigeria, had barely started its educational revolution. Its 1959 primary school population of 250,000 has since been doubled and is still climbing steeply (see chapter 9, pp. 244–6). Secondary education has, in all Regions, made its big leap forward after independence. There were 115 secondary schools in Nigeria in 1959, a number which has since doubled. At independence there was one university: now there are five.

Next to agriculture, education is Nigeria's biggest industry. It absorbs over a third of regional budgets and a prominent slice of foreign aid. What the government and the missions cannot provide between them is supplied by hundreds of private institutions, ranging from some of the eminent and venerable grammar schools to travesties on the lines of Dotheboys Hall. For those who cannot go to school at all, there is a booming industry in correspondence courses and evening classes. Many more Nigerians study at home for the English General Certificate of Education than do at school for the West African School Certificate. For every external student who passes, scores fail.

In Southern Nigeria, the rush to provide more schools has gone too far too fast. The strain imposed on human and financial resources by universal free primary education almost broke the system in the Western Region as soon as it was launched. In both West and East, the courses had later to be cut down from eight to seven, and finally to six years. The Nigerian primary school has an enormous range. There are contemporary 'model' schools for the children of the elite in Lagos, Ibadan or Kaduna. But the 'bush' or slum school often has scarcely a textbook in sight; unqualified and demoralised teachers are frequently kept waiting several months for their pay because of bureaucratic muddles. The average 'Standard VI' product—the youth who forms the backbone of the 'applicants' class—is precariously literate, with a shaky grasp of English.

The problem of standards has also beset higher education. A basic dilemma arose as early as 1929, when the government faced violent nationalist criticism for suggesting a Nigerian School Certificate to replace the Oxford and Cambridge certificate then in use. This conflict between the requirements of nationalist individuality and the need to maintain universal standards has now been partially resolved. The West African Examinations Council, with headquarters in Accra and Lagos, now sets West African exams but in close collaboration with the Oxford, Cambridge and London boards. It has produced excellent new syllabuses, substituting West African history for that of the British Commonwealth and including Nigerian titles in its set books for English. Primary school syllabuses, the responsibility of the regional ministries of Education, have also been successfully 'Nigerianised'.

Nigeria now has five universities: two federal institutions, at Ibadan and Lagos, and regional ones in the North (Ahmadu Bello University, Zaria), in the West (University of Ife), and in the East (University of Nigeria, Nsukka). While the elegant white buildings of the Ibadan campus have had seventeen years to blend with the luxuriant forest landscape, the other sites still look raw, though in spacious and attractive surroundings. The students are older and more serious than their British or American counterparts, much

more politically conscious, though slow to demonstrate. Most
have worked for some years before entering college. Almost all try
to find vacation work (it is not easy to find) and many have to
work for their living even in term time. This, combined with the
unevenness of educational backgrounds, makes it creditable that
the graduation failure rate is so low (between 15 and 20 per cent).

The universities' most publicised problem has been tribal
conflicts, culminating in the international row that nearly broke
apart Lagos University in 1965 over the replacement of an Ibo
by a Yoruba vice-chancellor. The other universities were soon to
be overtaken by the same tribal hurricane. During the upheavals
of 1966 the universities became tribalised: the Ibo fled from Zaria,
the Northerners were hustled out of Nsukka and the non-Yoruba
melted away from Ibadan. When he resigned as vice-chancellor of
Ibadan, Dr Kenneth Dike, an Ibo, explained mildly that the
university's interest would be better served by a vice-chancellor
who had the fullest support of the people of the Region. Addressing a congregation at the graduation of 500 students, he added less
mildly that 'the educated Nigerian is the worst peddlar of tribalism'.[26]

The universities have never quite solved the problem of what
they are for. Their dilemma was expressed by Azikiwe, founder of
the University of Nigeria, Nsukka, on foundation day. 'We cannot
afford to continue to produce an upper class of parasites who shall
prey upon a stagnant and sterile class of workers and peasants.'
This might have been taken as a dig at Ibadan, the doyen of the
universities, where the emphasis had been classical and British.
Nsukka was a real 'campus' after the American fashion. However,
all the universities have made efforts to become more relevant.
There are schools of business administration and engineering at
both Lagos and Nsukka, institutes of administration at Zaria and
Ife. Ibadan has a large and active extramural department, while
both Ife and Ibadan have schools of African studies. What is disappointing is the response from the students. While arts courses are
over-subscribed, the 'useful' schools lack candidates—a reflection
of the white-collar mentality which pervades Nigerian educational

attitudes. It is a product partly of the liberal educational back-ground of British administrators, partly of the colonial tendency to identify physical work with meniality. With it goes the cult of the certificate, boom of the colonially-stressed idea that a piece of paper is as essential as a collar and tie for lifting you out of your world into theirs. A notable Nigerian protestant against the white-collar mentality is Tai Solarin, a Western Region teacher who, with his English-born wife, founded Mayflower School. The boys and girls at Mayflower built their own dormitories. They make cocoa from home-grown beans and breed their own pigs. Solarin, a popular columnist as well as teacher, wants not only a new kind of school but a new kind of Nigeria. His fiercest crusade is against the grammar school—'the prestige education . . . which holds us to ransom today . . . a useless school, fashioned for a colonial period which has died'.[27]

Another element of imbalance in education is that Nigerian women have been left far behind. Their backwardness, as in other developing countries, has kept the whole society back. In village life, a woman's responsibility for trade assures her an independence and status, however many other wives she has to share her husband with. But education has come much later to her than in other societies, such as Ghana's where there are matriarchal traditions. This backwardness has been especially marked in the North, where it is still reinforced by Moslem feeling. Few episodes more forcefully illustrated the contradictions in Nigerian culture than the marriage of the Federal Prime Minister's daughter in 1963, amid much pomp and ceremony, at the age of thirteen. Since then, the North has produced its first woman lawyer. In the South, women have invaded all the pro-fessions, but they are still pioneers.

THE CIVIL SERVICE

Nigerians owe a great deal to their civil service. It made the essential difference between the Nigeria of 1966 and the Congo of

1960. When the politicians were abruptly removed from the scene, the civil servants took over; permanent secretaries became virtual ministers. During the many chaotic interludes of 1966, they kept the administration ticking over. Indeed, had not the second coup of July supervened, they would have produced an entirely new and improved development plan for the whole country.

The civil servants have not been wholly untainted by corruption. It is often said in Nigeria that the politicians could not have got away with the plunder they did without expert departmental help. ('Someone must have shown them how to do it.') After the coup, the very fact that the military rulers depended so heavily on the civil servants enabled them to escape the full weight of anti-corruption inquiries launched by the new regime. If an unsavoury tale is later told, the civil servants may claim that they had little alternative. The commission investigating corruption in the West in 1962 singled out for praise 'some bold and courageous civil servants who stuck to their guns with remarkable fortitude in the face of circumstances of a trying order'.[28]

It was probably senior federal civil servants who prevented national disintegration in the closing months of 1966. Partly, no doubt, because they had a vested interest in unity, most of them managed to remain Nigerians long after almost everyone else had descended into tribalism. Foreign service officers kept up the usual appearances; even after the massacres of Ibo by Northerners in September–October, Ibo and Northerners continued to work together and even attended the same parties. However, civil service standards and morale had declined noticeably under the political stresses of the Balewa regime. In the tortured Western Region in particular, civil servants were being posted, demoted and dismissed, while others were promoted, at the whim of power-crazed and irresponsible politicians. In all the Regions, the widespread inflation of the census figures in 1962 and 1963 at the behest of politicians was an exercise which involved civil servants; it seemed a landmark in the moral decline of the service.

The most obvious victims of the social and political ills were the public corporations into whose hands the railways, the airways, the ports and electric power were entrusted. The object had been to remove these services from day-to-day politics and separate their finances from the general budget. The system worked badly from the start. Chairmanship of corporations quickly became key political appointments. This meant in effect tribal appointments, as incumbents were expected to staff their corporations, from manager to office boy, with members of their own tribe. The result was the resentment of other groups, as well as gross and hopeless inefficiency. A columnist in the *Morning Post* complained: 'These corporations have proved the most fertile grounds for nepotism and corruption, breeding as they must in their turn the worst forms of inefficiency and public immorality, and therefore the most hideous form of public discontent.'[29]

The Nigerian railway corporation came in for the most widespread criticism. Its chairman until almost the end of the Balewa regime was the Ibo physician Dr Ikejiani, a man widely held to have systematically filled the railways with Ibo, down to the signalmen and station clerks in the remote Hausa North. When, at last, the Railways Board was dissolved in 1965 the newly-appointed Minister of Transport commented that he had 'inherited not a boon but a bane. The financial situation is so serious that the Corporation cannot find money to pay its way and the bank will not grant any more advance unless the railways obtain a government guarantee.' The corporation was losing £1·2 million a year for no good reason; because of bad maintenance only half its fleet of engines was in service, with the result that only a third of normal traffic was being carried.

Social services are necessarily rudimentary. However, there are some fine landmarks. The teaching hospitals of Lagos University and Ibadan University are among the most modern in the world, with appropriate medical and nursing standards. Lagos also has a modern maternity hospital, a children's hospital, an infectious diseases hospital, a dental clinic and a network of health clinics. Lagos water is safe to drink and the city council has an active and enlightened health department. However, even Lagos still lacks a sewage system. Bourgeois houses have septic tanks in their gardens, while the rest of Lagos makes do with night-soil workers and their malodorous carts. Even in Lagos, the health services are thin for the patient with no strings to pull; and even in Lagos babies have died in their mothers' arms while waiting their turn for attention. In the rest of Nigeria the government provided, in 1963, 200 general hospitals, 37 specialist hospitals, 32 infectious diseases hospitals, 1,100 maternity clinics and 1,500 dispensaries. This service, thinly spread among 50 million people, was supplemented by private and mission hospitals and by an extensive background of native medicine.

For all too obvious reasons there is no unemployment benefit in Nigeria. Many large firms run pension schemes for their employees; for the rest the government has a compulsory National Provident Fund. Employers and employees each contribute 5 per cent of earnings, up to a maximum of £2 a month, in return for retirement, invalidity and survival benefits. The scheme has been unpopular. Workers could not understand why the Fund did not publish accounts (the administrators explained that such systems do not usually publish accounts, but in the end was forced to publish that they had collected £14·7 million in the first four years). The workers grumbled that it did not pay unemployment benefit: a worker had to be out of work for two years before he could withdraw his contributions. There was, naturally, a feeling that it was all a conspiracy, in which the money was somehow corruptly dissipated.

THE PRESS

Perhaps the most widely praised aspect of Nigerian amenities is the press. Its freedom, variety and liveliness have long been the envy of other African countries who have had, at best, a competently assembled government sheet and, at worst, the muzzled press of Nkrumah. The Nigerian press has a long history. At the turn of the

53

century the *Lagos Weekly Record* of John Payne Jackson, a nationalist of Liberian origins, was only one of a number of radical sheets. Ernest Ikoli, another of the early editors, recalls that in those days 'a newspaper's popularity was often measured by the intensity of its assault on the only target that was available'[30]—that is, the British authorities. Nationalist editorials of those days were couched in measured, stately prose and kept a careful weather eye on the laws of libel and sedition. The *Daily Times*, today's mass-circulation tabloid, began publication in 1926.

The impact of mass journalism of the British pattern came soon after the Second World War. Nigeria is a promising terrain for a Northcliffe-style press revolution: mass literacy is booming as fast, and in comparable numbers, as it did in the England of Northcliffe's day. In 1947 the London *Daily Mirror* won a fight with the London *Daily Telegraph* for the Lagos *Daily Times*. The *Mirror* organisation, pioneering new distribution techniques by road, rail, river and air, built up the *Daily Times* to its present circulation of 100,000. The nationalist and the mass-circulation tradition were combined in Azikiwe's *West African Pilot*, a paper which launched him as a politician and which still represents radicalism from an Ibo point of view. Lord Thompson was in the fray briefly with his *Daily Express*, but the hidden pitfalls of Nigerian politics baffled him and the paper folded in 1965. The Federal government also runs the *Morning Post*. None of these makes a profit, or has a circulation approaching that of the profitable *Daily Times*.

In a milieu where the printed word still has the prestige of rarity and novelty, the press plays a disproportionate role. Cecil King, with his *Daily Times*, has recognised this and given the paper the improbable role of a *Mirror* in presentation and a *Times* in being a newspaper of record. However, the *Daily Times* is only relatively good; general journalistic standards are low. Writers are poorly paid and often ill-educated. No one yet knows how a free and vigorous press can be made to thrive in Africa, where both lack of local capital and political factors militate against it. In

Nigeria the future may lie with regional government papers. These are of a technically high standard in the West and the North, but they suffer even more than the 'national' dailies from lack of trained journalists.

RELIGION

Nigerians are a very religious people, displaying much of their history, and much of its variety, in their religion. Perhaps 45 per cent are Moslem, 30 per cent pagan and 25 per cent Christian.* The first Northern ruler had been converted to Islam by the end of the eleventh century. Dan Fodio, the reformer who united much of the North in the nineteenth century, was a religious reformer fighting a Holy War; the fiercest resistance he met, in Bornu, was heroically led by an equally devout Moslem, El Kanemi (see chapter 3, pp. 74–6). Today, Islam is the religion of 75 per cent of the Northerners and 33 per cent of the Westerners. Nigeria celebrates both Moslem and Christian holidays: Lagos looks like a Moslem city for the Idul Kabir holiday, when it swarms with rams for the traditional slaughter, and like a Christian city at Christmas or Easter, when its many churches are even fuller than they are on ordinary Sundays.

The Christians are disproportionately influential because of their unique role in education. In the largely Moslem North the best-educated group is that of the pagan Middle Belt, because it has been the only area where missionary schools were allowed in sufficient numbers to make an impact. The Catholics are especially strong in the Eastern Region where, in remoter areas, children following any white stranger are still apt to shout after him: 'Father!' The West is largely Protestant country. A long-planned union of Protestant churches, grouping the Baptists, Methodists and Anglicans, was finally scheduled for consummation in 1965, but at the last minute the negotiations broke down once more over

* The proportions are from the 1952–3 census, as details are not available from the 1963 census.

the pooling of the missions' very considerable property. The missions have lost little of their old momentum. Their schools and hospitals continue to increase. However, there is growing pressure for governments to assume control over the mission schools— and this will be done when resources are available. The Missionary Society and the Baptists still run the only nation-wide chain of bookshops; in fact, in most towns theirs are the only comprehensive bookshops.

Nationalism has had a great effect on Nigerian religion. In the 1880s the Liberian-born nationalist Edward Blyden was fiercely criticising the condescension of white missionaries and their intolerance of African customs, such as polygamy. Under his influence, the United Native African Church seceded from the Anglican Church in 1891. It was followed by many other groups, some of whom, like the Order of the Seraphim and Cherubim, are still strong. Some African churches hold bizarre processions, often at dead of night, with white-robed worshippers, lanterns swinging and bells ringing. Their thatched churches are a prominent feature of Victoria beach at Lagos, where hymns are sung to high-life rhythms. One bearded prophet features in Wole Soyinka's play, *The Trials of Brother Jero*: 'I am a prophet. A prophet by birth and by inclination. You have probably seen many of us in the streets, many with their own churches, many inland, many on the coast, many leading processions, many looking for processions to lead, many curing the deaf, many raising the dead.'[31]

ART AND LEISURE

Nigerians make varied and exuberant use of their leisure. When there is music, even if no more than a drum, children barely a year old dance in time and with skill. Nigerian towns abound in 'high-life' bars, where that peculiarly West African music, more danceable than calypso, is played through much of the night, often by internationally-famous band leaders. A more traditional version, with a more intellectual appeal, is the 'juju music' of Yorubaland, which has something of a religious ritual about its protracted numbers. The words of high-life songs—highly irreverent on either a sexual or a political plane—are an essential part of the fun.

Football, the national sport, is played throughout the year; cricket might perhaps have suited the climate more, but not the temperament. Nigerians are enthusiastic gamblers and pools firms are a big industry. The betting is on English matches. Nigerian matches are between 'house' teams: United African Company versus Ports Authority, John Holt's versus Posts and Telegraphs; there is not yet a league. In the towns and villages away from the capital, open-air wrestling is a traditionally popular sport, backed up by drumming and dancing. Upper-class Northerners are fine polo players, and horse racing is also much in favour.

In both musical and dramatic entertainment, the Yoruba appear to outshine the others. Most of the high-life 'kings' are Yoruba. Yoruba dance troupes go on tour through other Regions. Spectacles at a much more sophisticated level are also available. The Ogunde Concert Party is Nigeria's most famous itinerant group, offering political satire. Conducted in Yoruba and well supported with music and dancing, it is relentless in its attacks on authority and was at one time banned in its own Region. Folk operas, notably those of Duro Ladipo, have also attracted audiences and have been successful as a cultural export to Europe.

Sculpture, not painting, is the traditional African form of representational art. Excellent figures in wood, ivory or metal are still made, though there is little sign today of the greatness of Ife and Benin bronze work of the classical period (see chapter 3, p. 68). A former blacksmith in Oshogbo produces representational plaques of exceptional charm—and growing commercial success—by using hammer and nail on flat aluminium roofing sheets.

Nigeria is as prolific in literature as one would expect from a country of its size and cultural variety. All three major languages—Hausa, Yoruba and Ibo—have a viable vernacular literature of stories, histories and poems. Onitsha market, in the Eastern

Region, is famous for its popular romances and erotic handbooks, either in Ibo or in ramshackle English, usually illustrated by a picture of the author and published by the printer. The playwright J. P. Clarke and novelists Cyprian Ekwensi and Amos Tutuola bridge the gap between traditional narrative and modern literature of an international standard. At the highest level, Chinua Achebe writes novels and Wole Soyinka writes plays of wholly international standard, though their themes are strongly local. In *Things Fall Apart* and its sequel *No Longer at Ease* Achebe brings a coolly objective approach and a quiet mastery of style to the impact of modern life in village and city. In *A Man of the People* he enjoys unpretentious fun at the expense of Nigerian politicians. Wole Soyinka's *The Road* is a play about death, against the background of the extremely dangerous ninety miles between Lagos and Ibadan. But Soyinka's real métier is comic satire, his targets ranging from the pompous village intellectual of *The Lion and the Jewel*, through the Nkrumah-style dictator of *Kongi's Harvest*, to the 'lipstick-coated' telephone voice of the English landlady who asks, in "Telephone Conversation": 'How dark?'

> 'You mean—like plain or milk chocolate?'
> Her assent was clinical, crushing in its light
> Impersonality. Rapidly, wave-length adjusted,
> I chose. 'West African sepia'—and as afterthought,
> 'Down in my passport.' Silence for spectroscopic
> Flight of fancy, till truthfulness clanged her accent
> Hard on the mouthpiece. 'WHAT'S THAT?' conceding
> 'DON'T KNOW WHAT THAT IS'. 'Like brunette.'
> 'THAT'S DARK, ISN'T IT?' 'Not altogether.
> Facially, I am brunette, but madam, you should see
> The rest of me. Palm of my hand, soles of my feet
> Are a peroxide blonde. Friction, caused—
> Foolishly madam—by sitting down, has turned
> My bottom raven black. . . .'[32]

3. How Many Histories?

In the first place, as the title 'Royal Niger Company's Territories' is not only inconvenient to use, but to some extent mis-
leading, it may be permissible to coin a shorter title for the
agglomeration of pagan and Mohammedan states which have
been brought by the exertions of the Royal Niger Company
within the confines of a British Protectorate and thus need for
the first time in their history to be described as an entity by some
general name. . . . The name 'Nigeria', applying to no other
portion of Africa, may, without offence to any neighbours, be
accepted as coextensive with the territories over which the Royal
Niger Company has extended British influence, and may serve to
differentiate them equally from the British colonies of Lagos and
the Niger Protectorate on the coast and from the French territories of the Upper Niger.—*The Times*, 1897.[1]

How many histories has Nigeria? The basic division is between
North and South. The history of the North, like its geography, is of
wide horizons and large units. Until modern times the North
looked northwards, overland across the Sahara. That is where its
people came from in the first place, then its trade and finally its
Islamic religion. All came across desert routes which dwindled in
importance only when European influence from the South, from
across the sea, began to replace Arab influence from the North,
across the desert. These ancient desert routes may be given new
life, in a pan-African context, in our own time: a desert highway
from Tripoli may restore to Kano something of its lost importance
as a crossroads of trade.

The South—land of forests, swamps and creeks—naturally has
a more fragmented history. Although many of the Southern tribes,
like the Northern, probably migrated originally from the North of

59

Africa, in historical times change has tended to come from Europe. Between North and South there was no formal or constitutional link—though wars, conquests and reconquests, trade and religious proselytisation constituted a vital intercourse—until 1914. In that year Sir Frederick (later Lord) Lugard amalgamated the Protectorates of Northern and Southern Nigeria and thereby became the first British Governor-General of the whole country. Seventeen years earlier Flora Shaw, who was to become Lady Lugard, had first suggested the name 'Nigeria' in the article in *The Times* quoted above. Even today, the northbound traveller finds Ilorin a kind of frontier town. Southern sights—a sea of aluminium roofs and the top-heavy head-ties of Yoruba women—blend with Northern sights—mosques, white stone houses, donkeys and the plain baft robes of the Hausa.

The North-South division is only an umbrella covering many subdivisions. In the North, the kingdom of Kanem-Bornu and its dependencies, known to Arab geographers from the ninth century onwards, has a separate story from that of the seven Hausa states which were flourishing in the sixteenth century and which still determine the outlines of Northern administrative provinces. Again, the Tiv, the Idoma, the Jukun and their neighbours in the Middle Belt have a separate history, and their separateness has survived. In the South, the extensive Oyo empire of the sixteenth to nineteenth centuries and its Yoruba successor states have a different story from that of the Benin and Warri kingdoms. Another history is that of the rise of the commercial city-states of the Niger Delta in the eighteenth century, and their complex relationships with their own hinterland on the one hand and with the British merchants on the other.

Multiplicity of themes characterises Nigeria's history as much as it does Britain's. However, the Northumbrians, Wessexmen, East Anglians and Cornishmen—and the Scots and Welsh as well—have held together in a single state for centuries while Nigeria is as yet scarcely weaned. The results are obvious. 'Tribalism' continues to bedevil the politics of a nation in which the people still think of

themselves as Ibo, Yoruba, Hausa or even Ijebu, Aro or other
tribal sub-group, rather than Nigerian.

NOK CULTURE

In Nigerian pre-history the Nok culture still stands alone, as there
is virtually nothing between its ending in the third century and the
emergence of the Kanem-Bornu empire in the ninth century. The
Nok culture was discovered by accident in 1936, when a finely-
sculptured monkey's head was dug up in a tin mine. Eight years
later, a terra-cotta figure of a human head was found twenty-five
feet down another tin mine in the hills near Jemaa. The society
which has been revealed near the geographical centre of today's
Nigeria flourished at the beginning of the metal age, 500 BC to
AD 200, and was one that knew of iron smelting and smithing and
the use of flat stones and hoes for swamp cultivation. The Nok area
so far discovered stretches 300 miles by 100 miles, lying across the
Niger and Benue valleys, mostly north of the confluence. The
archaeologist Bernard Fagg concluded that the Nok people appear
likely to have been the ancestors of the present population of this
part of Nigeria and 'appear to have enjoyed an economy and way of
life nearly, if not quite, as advanced as that of the present inhabitants'.[2] Fagg found in the style of the Nok figurines striking simi-
larities, especially in the eyes, to modern Yoruba wood carving, and
also to the traditional Ife and Benin bronzes.

EARLY BEGINNINGS

The physical origin of the Nigerian peoples is lost in obscurity. The
Hausa, Kanuri and Yoruba all have fairly consistent legends of
origin, pointing to a migratory period. All indicate a northern or
north-eastern origin, from the regions of the Sahara and the Nile
valley. One writer had dismissed as 'a doubtful hypothesis, developed at a time when dispersionist anthropology, and the idea of
the white people as the carriers of civilisation, were much in vogue',
the idea that it was the Berbers, Arabs and other white people who

61

played a significant part in the forming of the Sudanic states.[3] The ninth-century Arab writer Al-Ya'kubi recorded that 'the Blacks who went westwards towards the Maghreb [had] divided the country, so that they now have a number of kingdoms. The first of their kingdoms is that of Zaghawa, and they inhabit a territory which is called Kanem. Their dwellings are reed huts, and they do not possess any cities.'[4]

The legend of the origin of Daura, thought to be the earliest of the seven Hausa kingdoms, tells how Abuyazidu, Prince of Baghdad, quarrelled with the King and, 'with twenty companies', journeyed south as far as Bornu. The King of Bornu, seeing the strength of his forces, decided on a ruse: he gave the visitor his daughter Magira in marriage and later asked for the loan of his horsemen for a war, secretly planning to kill him. But Magira warned her husband and they both left and travelled westwards. Abuyazidu left his wife with child at a place called Gabas Ta Buram, and proceeded to Daura. There he killed a snake which had prevented people from drawing water at the well and thereby won the hand of the Queen. Their son Bawo had six sons who later became the kings of the respective Hausa states: Daura, Kano, Zazzau, Gobir, Katsina, Rano and Biram. Thomas Hodgkin speculates that an animal which Abuyazidu brought to Daura, 'which was like a horse and yet was not a horse', may record the introduction of the ass.[5]

The Yoruba have equally elaborate legends about their origin. According to one, their ancestors were driven out of Iraq and came to Yorubaland by way of Egypt and Ethiopia, leaving a portion of their people in every country as they passed. In Yorubaland itself, legends have traditionally been preserved by national historians, who tend to be descended from certain families, retained by the Alafins of Oyo. These traditions ascribe the Yoruba ancestry to a king of Mecca, one of whose children was Oduduwa, the father of the Yoruba. Also descended from the same king were the kings of the Gogobir and of the Kukuwa, two tribes of the Hausa country—a circumstance which is held to account for the similar tribal marks on Yoruba and Hausa today. Oduduwa is said to have relapsed into idolatry but one Braima, the son of Oduduwa's idolatrous priest, became a Moslem and his followers slew the priest. Oduduwa travelled to Ile-Ife, which is still revered as the 'cradle' of the Yoruba. The nineteenth-century Yoruba historian Samuel Johnson remarks that, while the theory of the Mecca origin is certainly not valid, the Yoruba must have come originally from the East, 'as their habits, manners, customs, etcetera, all go to prove'.[6]

THE COMING OF ISLAM

Nigeria entered the mainstream of history in the twelfth century, with the conversion to Islam of Ummejilami, the ruler of Kanem. By that time the Kanem-Bornu state was an extensive and powerful divine-hereditary kingdom, with an elaborate palace hierarchy within which the Queen Mother had a position of special power. An official historian said of one of the twelfth-century sultans of Bornu that 'his horses numbered 100,000—his soldiers were 120,000, not counting mercenaries. . . . Among his noble acts were pilgrimages to the sacred house of God on two occasions. On his first pilgrimage he left in Egypt 300 slaves, and on his second a like number.'[7] Kanem's capital was at Njimi, but the ruler remained a nomad, like the English kings in the early Middle Ages. During the twelfth and thirteenth centuries the Kanem-Bornu empire extended as far as Kano in the west and Wadali in the east. It began to decline in the fourteenth century after conflicts within the dynasty.

Of the Hausa states, it was the walled, commercial city of Kano which first rose to prominence, in the twelfth century. It was converted to Islam in the fourteenth century, at the time when Oyo and Benin were emerging in the South. The other Hausa states rose to prominence in the fifteenth century, when Kanem-Bornu was already in relative decline. This was the period of southward penetration into Hausaland of the pasture-hungry Fulani—light-skinned nomads who brought their Islamic culture with their cattle from across the desert. The nineteenth-century *Kano Chronicle* recalls that in the fifteenth century 'the Fulani came to Hausaland from Mali, bringing with them books on divinity and etymology. Formerly our doctors had, in addition to the Koran, only the books of the Law and the Tradition (Hadith).' The *Chronicle* adds that Kano's fifteenth-century ruler extended the walls and built the market which still functions today. He 'appointed Durman to go round the dwellings of the Indabawa and take every first-born virgin for him. He was the first Sarki to have a thousand wives. . . . In his time occurred the war with Katsina. It lasted eleven years, without either side winning. He ruled thirty-seven years.'[8]

The kingdoms of Nupe and Jukun, ruled by pagan dynasties of divine kings, emerged in the fifteenth century, while the following century saw a renaissance of Bornu and the organisation of the second Kanem-Bornu empire. The Spanish traveller Leo Africanus writes of Bornu in the sixteenth century as third in importance among the major states of the Sudan, after Gao and Gaoga. Kanem-Bornu lived mainly by its trade with visiting North African merchants, who bought slaves and horses. The seventeenth century saw a bitter struggle between Kano and Katsina for control of the trans-Saharan trade.

YORUBA KINGDOMS

To the South, the great Yoruba kingdom of Oyo emerged in the late thirteenth century. Little definite is known of its beginnings. Samuel Johnson, the Anglican pastor at Oyo who, in the late nineteenth century, wrote *History of the Yorubas*, still the only comprehensive account of their history, admitted that there was no clear dividing line between legend and fact. All indications are that Ile-Ife, near the modern town of Ife, was the cultural and probably also the political source of the empire. The most remarkable survival from the Ife kingdom are its unique bronzes and terracotta figures. These are exquisite statuettes, executed in a naturalistic style which marks them out from the more formalistic and symbolised art of surrounding cultures. They were probably cast in the twelfth and thirteenth centuries.

Ife, with the Ifa religious oracle, long afterwards retained its position as the spiritual capital of Yorubaland. The Portuguese explorer Pacheco, describing visits to Benin in the fifteenth century, says of the Oni (king) of Ife, that 'he is considered among the Negroes as the Pope is among us'.[9] Even today the Oni of Ife has a prestige pre-eminent among obas, out of proportion to his temporal power.

After its period of military expansion in the fifteenth century the Oyo empire covered the whole of Yorubaland—bounded in the west by modern Togo, in the east by Benin and in the south by the Atlantic. Among its celebrated kings was Shango whom the Yoruba deified as the god of thunder and lightning, which he still is today. Accounts of Shango tell of 'volumes of smoke issuing from his mouth and nostrils'[10] and he was said to have had one hundred and sixty people slain in a fit of anger. He was credited with the knowledge of making preparations to attract lightning; his house was actually struck by lightning and many of his family were killed after one of his experiments. Shango was so upset by this that he hanged himself from a tree.

Suicide plays an important part in Oyo's royal tradition. To ensure the election of a successor by the 'wise men', the eldest son of a dead Alafin (king) had to commit suicide. The wise men—called *Oyo Mesi*, the seven chief counsellors chosen from among the royal family—could inform the Alafin 'we reject you', or alternatively give him a symbolic present of a parrot's egg. He must die the same day. The *Oyo Mesi* were at the head of an elaborate bureaucracy. The *Bosorun* was the prime minister, while the *Kakanfo* was the commander of the army (also eligible for the gift of a parrot's egg, in the event of military defeat). Provincial kings held their kingdoms under feudalistic titles from the Alafin. Captain John Adams, writing of his voyages in the late eighteenth century, tells of reports that the Alafin of Oyo had 'an organised army amounting to 100,000 men, composed of infantry and cavalry'.

6—N

Then, as today, the cloth manufactured at Oyo was apparently 'superior, both for the variety, pattern, colour, and dimensions, to any made in the neighbouring states'.[11]

BENIN KINGDOM

Even more extensive and powerful was the Benin kingdom. A legend of the origin of the second kingdom in the late twelfth century tells how the Benin people, preferring a republican form of government to the succession of their last king's heir, sent ambassadors to the Yoruba kingom of Ife, asking for a wise prince to be sent as their ruler. To test the reliability of the Binis, Oduduwa, the ruler of Ife, sent seven lice to the chiefs of Benin, to be cared for and brought back after three years. The lice came back sleek and fat, and this encouraged Oduduwa to send his son Oranminyan. The son married the beautiful daughter of a local chief, but he found Benin altogether too much for him. According to the Benin historian Egharevba, 'after some years residence here, he called a meeting of the people and renounced his office, remarking that the country was a land of vexation—*Ile Ibinu*, by which name the country was known afterwards—and that only a child born, trained and educated in the arts and mysteries of the land could reign over the people. He caused his son . . . to be made Oba (king) in his place, and returned to his native land, Ife.'[12] The son, Oranminyan, left at Benin, became Oba Eweka i, the first of a line of thirty-six Benin obas. He also left another son at Oyo, who became the first alafin (king) there.

The Benin kingdom entered its great period in the fifteenth century under Oba Ewuare the Great. It is remembered of him that as well as being 'a great magician, physician, traveller and warrior . . . powerful, courageous and sagacious', he also 'made good roads in Benin City and . . . the town rose to prominence and gained the name of city during his reign'.[13] Benin's influence in this period extended to Sierra Leone and to the Congo river; its boundaries stretched from the Niger in the east to Porto Novo in the west.

Both Lagos and Badagry were its colonies. When the Portuguese arrived on the coast, it was Oba Ewuare who 'discovered' them, rather than the other way round. He sent a messenger asking the Portuguese to bring their missionaries into the town, a request of which the Portuguese quickly took advantage to organise the export of slaves. Later the Oba sent his own ambassador direct to the King of Portugal, and the men in the Lisbon court found him 'a man of good speech and natural wisdom'.

Benin City seemed 'very great' to a seventeenth century Dutch traveller: 'When you enter it you go into a great, broad street, not paved, which seems to be seven or eight times broader than Warmoes Street in Amsterdam. . . . The houses in this town stand in good order, one close and even with the other, as the houses in Holland stand.' The king every year 'goes twice out of his court and visits the town, at which times he shows all his power and magnificence and all the bravery he can, and then is conveyed and accompanied by all his wives, which are about 600 in number, but they are not all his wedded wives'. This traveller found Benin people 'very reasonable, and will do no wrong one to the other, neither will they take anything from strangers, for if they do they should afterwards be put to death, for they lightly judge a man to die for doing any wrong to a stranger'.[14] The Dutch geographer Dapper elaborated the point that 'these Negroes are much more civilised than others on this coast. They are people who have good laws and a well-organised police; who live on good terms with the Dutch and other foreigners who come to trade among them, and showed them a thousand marks of friendship. Deceiving and drunkenness are not their principal faults but rather lechery.'[15] In Benin the Dutch sold cloth of gold, of silver and of scarlet, violet embroidery silk, coarse flannel, bracelets, drinking vessels, mirrors, iron bars, beads, candied oranges, lemons and other green fruits. They bought 'striped cotton garments which are retailed on the Gold Coast, blue cloths which are sold on the rivers of Gabon and Angola', jasper stones, leopard skins, pepper and female slaves, 'for they refuse to sell men'.[16]

Like Ife, Benin in its heyday is now remembered largely for its carvings. As early as the thirteenth century Oba Ogualo had sent to the Oni of Ife for a brass smith. Ewuare the Great encouraged both wood and ivory carving. The astonishing variety of Benin sculpture is difficult to appreciate today because so much of it is scattered in far-flung museums. It has been estimated that in 1897 alone as many as 2,500 bronze plaques and ornaments were removed from the oba's palace, and Benin carvings have since fetched very high prices in auctions. The most famous carvings— an oba and his attendants, a pair of acrobats swinging from ropes on a tree, a pillar in the oba's palace ornately decorated with figures, a Portuguese soldier levelling a rifle—have a striking serenity and modernity of approach and design.

THE COMING OF EUROPEANS

Europeans began to affect the Nigerian scene in the fifteenth century. Herodotus has written of a Phoenician expedition round Africa in about 500 BC and the Carthaginian Hanno travelled to West Africa about the same time. From the eleventh century AD Arabs were exploring overland. The first serious visitors were the fifteenth-century Portuguese, looking for gold and the sea route to India. Henry the Navigator equipped an expedition and by 1462 the whole coast was open to trade. By 1471 the Portuguese were obtaining gold at Minna (Elmina) in the Gold Coast (Ghana) and pepper at Benin. Although King John II declared himself 'Lord of Guinea' in 1483, he had no political power: his traders merely built forts and a slave depot. At Gwato, on the Benin empire's coast, they built themselves a fort: here they acquired slaves, whom they later bartered for gold at Minna. The depth of Portugal's spiritual influence was doubted by one of their sixteenth century writers. 'As the King of Benin was very much under the influence of his idolatries, and sought the priests rather to make himself powerful against his neighbours with our favour than from a desire for baptism, he profited little from the ministrations of those sent thither.'[17]

The sixteenth century saw the end of the Portuguese monopoly of West African trade—and the transition from pepper to slaves as the main commodity. A late example of the hazards of the pepper trade is provided by the voyage of Captain Thomas Wyndham to Benin in 1553. The Oba promised to fill Wyndham's ships with pepper and actually collected eighty tons of it in his warehouse. But meanwhile the crew had drunk too much palm wine and most of them died of fever, forcing Wyndham to depart hastily without his pepper.

Slaves became profitable after the discovery of the New World had established a seemingly insatiable demand for workers on the plantations. Slavery was not new to Africa, but it had existed primarily in its domestic form—involving rights as well as duties. In Bornu the kings sent slaves to govern their provinces and Hausa kings also often ruled through slaves. In Yorubaland, slaves of the alafin often attained great power. It was the Europeans who turned slavery into an industry and introduced such well-documented barbarities as the rigours of the 'Middle Passage' (across the Atlantic). In return for copper bars, pewter tankards, blue linen, spirits and other imports, perhaps 24 million slaves were exported from West Africa and Angola in the sixteenth, seventeenth and eighteenth centuries. Some 22,000 were shipped annually from Nigerian ports alone in the seventeenth century.

The Europeans could not capture the slaves for themselves, but depended on African middlemen who dealt with the interior. This middleman trade deeply marked Southern Nigerian history, both in the slave era and in the palm-oil era which replaced it in the nineteenth century. It is responsible for the rise of the trading city-states of the Niger Delta—highly organised and often despotically governed commercial communities which, in their heyday, became wealthy and powerful. At first they provided the European traders with an indispensable service but later the Europeans sought to cut out these middlemen. In one case it was the other way round: a middleman tried to export direct to England. The ensuing quarrels hastened the start of British colonisation.

The Delta was originally peopled by fishermen, largely of the Ijaw tribe, but the ramifications of the new slave trade stretched well back into the Ibo hinterland. The Aro, a branch of the Ibo who were guardians of the sacred Arochuku oracle, shrewdly exploited their spiritual power to monopolise the primary trade in slaves. Apart from the freedom of movement in a warlike and fragmented area which their spiritual position gave them, their oracle had a convenient way of sentencing large numbers of people to be sacrificed to it. These sacrifices were put to a more lucrative use than death.

Bonny, a village at the mouth of one of the larger Delta channels, rose to pre-eminence, first in the slave trade and later in the oil trade. (It declined disastrously in the early twentieth century, but in our own time is emerging once more under the impact of a new kind of oil.) Bonny's royal house of Pepple has reigned continously from the eighteenth century. Of King Opubu, the British trader Richard Jackson wrote in 1826 that:

> without the assistance of the slightest education, [he] transacts business with 13 vessels now lying here (and often there are many more), all the concerns of which, however minute and complicated, he carefully bears in his rememberance, never forgetting what he promises to do for them, nor omitting to send for what they promise him; and traffic with them naturally leading to the despatch of trade with the interior, by bartering their merchandise for oil, ivory and slaves, all passing through his hands and under his own observation—one cannot sufficiently eulogise his extraordinary ability. In fact his generally admitted correctness in all points of business excited the wonder and claims of all who knew him.[18]

The divine prerogatives of the Pepples buttressed the power of their prosperous family slaving business (such a firm was known as a 'House') which was itself organised by prominent slaves. Some of these slaves became powerful and eventually challenged the monarchy itself. When King Opubu died in 1830, his son and sucessor, William Dappa, was a minor. Alali, the slave who was head of the Opubu House, became regent, and there was a period of rivalry between the prince and the regent.

This came at a time of transition and confusion in what had been a well-organised trade. For reasons that combined religious morality with good commercial sense, the British had now outlawed slavery and were trying to enforce the ban against their more backward European neighbours. In 1836 a British ship entered Bonny and seized four Spanish ships suspected of slaving. The Regent Alali was outraged. The British tried explaining to him that a new treaty with Spain gave them the power to search ships. Unfortunately, the only man who could interpret the text of this treaty to the regent was one Capsios, leader of the Spanish traders. 'This gentleman deliberately misrepresented the document to the Bonny chief. He went further. In order to arouse the suspicions of the regent he insinuated that the document might be a forgery, in spite of British protestations that it was the correct copy of the treaty.'[19]

Spanish intrigue won the day, and Alali arrested the commander of the British ship. But after a show of force the British made him sign a one-sided treaty, forbidding him to imprison a British subject. The regent's continued support of the slavers, at the expense not only of morality but of the smooth passage of the British oil trade, finally damned him in British eyes. Commander Craigie duly arrived in Bonny and, when the regent refused to meet him, he opened negotiations with the hitherto powerless prince. The regent had to sign a document accepting the terms of his deposition, and William Dappa Pepple became the effective ruler. He was as astute, both in trade and politics, as his father had been. Inevitably, it was not long before he also quarrelled with the British. He tried to regain his freedom of commercial manoeuvre but he was living in the wrong era. The appointment in 1849 of John Beecroft as British consul, based at Fernando Po, was the end of such freedom and the consul quickly came to be regarded as 'the de facto governor of the Bights of Benin and Biafra'.[20] Beecroft accused

King Pepple of trying to resume 'the abominable traffic of selling your fellow men'. By a ruse, he captured the king at Fernando Po, exiled him to Ascension Island and later to London. In 1861, King Pepple returned, a devout Christian but a broken ruler.

King Jaja of Opobo belongs entirely to the oil era. Like slaves, oil had to be purchased in the interior and Delta politics continued to hinge on control of the access. Jaja was not an Efik of the Delta but an Ibo of the interior. He was sold as a slave to a Bonny chief who, 'finding him insubordinate and headstrong, made a gift of him to Madu, a chief of the Anna Pepple House'.[21] Eventually he was elected head of this House and he concentrated on building up its trade, shrewdly cultivating the interior chiefs as assiduously as the European traders did. When a feud developed with the rival House of Manilla, Jaja left Bonny and, by a masterstroke of enterprise, established himself on a new site where he could dominate the interior trade, virtually sealing it off from Bonny. He became 'king' of the new state of Opobo (though to this day the Bonny people do not recognise him as such). This time the British, who were as furious as the Bonny rulers, were ineffectual. They placed an embargo on trade with Opobo, but this only rebounded to the disadvantage of their own traders and some of these traders were quick to side with Jaja.

After Jaja's de facto victory, the British tried to negotiate a protection treaty with him. Jaja insisted on a definition of protection and was duly informed by Consul Hewitt: 'The Queen does not want to take your country or your markets, but at the same time she is anxious that no other nations should take them. She undertakes to extend her gracious power and protection which will leave your country still under your government; she has no wish to disturb your rule.'[22] Jaja insisted the protection clause be left out of the treaty. When the oil price began to decline, he tried to bypass the merchants by shipping direct to England; in return the merchants grouped themselves into a syndicate; in his turn, Jaja offered a monopoly of all the trade to one trader at the expense of the others. In the end the British consul conveyed him to Accra, where he was tried and condemned to five years deportation to the West Indies, with an allowance of about £800 a year. He did not live to return to his country.

As the slave trade gave way to the palm oil trade, the middlemen gave way to Europeans with increasing appetites for trading direct in the interior. The essential step was to find a highway—and the only highway was the Niger. When the African Association was founded in 1788 to explore the hinterland for the joint benefit of missionaries, scientists and traders, it was still believed that the Niger flowed westwards, as an early Spanish account had claimed. After several abortive and tragic attempts by the Association's explorers, the young Scottish doctor, Mungo Park, travelled up the Gambia river in 1795. He was robbed, imprisoned, sick with fever, famished and deserted by his followers. But at last he came through some marshy ground, 'and looking forward I saw with infinite pleasure the great object of my mission; the long sought-for, majestic Niger, glittering in the morning sun, as broad as the Thames at Westminster and flowing slowly to the *Eastward*'.[23]

The next achievement—to find out where the Niger flowed into the sea—was not to be made until 1830, when the brothers Richard and John Lander, travelling overland from Badagry to Yauri, sailed downstream on the Niger. They came near to failure at Asaba, where they were captured by Ibo. But their captors agreed, in the hope of ransom, to deliver them to the master of an English brig, and captors and captives set sail downstream. The Landers were overjoyed to find the brig in question anchored, unknown to its captain, at the mouth of the Niger. This discovery was promptly put to commercial use. The Liverpool trader, MacGregor Laird, set up a company to explore the river. In 1841 the Society for the Extinction of the Slave Trade and for the Civilisation of Africa financed the famous Niger Expedition, which set sail in three ships, aiming to conclude treaties with the local chiefs and establish a model farm. On board was Samuel Crowther, the freed slave who later became Bishop on the Niger. They carried quinine, but used

73

it only when patients showed signs of recovery: more than a third of the members died of malaria. Even the crops on the model farm failed to thrive.

This setback, both to trade and to evangelism, was only temporary. By 1848 the Wesleyan Methodist Society and the Church Missionary Society had missions at Badagry and Abeokuta. By 1918 there were as many as fifteen American and European groups in the South and the Middle Belt, consisting of 600 European and 5,000 Nigerian missionaries, responsible for 3,000 churches and some 800,000 communicants. The relatively unorganised Ibo and Ibibio of the South-East and the pagans of the Middle Belt proved more receptive than the closely-knit and more traditionalist society of the Yoruba. At Abeokuta, trade quickly followed the mission and within a year of its establishment in 1848 the large trading firm of Thomas Hutton had set up a 'factory' (trading post). To the east, the explorer Baikie's Niger expedition in 1854 had facilitated the founding of one of West Africa's most successful missions—the Niger mission. This was the first to start off as an entirely Africanised mission. It established its headquarters at Lokoja and Onitsha, both places where the traders, too, made a base.

DAN FODIO'S CRUSADE

The nineteenth century wove together the three hitherto separate strands of Nigerian history: the Moslem North, the forest kingdoms of the South, and the British. In the North, the holy war of the Moslems united the Hausa country at a single stroke. The British, lying off the Southern ports and creeks, were steadily, sometimes imperceptibly, transforming their influence from commercial dominance to political power. Caught between the two pressures, the old Yoruba and Benin kingdoms went through a critical period of strife, warfare and, finally, decline.

Fulani settlement had been going on in the Hausa towns for the past four hundred years. The 'town' Fulani—so called to distinguish them from the nomadic 'cattle' Fulani—formed an intellectual elite. One of these, a teacher called Othman Dan Fodio, became a reforming preacher and writer. He attacked not only the laxity of the Islamic religious practice but also oppressive taxation in the Hausa states. He was a tutor to the children of Nafata, the King of Gobir, but his doctrines forced him in 1804 to flee from the court to Gudu, and it was there that the *jihad* was launched. It swept most of the Hausa kings off their thrones and established Fulani hegemony over all of Northern Nigeria except Bornu and the pagan areas of the Middle Belt. Like all crusades, its motives were not exclusively religious. The Fulani had the solidarity of an elite among the Hausa communities, but the revolt had the characteristics of a common man's (i.e. ordinary Hausa's) protest against oppressive government. The Fulani won their first battles against heavy odds and, by 1807, Zaria, Kano and other states had been subjugated.

It was a remarkably intellectual crusade. Dan Fodio expressed advanced views on women in a treatise denouncing the 'impious practices which affect this Hausa country'. He complained that 'most of our educated men leave their wives, their daughters and their captives morally abandoned, like beasts, without teaching them what God prescribed should be taught them'. While warning women not to be deceived by 'those who stress obedience to your husbands without telling you of obedience to God and to his Messenger', he nevertheless concluded that 'the woman owes submission to her husband, publicly as well as in intimacy . . . at least so long as he does not command what God condemns'.[24] Dan Fodio's son, Sultan Bello, who took secular control of the state, 'was much occupied with composition, and whenever he composed anything he used to issue it to the people, and read it to them, then become occupied with another composition'.[25] The explorer Clapperton in 1824 found Sultan Bello 'excessively polite', but a little daunting intellectually. 'He asks me a great many questions about Europe, and our religious distinctions. He was acquainted with the names of some of the more ancient sects and asked whether we were Nestorians or Soconians. To extricate myself from the embarrassment occasioned by this question I bluntly replied we were called Protestants.'[26]

The fiercest resistance to the *jihad* came from Bornu, where the fighting against the Fulani armies was organised by a man not unlike Dan Fodio himself—El Kanemi, a Moslem scholar who took command of the army and later took over power in the state. El Kanemi's defence was intellectual as well as military. He wrote to Sultan Bello to ask him 'why you are fighting us and enslaving our free people. If you say you have done this to us because of our paganism, then I say we are innocent of paganism, and it is far from our compound.' He brushed aside the complaint about 'the practice of the Emirs of riding to certain places for the purpose of making arms and giving sacrifices there'. His defence was that this did not make them pagans 'since not one of them claims that it is particularly efficacious'. Sultan Bello replied spiritedly that he had heard reports of Bornu 'that they make sacrifices to rocks and trees and regard the river as the Copts did the Nile in the days of the Jahiliya'. [27]

With remarkable speed after its establishment, the Fulani empire began to push southwards. The *jihad* had coincided with the already fairly well-established decline of the Oyo empire. In 1817, Afonja, the Yoruba governor (*Kakaufo*) of Ilorin, had tried to assert his independence. With the assistance of a local Fulani, Malam Alimi, and his band of Hausa and Fulani mercenaries, Afonja succeeded in winning his independence. Alimi was not sufficiently ambitious to pursue his advantage, but his son, Abdusalami, defeated Afonja and thus became the first Fulani Emir of Ilorin. This foothold was soon exploited. In 1837, the Ilorin sacked Old Oyo, capital of the ancient Oyo empire. Three years later they were themselves defeated at Oshogbo. The further southward progress of the *jihad* was arrested by the advent of the British. In Nigeria's First Republic, many Southerners feared that the departure of the British had opened the way for its continuance.

RISE OF MODERN COMMERCE

In the South the trade in slaves was yielding, for sound commercial as well as moral reasons, to the trade in palm oil. Its two centres were the Delta in the East and Lagos in the West. Just as Consul Beecroft had trouble securing the supply routes in the Delta, so he became involved in the turbulent politics of the Lagos hinterland. In 1851 he deposed Kosoko, the slave-trading King of Lagos, and substituted his more amenable uncle, Akitoye. The excuse was Kosoko's unremittent slaving; the real reason was Akitoye's greater pliability. Having interfered, it was no longer easy for the British to withdraw. Kosoko continued to harass the hinterland. Moreover, warfare among the Agba, a branch of the Yoruba, threatened the supply route from Abeokuta. The Foreign Office now instructed its consul to annex Lagos 'to secure for ever the free population of Lagos from the slave-traders and kidnappers who formerly oppressed them; to protect and develop the important trade of which their town is the seat; and to exercise an influence on the surrounding tribes which may, it is hoped, be permanently beneficial to the African race'.[28]

That was how King Docemo came to cede Lagos in 1861 to Acting-Consul McKoskry, in return for a pension of £1,030 a year. The incoming consul, Sir Richard Burton, described the scene— a classic episode in the acquisition of empire.

A flag-ship was slipped and rigged near the British Consulate, and Commander Bedington landed with his marines. A crowd of people and some chiefs were assembled at the palaver-house. The king, when civilly asked to sign away his kingdom, consented and refused, as the negro will, in the same breath. On the next day he affixed his mark, for of course he cannot write. . . . Without awaiting, however, the ceremony of signature, possession, nine tenths of the law, was at once entered upon. The 'Captain' read out the English proclamation very intelligibly to the natives, confirming 'the cession of Lagos and its dependencies'—a pleasantly vague frontier. Then followed a touching

77

scene. One Union Jack was hoisted in the town, another on the beach. *Prometheus Vinctus* saluted with 21 guns. The marines presented arms; three hundred fetish, or sanctified boys, as the convert people call them, sang a hymn, headed by their missionaries. And as we Englishmen must celebrate every event with a dinner . . . forty-four Oyinbos, Europeans, and Africo-Europeans, officials and merchants, sat down to meat upon the quarter-deck of the *Prometheus*, and by their brilliant speeches and loyal toasts added, as the phrase is, *éclat* to the great event.[29]

The Oyo empire of the Yoruba was now in full decline; its influence was to be replaced by that of a number of successor states. Ibadan developed as a refugees' city from its beginnings as a war camp in 1829, and found itself a main bulwark against further Ilorin progress to the South. Another bulwark was the town of Abeokuta, also a refugees' town, founded by the Yoruba group known as the Egba. An exacerbating factor in the apparently incessant warfare in this area was the continuing demand for slaves and the increasing difficulty of providing them. The Yoruba had for a century been merchants and brokers, buying slaves from the Hausa and selling to the Europeans at Porto Novo on the Slave Coast. The Fulani occupation of Ilorin cut off this source, and there was pressure to find slaves nearer at hand.

After the annexation of Lagos, its British Governor inevitably played his part in the wars and rivalries of the interior. When the Egba people blocked the roads between Lagos and Ibadan, Governor Glover retaliated by blockading their supplies. By 1871 Lagos was financially self-sufficient, with half a million pounds worth of trade annually. It could not afford to let the rivalry of two sets of middlemen interfere with business. By now there was a new climate of opinion in Britain about Africa. Competition with the French and the Germans necessitated firmer political action—and the opening up of the Niger had made this possible. By the time the British had established a consulate at Lokoja, at the confluence of the Niger and Benue rivers, in 1860, the trade of the Delta was worth over a million pounds a year to Britain.

But conditions were still not satisfactory for further consolidation. By 1878 four separate companies were established in the Delta area alone, none of them able to organise effective protection against raids. Such competition was wasteful, in view of the increasingly tempting opportunities for penetration in depth of the Niger hinterland. The way was open for a unifier and a convinced imperialist, a role filled by Taubman Goldie. This officer of the Royal Engineers arrived in the Delta in a steam launch in 1877, intending to sail up the Benue. The voyage was cut short by the death of his brother who was accompanying him, but 'on the journey back I conceived the ambition of adding the Region to the British Empire'.[30]

On a second visit, Goldie set about uniting the four companies into the United Africa Company. The company was given power to make treaties and it had its own fleet of gun boats. Subscribed capital began at £100,000, but later, to meet the challenge of the French companies, Goldie increased it to £1 million by offering shares to the public. For Sir Taubman Goldie (as he later became) unification of trading interests was only a means to an end. Declaring that his company 'was not actuated by purely commercial motives', he wrote to the Foreign Office that they were 'Englishmen first and investors afterwards'.[31] Goldie argued that 'with old established markets closing to our many factories, with India producing cotton fabrics not only for her own use but for export, it would be suicidal to abandon to our rival powers the only great remaining underdeveloped opening for British goods'.[32]

Goldie has been called the founder of modern Nigeria. The pressure of German and French competition, culminating in the establishment of a German protectorate over Cameroon in 1884, had eased the following year, when the Berlin Conference recognised British influence in its areas in return for its recognition of King Leopold of Belgium's rights in the Congo. In 1886 the Niger Company, as it was then called, was granted a royal charter giving

79

it political authority over the areas it controlled. It conquered Nupe and Ilorin in 1898, and founded the West African Frontier Force to protect its acquisitions from the French. Not until 1900 did the British government take over all the Company's territories and establish the Niger Coast Protectorate, the Lagos Colony Protectorate, and the Protectorate of Northern Nigeria.

The Benin empire was the last to hold out against the British in Southern Nigeria. In 1892, Oba Ovenramwen had signed a treaty accepting British protection and promising to outlaw human sacrifices and slavery. But five years later the British were complaining that the treaty was not being honoured. Acting-Consul Phillips set off to visit the Oba, but carelessly arrived during the Ague festival, during which an Oba was not supposed to see a non-Bini. In the affray that followed, Phillips and five of his party were killed, as well as most of their escort of 200 men. Within six weeks a punitive expedition of 1,500 men burnt the town. More than 2,000 of its bronze carvings were taken to Europe, and the Oba was deported to Calabar.

THE COMING OF LUGARD

After the government had taken over from the Niger Company in 1900, Sir Frederick Lugard became High Commissioner in the North. It has been said of him that 'a colonial governor can seldom have been appointed to a territory so much of which had never even been viewed by himself or any other European'.[33] Thomas Hodgkin has found much in common between the two great empire-building movements which marked the beginning and the end of the century—the Fulani and the British. 'Both succeeded in imposing, by a combination of diplomacy and military force, the authority of a single government over a large, politically heterogeneous nation. Both derived their dynamic from a missionary impulse.' [34]

Lugard has marked subsequent Nigerian history by his introduction of 'indirect rule'—the system of governing through established institutions and hierarchies instead of attempting to build new ones. In fact, given the resources at his disposal and the size of the area, he had little alternative. In his first annual report, he explained: 'The Fulani rule has been maintained as an experiment, for I am anxious to prove to this people that we have no hostility to them, and only insist on good government and justice, and I am anxious to utilise, if possible, their wonderful intelligence for they are born rulers.'[35] He undertook expeditions against Bornu, Yola Benue, Sokoto and Gwandu. The last two offered the stiffest opposition. The Sultan of Sokoto wrote to him: 'From us to you. I do not consent that anyone from you shall ever dwell with us. . . . Between us and you there are no dealings except as between Moslems and unbelievers, war, as God Almighty has enjoined on us. . . .'[36] When Lugard finally encountered the Sultan he had a pathetically small force at his disposal. But he had a trump card; in the style of Hilaire Belloc:

> Whatever happens we have got
> The Maxim gun and they have not.

4. From Colony to Nation

Each step of our constitutional advance has been purposefully
and peacefully planned, with full and open consultation, not only
between representatives of all the various interests in Nigeria, but
in harmonious co-operation with the administering power.
   —Sir Abubakar Tafawa Balewa, Independence Day, 1960.[1]

The defects in British administration have turned out to be a
blessing in disguise. For if British rule had been less inept than it
was, the opportunity for Nigerians to demonstrate that they are
qualified to manage their own affairs would have been corres-
pondingly reduced.—Chief Obafemi Awolowo, 1960.[2]

NIGERIA'S COLONIAL EXPERIENCE has been short and remarkably free from violence. Resistance there was: it began on the day
the British arrived and continued to the day they left. But once the
colony had been 'pacified', most of the protests were unviolent and
unheroic: there was neither a Mau-Mau uprising nor a Gandhi.
Even compared with the Gold Coast, whose colonial experience
was similar, the fight for freedom was sedate. When it was over,
Chief Awolowo regretted that 'our struggles for independence have
produced no martyr—no single national hero who is held in
reverence and affection by the vast majority of people in Nigeria'.[3]
   It was not that Nigerians failed to resent their colonial status,
nor did they lack potential heroes. Their weight of numbers and
diversity, the smallness of their educated elite, and the tardiness of
the colonial power in laying the foundations of a recognisable and
viable state, conspired to delay the assembly of the essential
ingredients of militant nationalism. By the time these came to the
boil, their usefulness was almost over: the winds of change were
already blowing on the government as well as on the governed. A

more basic reason for the relative gentleness of the struggle in West as opposed to East Africa was the absence of white settlers. It had always been colonial policy in West Africa to discourage settlers and, in any case, the climate was hardly tempting to the immigrant farmer.

What battle there was, was fought largely in words—and mostly moderate ones. When Herbert Macaulay founded the first nationalist party in Lagos in 1923, he based his newspaper attacks on the government on the rights of the people of Lagos as British subjects. He appealed to 'the manifold blessings of Pax Britannica' and used to end his articles with 'God save the King'.[4] Macaulay was the grandson of Samuel Crowther, a repatriated slave who had later become Bishop on the Niger. 'If ever there was a black English gentleman of his era, it was Herbert Macaulay', recalled Chief Anthony Enahoro, who had been a youthful admirer of his. 'Always impeccably dressed in starched, spotlessly white suit, black bow-tie knotted painstakingly, white buck shoes and sporting a white panama hat, he was the object of much adulation by the populace. One imagined he typified the term "Victorian gentleman".'[5]

The nationalist temperature rose in the late 1940s, when the post-war mood of freedom was felt more strongly by the nationalists than by the government. 'I hate the Union Jack with all my heart because it divides the people wherever it goes. . . . It is a symbol of persecution, of domination, a symbol of exploitation . . . of brutality. . . . We have passed the age of petition . . . the age of resolution, the age of diplomacy. This is the age of action—plain, blunt and positive action.'[6] That, from Mallam Abdallah, president of the radical Zikist Movement, was about as far as extreme words went. For that speech, made in 1949, Abdallah and his followers were punished—some fined, others sentenced to short terms of imprisonment. In the same year, twenty-one coal miners were shot dead by the police during a strike in Enugu, and four years later thirty-six people died in a riot in Kano. The Enugu trouble had been over wages rather than freedom and the shooting was fortuitously caused by a panicky British police officer. The Kano riot had not been exactly against the British, but was part of an argument between Northern and Southern politicians over the appropriate date for independence.

Incautious journalists sometimes went to prison for short periods. Anthony Enahoro, when he was editor of the Mid-West *Daily Comet*, was twice gaoled for seditious writing. But the principal nationalist figure of the time, Nnamdi Azikiwe, a proprietor of radical newspapers, the 'Lion of Africa', whose eloquence kept nationalism on the boil for two decades, rarely forgot basic editorial discretion. The nearest he ever got to gaol was in 1936, in his earliest days as a journalist, when he was editor of the Accra *African Morning Post*. Having been convicted for seditious publication, he successfully appealed on the ground that the prosecution had forgotten to prove he was editor on the day in question.

Azikiwe never advocated civil disobedience; nor did the other outstanding post-war nationalist leader, his rival Chief Awolowo. He, too, never went to gaol in the pre-independence period, though, ironically, he was gaoled for treasonable felony three years after independence. The Northern leader, the Sardauna of Sokoto, and his colleagues in the Northern Peoples Congress, actually opposed the agitation of Southern politicians for an early date for self-government, on the grounds that the North was not yet ready for it.

Nigeria's size and diversity made it harder than it was elsewhere for educated people to identify themselves with a 'nation'. In 1920 the Governor, Sir Hugh Clifford, made the point somewhat unkindly:

> It can only be described as farcical to suppose that . . . continental Nigeria can be represented by a handful of gentlemen drawn from a half-dozen coast towns—men born and bred in British-administered towns situated on the sea shore who, in the safety of British protection, have peacefully pursued their studies under British teachers, in British schools, in order to enable them to become ministers of the Christian religion or learned in the laws of England, whose eyes are fixed, not upon African native

history or tradition or policy, nor upon their own tribal obligations and duties to their Natural Rulers which immemorial
custom should impose on them, but upon political theories
evolved by Europeans to fit a wholly different environment, for
the government of peoples who have arrived at a wholly different
stage of civilisation.[7]

Even more unkindly, Sir Hugh went on:

Imagine what these gentlemen's experience would be if, instead
of travelling peacefully to Liverpool in a British ship they could
be deposited . . . among the cannibals of the Mame Hills . . . the
determinedly unsocial Mumuyes of the Muri Province or the
equally naked warriors of the Ibo country, and there left to explain
their claims to be recognised as the accredited representatives of
these their 'fellow nationals'.[8]

After the Second World War decolonisation was in vogue, and the
British scarcely resisted constitutional change. There began a more
or less gentlemanly tug-of-war between the government and the
small but rapidly growing minority among the governed who were
politically conscious. By the early 1950s, the argument was not
about whether independence would be granted, but about what
kind of independence and when.

The outstanding colonialists were scarcely more forbidding than
the nationalists, though few of them could claim to have been ahead
of their time. Lord Lugard, the first Governor of the whole of
Nigeria, warned at the beginning of the century that 'the preaching
of equality of Europeans and natives, however true from a doctrinal
point of view, is apt to be misapplied by people in a low stage of
development, and interpreted as an abolition of class distinction'.[9]
However, Lugard ruled with a relatively light touch. His policy
of indirect rule—preserving what he found in chiefly institutions
and local government hierarchies—ensured a smooth transition to
the British regime which in turn facilitated the transition to self-
government. Even more important, Lugard united the Northern

and Southern portions of Nigeria—albeit imperfectly—in 1914, and thus laid the first foundations of the modern Nigeria.

In the more heated post-war period, Sir Arthur Richards, who was Governor between 1943 and 1947, 'seemed to have a special knack for antagonising educated elements; in Nigeria, at least, his name is at the bottom of their popularity list'.[10] However, during Richards's period of office the Labour Party came to power in Britain and in 1947 sent out a younger and more modern Governor, Sir John Macpherson. For good measure they also sent 'one of the most liberal Nigerian Chief Secretaries'[11]—Hugh (later Sir Hugh) Foot. Macpherson almost immediately took steps to review the unpopular constitution introduced by Richards. Foot seemed to Chief Awolowo 'an official very much after my heart. He was a very honest and affable person; an exceptionally able and brilliant administrator, and a powerful and almost irresistible orator.'[12] After Macpherson came the last Governor (or Governor-General, as the post was to become under the 1954 constitution), Sir James Robertson. He 'proved to be the best type for the job. A warm Scotsman, practical, businesslike, and genial, he saw Nigeria through the last phase with as much success as any man could have had in the circumstances.'[13]

For all the reasonableness on both sides, for all the lack of bitterness, the product which emerged from a decade of negotiations between government and governed was far from satisfactory. Nigeria became independent with a federal structure which, within two years, was shaken by an emergency and, within five, had broken down in disorder, to be finally overthrown by two military coups and a civil war. Southern politicians, frustrated by the built-in domination of the more populous but also more backward Northern Region, increasingly blamed the British for having 'arranged it all' on the old 'divide and rule' principle. There is still a widespread feeling among Southern Nigerians that the British deliberately left the North in a dominating position because they found its conservatism both congenial and useful.

Specific criticisms of the edifice the British left behind are two:

that it was federal rather than unitary, and that, being federal, it broke the basic rules of federalism by allowing one part to dominate the rest. The weakness of the first charge is that it was not the British but the Nigerian politicians themselves who were the keenest federalists. 'Since the amalgamation [of Northern and Southern provinces of Nigeria] all the efforts of the British Government have been devoted to developing the country into a unitary state', complained Chief Awolowo in 1945. 'This is patently impossible; and it is astonishing that a nation with wide political experience like Great Britain fell into such a palpable error.'[14] Chief Awolowo had been arguing as early as 1941 'that the sheer territorial size of Nigeria necessitated the adoption of a federal form of constitution and hence the division of the country into regions, even if the inhabitants of Nigeria were linguistically or ethnically homogeneous'.[15] As late as 1951 the British introduced a new constitution which, though federal in form, was essentially unitary, in that all essential powers remained with the central government.[16] The drafting committee which drew it up reported that the problem which confronted it was unique. 'While other federations, the USA, Canada, Australia, etc., had been built by bringing together a number of independent states, they were engaged on the reverse process—that of the creation of a Federal Government by devolution.'[17]

The Nigerian constitutional historian, Kalu Ezera, admits that, after the constitutional conferences of 1953 and 1954, 'the problems were accentuated by the lack of effective leadership and vision of the Nigerian delegation. Once again it was proved that, to a large extent, the British administration held together the unity of Nigeria . . . It was Nigerian leaders with only the reluctant consent of the British Government, that created "three states and two territories" for Nigeria.'[18] After the conference Azikiwe's *West African Pilot* concluded that 'the revised constitution is the handiwork of Nigerians. Whatever may be the faults of the British, they cannot be accused of having influenced the decisions.'[19]

Given that Nigeria had to be federal, what was the right kind of federation? It is arguable that Britain's very preoccupation with unity led it into supporting the wrong kind. Of the three major Nigerian political parties, two—the National Council of Nigerian Citizens and the Action Group—advocated the division of Nigeria into more than three states. In 1943, Azikiwe, a late convert to federalism, was asking for twenty-five provinces or eight 'protectorates'. In 1947 Awolowo, the leading federalist, advocated a federation of eight states. In 1957 Azikiwe's party was asking for fourteen states, based on the existing provincial boundaries. Ezera, while approving the British role in these long negotiations, admits that a big obstacle in the creation of more states was 'the British official attitude which, in its formalistic concern for the unity of Nigeria, had hitherto been strongly opposed to what it regarded as "fragmentation" of the country—a view which had been held and restated by successive Colonial Secretaries'.[20] The nearest the British came to considering more states than three was the appointment of the Minorities Commission on the eve of independence in 1958. But this was concerned with the fears of minority groups rather than the political balance of the Federation. The Commission decided that such claims did not at that time warrant the creation of more states. The argument about more states than three (or four, as they later became) was never settled in the First Republic, but remained a nagging issue in politics.

With hindsight, it is tempting to argue that the British should have left either a unitary system, or a federation whose parts were more equal in size. However, it is more than doubtful if the Northerners could have been persuaded to enter a federation with the better-educated and more thrustful non-Moslem Southerners, unless the North's numerical strength were reflected in political power. Without hindsight, the arrangement must have seemed to the British a nice balance between the more dynamic (and therefore less predictable) South and the more backward (but apparently more stable) North. What nobody foresaw was that politics in an underdeveloped country might become too ruthless for so delicate an arrangement to work.

88

TOWARDS UNITY

In the haphazard method of its conquest and in the largely prag-
matic evolution of its administration, Nigeria was not untypical of
the proverbial absentmindedness with which the British acquired
their empire. The original motive had been to stop the Germans
from annexing the area; after that, pacification was essential for the
security of trade. The system of indirect rule which Lord Lugard
practised in the North was for a time extended to the South—
though here there were difficulties. In the South-West (later the
Western Region), Yoruba society was sufficiently well-endowed
with chiefly institutions for the system to work. Yoruba obas, just
like the Fulani emirs of the North, could maintain the peace within
their jurisdiction, though their authority was far more fragmented
than that of the emirs. South-Eastern society (later the Eastern
Region) was less well-endowed with kings. Administrative chiefs
had to be specially created and these, with their inevitable association with the tax collector, proved instantly unpopular. The
'warrant chiefs', as they were called, provided the main targets for
the wrath of the women rioters at Aba in 1929. In this Ibo town
women were, and still are, the big traders: crowds of them, fearing
they would now be taxed, attacked officials and warrant chiefs
alike, demanding for good measure that 'all the white men should
go back to their country'.

Colonial policy varied as governments changed in London, and,
in the earlier period, according to the ideas of such individualists
on the spot as Lord Lugard. At the turn of the century the spirit
informing British policy was that of Chamberlain's 'new imperia-
lism'; its emphasis was on trade, the opening up of communications
to foster trade, and the levying of indirect rather than direct taxes
to pay for administration. A recent writer has drawn attention to a
marked conflict between this policy, which was successfully
carried out in Southern Nigeria between 1900 and 1914, and Lord
Lugard's indirect rule in the North.[21] The Southern administration, which included Lagos and the Yorubaland protectorates

after 1906, had about twenty Africans in the ninety senior posts: it was a 'golden age' for the civil service,[22] with all the apparatus necessary for a commercially-oriented government. Real administration, much more than Lugard's, was carried on by chiefs. In contrast to this system, Lugard's 'indirect rule' was one of military conquest. Governing an area too vast for effective administration, Lugard neglected to build civil departments or foster trade. Even his choice of administrative capital, Kaduna, was strategic rather than commercial.

It was to Lugard that the task fell of unifying the Northern and Southern portions of Nigeria in 1914. As a result, it was his methods and not those being practised in the South that prevailed. 'To cause the minimum of administrative disturbance'[23] he kept the gigantic North intact and kept the two administrations separate. This last decision clearly marked the future.

THE COLONIAL LEGACY

After the Second World War the political climate favoured the quick growth of representative institutions, and the experiment of indirect rule in the South was abandoned in favour of English-type local government, with county councils in the East and district councils in the West. These several and hybrid institutions survived throughout the First Republic and uniformity was never achieved. One reason why indirect rule was abandoned in the South was that it had provided no opportunity for educated young men to play a part in public affairs. The experiment with British-type councils largely solved this problem but created the far greater problem of corruption. Traditions of integrity in public service, rare and precarious enough anywhere, are not easily nurtured in colonial conditions, where the resources of the colonial power are felt to be unlimited. Corruption in Nigeria's local councils soon reached disastrous proportions, both in its financial aspect and in the political use made of local officials by regional governments during elections. Within three years of independence, scores of councils in both Eastern and Western Regions stood dissolved and were replaced by caretaker committees, sometimes as corrupt as the councils.

The profoundest of colonial legacies, that of education, had much in common with the 'let-well-alone' approach of indirect rule. Education has given Nigeria its most 'British' attributes—its schools and colleges, its language, its religion and many of the intangible intellectual and social attitudes of its people. In contrast to the French idea that civilisation is one and that it is French, including such things as *départments* and *cercles* as well as *lycées*, the British were content to make do as far as possible with what they found. While children in Dahomey or Cameroon were learning, from one notorious textbook at least, *'nos ancêtres etaient les Gaules, et ils avient les cheveux roux'*, Nigerian children were not even taught English until their education was already three or four years under way. Lord Lugard considered that 'the premature teaching of English . . . inevitably leads to utter disrespect for British and native ideals alike, and to a denationalised and dis-organised population'.[24] The result of these attitudes is apparent to a traveller today: if he hears an educated voice behind him in a bar in Dahomey he may have to turn round to see if it belongs to a Frenchman or a Dahomeyan—a thing he would rarely have to do in Lagos or Accra. However, the Lugard approach had its positive side. His system fostered cultural self-confidence which today puts Nigeria well ahead of the French-speaking African world in letters and the arts.

No one can accuse the British of having been over-enthusiastic, either in the quantity of education they provided or in the degree to which it was adapted to the needs of an embryonic nation. The vast Northern Region, which in 1960 had over half of Nigeria's population of nearly 50 million, had only forty-one secondary schools in that year (the whole of Nigeria had 883). The North produced its first university graduate nine years before independence; in 1960 Nigeria's two universities had 1,395 students enrolled. Education was, and to a large extent still is, dominated by missionaries. They, too, learnt something of the 'let-well-alone' philosophy. In the early days their teachers and priests banned dancing and sculptures as well as idolatry and polygamy. Later, they relaxed and adopted a more sophisticated cultural attitude. But Nigeria has not escaped the common experience in developing countries of semi-educated people being left 'between two cultures' —uprooted from village morality and too poor, both economically and spiritually, to adopt a new one.

The British, after all, had the orthodox colonial preoccupations: maintaining law and order, stimulating the supply of raw materials, creating demand for the sale of manufactures—and raising taxes to pay for the administration. Only in the last decade did the additional purpose creep in of preparing for self-government and independence. The main economic legacies were the introduction of more or less lucrative cash crops—groundnuts, cocoa, palm oil and cotton—the exploitation of timber and tin and the exploration for oil. There was no over-zealousness in building roads, railways or telecommunications, but these were quite equal to the needs of a colonial economy. Nigeria's economic inheritance from this regime was inevitably lop-sided. In times of high world prices, cash crops were encouraged at the expense of food crops, leaving independent Nigeria—at a time of low and still falling prices— with a shortage of food.

It is a truism that education and the advent of wealth stimulated the demand for independence. But what gave bite to that demand was another aspect of the colonial legacy—the growth, in the administration, of conciliar, then representative, then elective, and finally democratic procedures. Nigeria's first legislative council dates back as far as the annexation of Lagos in 1861. It had no power and it was in no sense representative; its function was to advise the Governor (who himself sat on it), and its eleven members included only two Africans. But it was a beginning. After the unification of the North and the South in 1914, Lugard set up a Nigerian Council of thirty-six members. Of these only thirteen were not government officials and of the thirteen only six were

Nigerians, nominated (not yet elected) to represent 'as far as may be'[25] their country. This was enough for the seed to germinate. The bargaining process, in which the nationalists asked for more and each time got less than they asked for but something, was about to begin.

EARLY NATIONALISM

If nationalism was resistance to the foreigner, it had an unbroken tradition from the very first appearance of the British. During the 'off-shore' stage of the European presence, the chiefs of Bonny and Opobo opposed penetration into the hinterland, to protect their commercial interests as middlemen. The occupation of Lagos, the first part of the 'on-shore' stage, was effected by force. So too was the British occupation of the Delta area, of the Ijebu and Yoruba areas, and of the Benin territories. In the North, too, it was the Maxim gun which enabled Lugard to reduce the last resistance.

The earliest organised protest was probably that of the palm-oil middlemen of Brass, in the Niger Delta, in 1895. When their interests were threatened by the expansion into the interior of the Royal Niger Company, they attacked and destroyed the Company's property with a force of 1,500 men. In 1918, the Egba people in Yorubaland, and in 1929, the women of Aba, revolted against taxation. These risings were put down by force: fifty of the Aba women were killed by the police in a punitive raid. Lagos, as the centre of sophistication, had the most unbroken tradition of protest. There was a tax revolt in 1895, a protest against the water rate in 1904 and a rumpus over the Land Acquisition Act in 1907. Lagos citizens formed a Peoples' Union as early as 1908.

The first Lagos leaders did not happen to be Nigerians at all. Edward Blyden, one of the earliest nationalist newspapermen, was born in the Virgin Islands. John Payne Jackson, who became editor of the *Lagos Weekly Record*, was a Liberian. In association with Patrick Campell, the head of a separatist Christian sect, and Ernest Ikoli, another journalist, Jackson launched the Nigerian Improvement Association in 1920. In the same year, the National

93

Congress of British West Africa was founded, as an attempt to lift nationalism on to a West African plane.

The National Congress did not advocate a single West African state, but merely a legislative council in each territory, half of whose members would be elected Africans. This seemed a far cry from the Nigerian Council of those days which, like its successors right down to the decade before independence, was only advisory. The Congress went further and demanded a House of Assembly, including 'financial representatives' elected by the people to control taxation, revenue and expenditure. It seems that, in spite of the sarcastic comments he made at the time, the Governor, Sir Hugh Clifford, took this recommendation to heart. The constitution of 1922 provided for the first Nigerian elections. It established a legislative council of forty-six members, of whom nineteen were unofficial. Only four of these were elected (three from Lagos and one from Calabar). Electors had to be adult males, British subjects, with an income of £100 and twelve months residence in their home town.

This early introductions of elections, limited though they were, stimulated political thought and activity. In the year after the new constitution came into force, Herbert Macaulay formed his Nigerian National Democratic Party (NNDP). It was a Lagos party, supported by chiefs and market women alike—but not by the more Westernised professional classes.[26] Already the seeds of later divisions had been sown. The more 'modern' people in Lagos, in alliance with the largely Christian, detribalised working class Ibo, formed a rival group in 1934: the Lagos Youth Movement, later called the Nigerian Youth Movement (NYM). The journalist Ernest Ikoli, a lawyer H. O. Davies, and a doctor J. C. Vaughan, were its architects. In 1937, another journalist, Nnamdi Azikiwe, joined the NYM and the following year it fought the Lagos Town Council election and won all three legislative council seats for Lagos. It formed branches in other towns and the *Daily Service* became its official mouthpiece. Only in 1941, when Azikiwe broke from it, did the NYM cease to have massive support.

One natural breeding ground for nationalism was provided by

94

the tribal associations. These social self-help groups, formed to look after members of particular communities both at home and in their travels, have an unbroken history and are still numerous and active today. The Ibibio Union, formed mainly to finance scholarship, dates back to 1928; the Ibo Union of Lagos, formed in 1939, became the Ibo Federal Union in 1944. At this stage a group of Yoruba students and professionals felt that Azikiwe, an Ibo, had given politics too 'tribal' a bias. Obafemi Awolowo, a Yoruba law student in London, formed his own pan-Yoruba movement—the *Egbe Omo Oduduwa* (Sons of the Society of Oduduwa), out of which the Action Group later grew. In 1948 the Ibo Federal Union became, with Azikiwe as president, the Ibo State Union—a body which came to play an important political role.

A part was also played by commercial and professional associations such as the Lagos Fishermen's Association, or the Palm Wine Sellers Organisation, which proliferated in the 1930s. Trade unions also helped. African clerks formed the Southern Nigerian Civil Servants' Union in 1912; the Mechanics Union and the Teachers' Union were born in the 1920s. Cultural groups, such as Azikiwe's Young Man's Literary Association, also played their part. Groups were also constantly formed to ventilate specific grievances. Opposition to an official plan to replace the Oxford and Cambridge school certificates with a Nigerian one—which looked too much like an admission of an inferior educational status—was organised through a National School Committee, and the official plan was duly abandoned. Activity at home was butressed by activity abroad: the West African Students' Union was active in London for twenty years from 1925.

THE RISE OF AZIKIWE

A new chapter in nationalist history began in 1937, with the return of Azikiwe. After his studies in the United States, he had spent three years in the Gold Coast as editor of the *African Morning Post*. Even before his return he had become a legend: that an Ibo boy (at a time when Yoruba were in the vanguard of development), the son of a clerk, should be the author of a book (*Liberia in World Affairs*), a graduate in political science, religion and philosophy, and editor of a nationalist newspaper, was enough to make him one. To all this was added Azikiwe's exceptional charm, handsome face and special gift for oratory, characterised by lavish use of 'long, technical, unusual and foreign-sounding words, calculated to dazzle the wholly unsophisticated audiences'.[27]

Azikiwe's story was very much an Ibo story—of the local boy who came home famous and wealthy after a long and arduous stay abroad. He was even born 'abroad'—at Zungeru in the Northern Region, where his father, a man from Onitsha in the Eastern Region, served as a clerk with the Nigeria Regiment. After early education at mission schools, Azikiwe had almost as much trouble as Chief Awolowo, who was to become his political rival, in finding enough money to study abroad. After three years as a government clerk and an abortive attempt at being a stowaway, he finally set off for the United States with £300 in his pocket—all that his father had been able to save and borrow. He has attributed his choice of America rather than Britain for his studies to the example of an early Gold Coast hero, Bishop Aggrey. The early experiences of a sensitive boy as the son of an African clerk in a British service probably also gave him an anti-British bias. He managed to attend Storer College in West Virginia and later went on to both Howard and Lincoln universities, working his way as a coal miner, casual labourer, dish-washer and even boxer. His encounters with penury and the distasteful racial atmosphere in the South led him at one stage to attempt suicide.

On his return to Nigeria, Azikiwe invested about £1,000 of his savings from his Accra editorship and another £4,000 borrowed from friends to establish the Zik Press Ltd, and he founded the *West African Pilot*—the daily paper which was to make itself and Azikiwe synonymous with nationalism for the next fifteen years. The *Pilot* boisterously championed every nationalist cause, highlighting every error or disgrace of the government, and at the same time lost no chance to enhance 'Zik's' personal fame and prestige. Typical of the *Pilot*'s causes was that of the Bristol Hotel incident of 1947, when a half-caste official of the Colonial Office, in Lagos as part of a delegation, was not allowed to take up his reserved accommodation because the hotel was for Europeans only. The resultant furore in the press temporarily united the nationalist movement, and the Governor was persuaded to outlaw all forms of discrimination. A more sensational newspaper story was that of an alleged attempt by the authorities to have Azikiwe assassinated—a story which was never substantiated. The passions aroused by this incident gave rise to the Zikist Movement, which began as a group dedicated to the personal defence of Azikiwe. It soon developed into a radical political body—so radical that the cautious Azikiwe himself soon declared that he was 'not a Zikist'.

The *Pilot*'s nationalism was, as the paper's name suggests, African rather than Nigerian, constantly reflecting Azikiwe's passionate preoccupation with the dignity of the African and the fallacy of the myths about European superiority. The paper was a success commercially as well as politically. It was the first paper to appeal to the growing class of clerks and artisans, students and teachers and, in general, to the young—mirroring its aspirations and formulating its ideas. It was also the first paper to appeal specifically to the Ibo, hitherto a neglected and 'backward' tribe in relation to the Yoruba. In this Ibo appeal lay the germs of later conflicts. For all Zik's universality of spirit, he was self-consciously Ibo, complete with the characteristic chip on the shoulder of a member of an underprivileged group who had 'made good'. Chief Awolowo, who was to become the champion of the Yoruba in face of the 'challenge', complained on one occasion that the *Pilot* even distorted its football reporting to favour the Ibo.

As if banished from the Garden of Eden, Nigerian nationalism was now steadily losing its innocence of tribal consciousness, and Ibo-Yoruba rivalry began to assume political proportions. In the year after Azikiwe's return, the Nigerian Youth Movement, of which he immediately took the lead, defeated Herbert Macaulay's

Nigerian National Democratic Party in the legislative council elections, gaining all three Lagos seats. However, Azikiwe's leadership soon came to be resented by a section of the Yoruba as being aggressively tribal. 'It seemed clear to me that [Azikiwe's] policy was to corrode the self respect of the Yoruba people as a group; to build up the Ibo as a "master race" ', thought Awolowo in 1940.[28] So the *Pilot* of Azikiwe and the *Daily Service* of Ernest Ikoli began a press war which was a microcosm of the coming struggle between the Ibo and the Yoruba.

POST-WAR NATIONALISM

The 1939–45 war gave immense new impetus to nationalism. Two Nigerian divisions served in the Middle East, East Africa, Burma and India, where they underwent the usual service propaganda about freedom and democracy. The 1940 Commonwealth Development and Welfare Act stipulated that trade unions should be formed—and in Nigeria the number of unions rose during the war from twelve (with less than 5,000 members) to eighty-five (with 30,000 members). The unions' wartime preoccupations were with the cost of living, which had quadrupled with no corresponding wage increase. Only European government staff were entitled to cost-of-living allowances. In 1945 seventeen unions, involving some 30,000 workers, went on strike for thirty-seven days, involving the post office, the railways and government technicians. At the end of it, an enquiry was promised. However, trade unions did not live up to their early promise as an effective political force. Then, as now, they were too fragmented, poor in bargaining power in conditions of massive unemployment, and weak in leadership.

After the war, as the government and the governor pushed and pulled one another in the direction of reform, the pace of change quickened. The government enacted no fewer than five new constitutions—each bringing Nigerians into greater participation in government, each bitterly criticised as not going far enough. This period saw the crystallisation of the political parties which were to dominate post-independence politics: the Ibo-dominated National Congress of Nigeria and the Cameroons (NCNC—later called the National Congress of Nigerian Citizens), the Yoruba Action Group and the Hausa-Fulani Northern People's Congress (NPC).

Sir Arthur Richards, who was Governor at the end of the war, belonged to the Churchill era and his temperament well reflected his prime minister's pledge that he had 'not become the King's First Minister to preside over the liquidation of the British Empire'. The constitution Richards introduced in 1946 was objectionable to nationalists both in the manner of its presentation and in its matter. It was drawn up without consultation. As soon as he read it Chief Awolowo pronounced that it 'retains some of the objectionable features of the old, contains unsavoury characteristics of its own, and falls short of expectation'.[29] The constitution referred to 'greater participation by Africans in discussion of their own affairs'. The word 'discussion' appalled the nationalists who felt that 'management' would have been appropriate. After much agitation 'management' was eventually substituted. The Richards constitution provided, for the first time, a legislative council for all Nigeria, plus three regional councils. On the one hand this gave Nigeria a unitary tendency, in that it integrated North and South in a common council; on the other hand it laid the first seeds of regionalism in setting up the regional councils. All the councils had 'unofficial' majorities, but the regional councils had no legislative power and could not appropriate revenue. Moreover, the 'unofficial' members included chiefs and emirs, whose comfortable, conservative presence always assured the government of a de facto majority. Nor was there any advance in the elective principle. Only Lagos and Calabar had elected seats. The nationalists condemned the whole arrangement as a calculated deception.

In the nationalist camp, the post-war years were Azikiwe's greatest. His popularity was solid among workers, clerks, artisans and teachers of all tribes and also among the non-Yoruba 'intelligentsia'. The origin of his party, the NCNC, goes back to a meeting in 1944 of the National Union of Students, under the chairmanship of Herbert Macaulay. It resolved to form a National Council of Nigeria, representing parties, tribal unions and trade unions, to work towards 'self-government within the British Empire'. Azikiwe was president and Macaulay general secretary. The Nigerian National Democratic Party (NNDP) soon affiliated and by January 1945 the National Council also had over eighty trade unions attached to it. The party's name was now changed to the National Council of Nigeria and the Cameroons. Its real fame began with the general strike of 1945, when an NCNC national tour raised £13,500 for the strikers. Three members of the party, including Azikiwe, were elected to the legislative council.

AWOLOWO AND THE ACTION GROUP

By this time it seemed clear to Awolowo from Azikiwe's statements 'and from [his] general political and journalistic manoeuvres over the years, that his great objective was to set himself up as a dictator over Nigeria and to make the Ibo nation the master race. It would appear, according to his reckoning, that the only obstacle in the path of his ambition was the Yoruba intelligentsia and these must be removed at all costs.'[30] Obafemi Awolowo, who became not merely the Yoruba's champion but a politician of a stature at least equal to Azikiwe's, is the son of an Ijebu (a sub-group of the Yoruba) farmer. He was orphaned in childhood and his higher education was long frustrated by lack of funds. It was not until 1944, when he was thirty-five, that he managed to get to London to study law. By this time he had already been editor of the *Nigerian Worker* and secretary of the Ibadan branch of the Nigerian Youth Movement. In London Awolowo resolved 'that before I again entered into politics I would see to it that Yorubas evolved an ethnic solidarity among themselves just as the Ibibios and the Ibos had done, in order to ensure a strong and harmonious federal union among the peoples of Nigeria'.[31] Five years after founding the *Egbe Omo Oduduwa* in London, the time seemed ripe for action at home.

The shortcomings of the 1946 constitution had been obvious to all and the newly-elected Labour government in Britain took early steps to liberalise it. The new Governor, Sir John Macpherson, immediately arranged to hasten Nigerianisation in the civil service, and set in motion an elaborate programme of popular consultation to determine what type of constitution Nigerians really wanted. This unprecedented grass-roots consultation began at the level of village councils, which sent representatives to divisional meetings which, in turn, acted as electoral colleges to select delegates to provincial conferences. The provincial conferences discussed the issues raised before sending representatives to the regional conference, where they were joined by all the regional parliamentarians. Finally came the general conference which had the final say. At each level, the first of fourteen questions put as the basis of discussion was: 'Do we wish to see a fully centralised system with all legislative and executive power concentrated at the centre or do we wish to develop a federal system . . . ?'

It was a foregone conclusion that the federalists would have their way. The spirit of regionalism seemed taken to its logical conclusion when the emirs of Zaria and Katsina warned the general conference that unless the Northern Region were allotted fifty per cent of the seats in the central legislature it would ask for separation from the rest of Nigeria on the arrangements existing before 1914.[32] However, the constitution that finally emerged was federal only in form. The regional assemblies could now legislate on nineteen specific subjects, but the central legislature was not thereby precluded from legislating on the same subjects. Real power still lay at the centre. In particular, regional bills were still subject to the approval of the Governor and his Council of Ministers. The main advance in the new constitution was the extension of the elective principle. All regional houses now had a majority of elected members, and members of the central legislature were elected through the regional assemblies. Outside Lagos and Calabar, where direct elections were held, a three-tiered electoral college system was introduced. All adult male taxpayers were now entitled to vote in the primary elections.

Like its predecessors, the Macpherson constitution was a compromise. It was bitterly attacked by Azikiwe and the NCNC on the grounds that the three-regional structure would artificially divide the country. Azikiwe preferred a division into more smaller units, on ethnic lines, and he also criticised the obviously conservative weighting in the electoral arrangements. In the event, the constitution was destined to be even more short-lived than its predecessors.

From the politicians' point of view, the extension of the elective element provided a new opportunity. In 1949, when Awolowo returned from London, the outline of the new Macpherson constitution was already known, and the NCNC had good prospects of forming a government in the West. The Nigerian Youth Movement was effective in Lagos only, while Awolowo's *Egbe* was too conservative to gather mass support. In that year, a meeting in Awolowo's house in Ibadan decided that, to win the election in the West, professional and other educated Yoruba had to be encouraged to return to their home towns and villages to muster support. To achieve this, a political wing of the *Egbe* was formed and this became known as the Action Group. It was not a radical party; in fact one of its first preoccupations was to gain the support of the obas.

THE NORTHERN PEOPLE'S CONGRESS

Two of Nigeria's main political strands—the nation-wide but Ibo-orientated NCNC and the more frankly Yoruba Action Group—were now woven. The third, the party of the North, was the last on the scene. The largely Moslem, tradition-bound society of Northern Nigeria was not—and still is not—the ideal breeding ground for a political party. However, the North's tiny minority of educated men were by no means immune from rebelliousness—against the British or against the conservatism of their own rulers.

The Northerners began with such relatively innocent cultural and social organisations as the Bauchi General Improvement

Union, or the Youth Circle at Sokoto, all of which flourished in the 1940s. In 1948 Dr A. R. B. Dikko, the Region's first doctor, and Abubakar Imam, editor of a Hausa newspaper, formed the Northern Nigeria Congress. At its inaugural meeting in Kano, three hundred delegates professed 'social and cultural objectives', but their real aims were the reform and democratisation of the country, and also to capture power for Northerners in the self-government process. The Congress changed its name to Northern People's Congress (NPC). The meeting was held in a suitably conservative atmosphere. However, when a District Officer recommended that the delegates proceed cautiously, a Sokoto schoolmaster, Mallam Aminu Kano, gave a reply which has since become famous: 'You may tell us to go by camel but we will go by airplane.'[33] The radical who made that reply did not stay long with the NPC. Aminu Kano's Northern Elements Progressive Union (NEPU) began in 1950 as a vanguard group within the NPC. But the following year it broke away and later remained the principal opposition group in the North.

By 1951 the NPC had sixty-five branches, with 6,000 members; it was now a fully-fledged political party, formed not against the British but as a Northern counterweight to the NCNC and the Action Group. This was to be the dominant theme of Nigerian politics until the end of the First Republic. The NPC, with political control of the most populous Region and therefore of the majority of seats in the Federal House, was able to dominate federal politics —but lived in perpetual fear that one day the South might unite and challenge that power. Sir Ahmadu Bello, the proud, imperiously handsome 'war prince' who was to become its leader became, ipso facto, Nigeria's most powerful politician.

The Sardauna was thought of in the South and abroad as a 'feudal' Moslem religious leader. He did indeed lay great stress on his descent from Othman Dan Fodio, the Fulani religious reformer and founder of the Sokoto empire, and on the fact that he saw his main mission as preserving the religion and traditions of the emirates. It is also true that towards the end of his life he became obsessed with religion and coveted the succession to the sultanship, held by his uncle. But the Sardauna was essentially a politician. The title means 'war prince'; the spiritual overlord of the Moslems was the Sultan. The Sardauna's conservatism was partly an insistence on the need to protect the essentials of Northern society against the threat of erosion and domination from the South. It was also partly a front—a gimmick, used in defiance of the Southern politicians. He was not nearly as reactionary as he liked to pretend. The North's policies on education, industrialisation and the stimulation of agriculture were not essentially different from those of the other Regions. In the year before independence the North enacted a new penal code; two years later it launched almost as ambitious a programme of educational expansion as had already been effected in the South. If the North was backward, it was because of its remoteness from the economic and cultural stimulation which the South experienced under British rule. The sheer size and poverty of the population, the thin spread of resources and the Moslem tendency to fatalism also played their part. All this was resolutely 'played down' under the Sardauna's brave front of defiance.

Like many of his colleagues among the North's small elite, the Sardauna was educated at the crack Katsina College, where the purest English in Nigeria was heard and where cricket, fives and polo were played. The boys, would-be teachers in the Moslem emirates, were enjoined by Governor Clifford at the official opening in 1922 to teach their future charges 'not only the lessons learned from books . . . but the way that good Muhammedans should live, the good manners, good behaviour and the courteous deportment without which mere book learning is of little worth'.[34] Bello was captain of fives, a game he continued to play throughout his life.

After three years of teaching at Sokoto Middle School, he became District Head of his native Rabah, and then served the Sokoto Native Authority at its head office. In 1944 the Sultan's court sentenced him to a spell of imprisonment for alleged discrepancies in a tax account, but it was rumoured that he had been framed and he was released on appeal. After completing a local government course in England he became secretary to the Sokoto Native Authority; he was also one of the founders of the Northern People's Congress. He became leader of the party in the regional House. Even after election to the Federal House in 1952 (central legislators were chosen from among the regional ones), he continued to concentrate on regional affairs. He became successively the regional Minister of Works, of Local Government and Community Development and, finally, in 1954, at the age of forty-five, Premier of the North. As Premier, the Sardauna was an even more convinced federalist than Awolowo. For him, a federal system was 'the only guarantee that the country will progress evenly all over, for *we* can spend the money we receive, and the money we raise, in the directions best suited to us. To show what I mean, you have only to consider the former backwardness of our educational and medical provision, compared with that of areas near Lagos.'[35]

SEARCH FOR A CONSTITUTION

For all Macpherson's good intentions, his 1951 constitution was destined to break down within two years. The new-found division of loyalties within each of the three major parties, as between the parliamentary group in Lagos on the one hand and the party headquarters in the Region on the other, made responsible government difficult. The constitution gave federal ministers no ministries to be responsible for. Nor was there any provision for a federal prime minister. The three dominant politicians, the Sardauna, Awolowo and Azikiwe, concentrated on the Regions, not the centre—the first two by preference and the last because he was defeated in an attempt to win a Lagos seat in the Federal House. He became leader of the opposition in the West (Lagos was at that time part of the Western Region). His absence from both the federal centre and his own Eastern Region threw the NCNC into disarray, and in 1953 a stalemate between the parliamentary party and a group of ministers resulted in the defeat of the appropriation bill in the Eastern House, and the eventual dissolution of the House. The Macpherson constitution seemed to have broken down at regional level.

At the federal level, things went no better. In 1953 Anthony Enahoro, an Action Group member, tabled a motion calling on the Federal House of Representatives to accept 'as a primary political objective the attainment of self-government for Nigeria in 1956'.[36] The leader of the NPC, the Sardauna, put a counter-motion, substituting for the phrase 'in 1956' the words 'as soon as practicable'.[37] Knowing that the preponderance of Northern members would inevitably result in their defeat, the Action Group and the NCNC together agreed to walk out of the House if the North used its majority to defeat the Enahoro motion. It did use it, and they did walk out.

That summer the conference which finally put Nigeria on the federal path met in London. It was a fiery meeting, illustrating both the unpredictable character of Nigerian politics and the strong centrifugal forces within it. The Action Group and the NCNC went to London in an alliance, both parties agreeing to demand self-government for 1956 (if not for the whole country then for the South at least) and agreeing that Nigeria should be federal. The NPC went with an eight-point plan that would, in effect, have made Nigeria into a loose confederation, co-operating only over the collection of customs revenue and over defence. However, in London the NCNC-Action Group alliance abruptly split on the question of Lagos: the Action Group wanted it for the Western Region while the NCNC wanted it to be federal territory. When Awolowo failed to get his way he openly threatened that the West would secede. He was persuaded to back down only by the firmness of the Colonial Secretary, who warned him that 'any attempt to secure the secession of the Western Region from the Federation would be regarded as an act of force'.[38] The NPC also abandoned its eight-point plan and it was agreed that the Southern Regions would be granted self-government in 1956.

THE NEW REGIONALISM

The 1953 conference did agree on the broad lines of the first truly federal constitution. Public and judicial services were to be regionalised, while revenue arrangements were to place the emphasis on the principle of 'derivation' as well as of 'need'. The resultant 1954 constitution deprived the central government of its right to approve regional legislation; its powers were restricted to a small list of federal subjects, including defence, foreign policy and communications. There was also a 'concurrent' legislative list, including commerce, agriculture, labour and industrial development. All other subjects were 'regional'. There were to be regional premiers but not yet a federal prime minister. The Governor-General was to run the Federal government. The new regionalism, while satisfying the major politicians, gave rise to misgivings. 'Economically as well as politically there will be three Nigerias', complained the influential weekly paper *West Africa*. It was feared that the Western Region, then the richest because of its cocoa, would become richer still in relation to the others. The disparity was likely to be further increased by the regionalisation of the marketing boards.

The 1954 constitution further advanced the elective element in politics, though uniformity was not achieved. In the Eastern Region universal suffrage for both men and women over twenty-one was introduced, while in the West only adult males who paid tax were to vote. The North continued to vote by the indirect college system, in which only adult taxpayers were entitled to vote and which was heavily weighted in favour of traditional interests.

The resulting federal elections of 1954 were Nigeria's first venture into democratic electioneering. It is now remembered mainly for the defeat of the Action Group in the West, its home territory. This was attributed partly to the non-Yoruba elements in the Mid-West areas who resented the frankly Yoruba orientation of the party, and partly to the loss of votes on account of rising taxes and an increasingly authoritarian tendency in the government. The elections produced the first embryo of the later political scene. No party won an absolute majority. The NPC, with 79 seats out of 184, went into coalition with the NCNC, which had won 61, leaving the Action Group in opposition.

Putting the finishing touches to the independence constitution produced no serious obstacles. At a quiet constitutional conference in 1957 the Colonial Secretary refused to draw what he called a 'blank cheque' for independence in 1959, but endorsed the dates for self-government. The Eastern and Western Regions became self-governing in 1957 and the North, in accordance with its own wishes, in 1959. It was also decided that there must be a Federal Prime Minister and Alhaji Abubakar Tafawa Balewa, the NPC's deputy leader and Federal Minister of Transport, became the first to occupy the post. No one was surprised that this post went to him and not to his party leader, the Sardauna: the latter had already stated publicly that he preferred to send 'his lieutenant' to Lagos.

Balewa was perhaps the only politician who survived office in the First Republic with a reputation as a national figure. In 1957, at forty-five, this slow-speaking, conservatively-minded yet palpably shrewd ex-schoolteacher seemed well suited, especially by his phlegmatic temperament, to hold the country together. In the North Balewa was an exception to the rule that leaders hailed from Fulani and aristocratic families. He was the son of an unimportant District Head in Bauchi, belonging to the Jere tribe, a branch of the Hausa. From local schools he graduated to Katsina College, the school through which many of his later political colleagues and opponents had also passed. He began teaching in Bauchi, studying privately at the same time for the Senior Teacher's Certificate. He was forty-three before he was able to attend the Institute of Education at London University. When he came back he said: 'I return to Nigeria with new eyes because I have seen people who lived without fear, who obeyed the law as part of their nature, who knew individual liberty.'

He was drawn inevitably into politics, as a member of the tiny class of educated people, at a time when, suddenly, legislators were needed. After a spell as education officer to the local Native

Authority (local government), he became a member of the first Northern House of Assembly and was unanimously elected from there to the Nigerian Legislative Council. As Minister of Works, he became one of the original group of central government ministers in 1952. Two years later, as Minister of Transport in the new Council of Ministers, he found himself the senior minister and leader of the biggest party in the House. Already he had been marked out by the British: his knighthood in the 1960 New Year Honours followed a CBE by some years.

The final five years of the pre-independence negotiations were dominated by the question of minorities, and by the related question of whether or not there should be more Regions. 'The spate of claims and counter-claims for separate states, the volley of allegations of oppression fired at a certain regional government, the exaggerated fears expressed by representatives of minorities against certain majority groups, and an apparent general feeling of insecurity' had, according to Azikiwe, placed the Colonial Secretary 'at a vantage point' in his stalling tactics over the date for independence at the 1957 conference.[39] In fact, as independence approached, it was becoming increasingly clear to minority groups in each Region that the parties soon to wield power drew their respective strengths from the majority groups in each case and the minorities might suffer as a result. Naturally, any 'separatist' ideas were on the whole opposed by the majority parties who could with justice point to the opportunism of some minority politicians whose chief aim appeared to be to carve an empire for themselves. On the other hand, supporting a minority group in someone else's Region could be a useful weapon against rival parties—a kind of electoral fifth column.

This was to be a dominant theme in later politics. For years the NCNC, in power in the Eastern Region, was to support the United Middle Belt Congress, which sought to carve out of the Northern Region the country of the Tiv and other non-Hausa groups. The NPC, in its turn, supported the Rivers State Movement, composed of non-Ibo elements in the Eastern Region, also anxious for a state of their own. Only the Action Group seemed to take the need for more Regions seriously enough to recommend that one should be carved out of its own Western Region. It campaigned in 1959 for a Mid-West Region, to be composed of the non-Yoruba elements—but on condition that the Middle Belt was also carved out of the North and the proposed COR State (Calabar-Ogoja Rivers) out of the East.

PREPARATIONS FOR INDEPENDENCE

The British were against the creation of more states. The Minorities Commission which toured the country in 1956–57 under Sir Henry Willink pointed to the difficulty of drawing boundaries and expressed the sanguine view that strong separatist feelings among minority groups were likely to be transient. It suggested only that the Niger Delta area (part of the Action Group's proposed Calabar-Ogoja Rivers State) should be designated a 'special area' to make sure it was not neglected. It also recommended the creation of special councils to look after minorities in both Calabar and the Mid-West.

The British government was able to use the agitation for more states as a bargaining point in the negotiations over the date for independence. Lennox Boyd, the Colonial Secretary, said he could not possibly agree to independence in 1960 'while small new governments, lacking experience, trained staff and a proper framework of administration were as yet unestablished'.[40] This forced the Action Group, as the only party immediately interested in new states, to yield. It could hardly afford to advocate delaying independence. In the end it was the Action Group which lost out in the battle for states: in 1963, when it was at the nadir of its fortunes, the Mid-West was carved out of the Western Region, without any corresponding move in the East or the North.

The 1957 Constitutional Conference found all the party leaders agreed on fundamentals. Pressed to agree to independence for the Federation in 1959, Lennox Boyd indicated that 1960 might, given the right conditions prevailing at the time, be acceptable to the British government. In the autumn of 1958, 114 Nigerian delegates and advisers assembled in London for the fourth time in eight years. Ezera recalls that 'this motley crowd, with the possible exception of party leaders, went to this London conference more for a holiday picnic on party patronage tickets than for a constitution-mongering negotiation about which they knew little or nothing'.[41] However, the meeting did accept the report of the Minorities Commission and, at its insistence, entrenched a long list of basic human rights in the constitution. With the minorities issue out of the way, or rather swept under the carpet, the most important issue in this and other conferences could at last be faced: the date for independence was fixed for October 1, 1960.

Already the political landscape of the future was clearly discernible. For five years the three party leaders had been premiers in their respective Regions: Azikiwe in the East (since 1954), Awolowo in the West and the Sardauna of Sokoto in the North. After the 1954 federal election the West had embarked on an ambitious programme of educational and economic reforms, including the introduction of universal free primary education and a lavish road programme. The East, under Azikiwe, had founded its new University of Nsukka and laid the foundations for industrial advance in the establishment of various statutory corporations. It is generally accepted that nothing like this rate of advance would have been achieved under colonial administration, in the absence of Nigerian political leaders.

The final pre-independence hurdle was the federal election of 1959. Kenneth Post, the historian of the election, concludes that it was relatively fair. 'Only where administrative and legal structures were already open to political pressures—the Native Courts and Native Administrations in the North being the most obvious examples—were there abuses.'[42] This is the seed of election-rigging techniques which were to flower later. Post stresses that British officials played a key role in limiting abuses and concludes: 'This was the result of a particular situation at a particular time, and these conditions will not occur again. In a sense, the Federal election of 1959 was the last great act of the British Raj.'[43]

The election was fought over personalities rather than politics, and the voting patterns were largely on a tribal basis. Both Azikiwe and the NCNC and, on a larger scale, Awolowo and the Action Group, tried to upset the pattern by gaining large numbers of seats outside their Regions of influence, in particular in the North. Both men covered many hundreds of miles by road, rail and water. Awolowo hired the services of an American public relations firm, which provided a helicopter that wrote 'Awo' in the sky. This was the beginning of big party spending in Nigeria, spending for which a lengthy period in office in a Region was naturally a prerequisite. As many as 80 per cent of the 9 million registered electors voted— a remarkable turnout in this first trial for universal suffrage. The last results came in seven days after the poll in Adamawa Province of the North, where the ballot boxes had been carried out on the heads of porters.

The results shattered the hopes of the Southern parties in the North. Between them, the Action Group and its allies and the NCNC captured a third of Northern votes, but, as the two parties were not in alliance and seats were allocated on a constituency basis, this presented no serious challenge to the NPC. The Action Group won only 25 of the 174 Northern seats, and the NCNC/NEPU only eight. Even in these constituencies, most members later crossed the carpet to the NPC.

Post may have been too sanguine in his conclusion about the fairness of the election. In the trial of Awolowo for treason in 1962–63, the prosecution based its case on the thesis that he had lost faith in the ballot box as a result of his experiences in the North in that election. Much of the evidence—the judge commented repeatedly on this—was concerned with the violent and mercenary nature of politics. One of the witnesses, Alhaji Ibrahim Imam, former head of the Bornu Youth Movement which was in alliance with the Action Group in the North, testified: 'In 1958 my house was attacked by members of the NPC. Five members of the Bornu

Youth Movement were killed, one inside my house and three somewhere else. I made a report to the police. No one was prosecuted for these murders.'[44] Later, Imam fled from his home town, Maiduguri, to Jos and reported that there 'the police invited me and told me it was not safe to stay in Jos and that I should go and stay in a place which is a stronghold of the Action Group'.[45] Later he went to live in Kaduna, after his house and property, which he valued at £15,000, had been destroyed by NPC thugs.

As in 1954, no party won an absolute majority in the Federal House as a result of the election. The NPC won 148 of the 312 seats in the House; the NCNC won 89 and the Action Group 75. Days of intense political bargaining followed the poll. According to the testimony he gave at his subsequent trial, Awolowo approached Azikiwe with an offer that their two parties should form a coalition. But Azikiwe declined. According to some reports he had agreed well in advance with the Sardauna that his party should continue in coalition with the NPC; Azikiwe also claimed later that at the same time as Awolowo approached him another Action Group delegation was in Kaduna, trying to negotiate with the NPC. This is a plausible story in the light of the later split in the Action Group.

Balewa now continued in office at the head of an NPC-NCNC coalition that was to last until the 1964 election. Awolowo became leader of the opposition in the Federal House. The game of political musical chairs, at each change leaving out one of the three major groups, had begun.

5. Birth and Weaning

As for me, my stiffest earthly assignment is ended and my major life's work is done. My country is now free, and I have been honoured to be its first indigenous Head of State. What more could one desire in life?

—Dr Nnamdi Azikiwe, November 1960.

THE INDEPENDENCE CELEBRATIONS were held in the days before such things began to be done economically. Nineteen-sixty was a vintage independence year: by October, the Ivory Coast, Niger, Upper Volta, Togo, Dahomey, Senegal, Chad, Mali, Madagascar, Gabon, the two Congos and the Central African Republic had all managed more or less splendid shows. Nigeria, with a population bigger than all of these put together, could afford to do better. Official guests from all continents were flown in at government expense, champagned and dined for periods ranging from a week to a month, and driven round the vast Federation in a fleet of specially imported Jaguars and Chevrolets. The guests ranged from 'heads of state and government, paramount rulers and chieftains, statesmen and politicians, nationalists and freedom fighters'[1] to the politicians' personal friends and, as had become customary on such occasions, a homely sprinkling of their former landladies. The visitors were well regaled. One guest at the durbar staged for Princess Alexandra at Maiduguri, in the Northern Region, 'sat stupefied by the pageantry of over 3,000 men and women, mostly mounted on horses, riding thirty or more abreast, some on camels (which at the end of the day staged a charge), some on foot and some in palanquins on Shuwa cows, the traditional conveyance for taking Shuwa brides to their husbands' homes'.[2]

The political temperature of the occasion was remarkably low, in marked contrast to the messianic fervour of Ghana's day in 1957, or to the defiant revolutionary zeal of Guinea's in 1958. The emphasis was on quiet constitutional dignity. At the state opening of Parliament, performed by Princess Alexandra on behalf of the Queen, a huge crowd watched without cheering as Prime Minister Balewa and his ministers entered the chamber. 'The ceremonies and speeches have tended to emphasise continuity, not change', *West Africa's* correspondent found.

> Even Sir James Robertson's assertion, in front of 20,000 people at the Racecourse, after he had been sworn in as Governor of independent Nigeria, that he would now act only on his Ministers' advice 'in all matters' cannot have meant much to most of his audience, while the warm cheering that greeted his remark—a remark underlined by the Prime Minister—that the Queen was now 'directly Queen of Nigeria' showed that the crowd was not in revolutionary mood. This is self-government without slogans and in the first week of celebrations I have heard no speech of the kind customary elsewhere on these occasions.[3]

In his Independence Day speech the Prime Minister stressed almost to the point of labouring his gratitude to the British: 'I pay tribute to the manner in which successive British governments have gradually transferred the burden of responsibility to our shoulders. . . . We are grateful to the British officers whom we have known, first as masters, and then as leaders, and finally as partners, but always as friends.'[4]

ATTITUDES TO THE BRITISH

However, other Nigerian leaders had more complex attitudes to the British—in which affection was only one ingredient. Azikiwe, appointed Governor-General in November 1960 of a country he could claim to have helped create, was in mellow mood, and in any case the 'gilded cage' of his new office, as he described it, put him outside politics. But his recollections of colonial Nigeria differed radically from those of Balewa—Azikiwe was to describe it later as 'a dingy prison'.[5] Nor did his new office make him immune from emotional outbursts, which showed the scars of an African who had lived through seamier sides of the 'white' world than had Balewa. In 1962, when an editorial in *The Times* of London speculated whether the Governor-General might be contemplating a return to politics, Azikiwe wrote a long, vituperative letter to the newspaper, accusing it and the rest of the British press of 'congenital racial snobbery'.[6] Awolowo, on the other hand, showed no such scars. 'We are a sister country to Britain and it is as such that we should behave and expect to be treated', he wrote in his autobiography.[7] In his most important speech of the 1959 federal election campaign he had denounced neutralism as 'an unmitigated disservice to humanity'.[8] However, he is a politician, and as leader of the Federal opposition he found the placid pro-Westernism of the Balewa government's early days an obvious target. When the remnants of the British presence became a political issue, he ranged himself solidly behind the protestants.

Few issues seem more important in the politics of a new country than that of the relationship with the former colonial power. This, above all, is felt to distinguish a 'radical' policy from a 'moderate' one, or a 'militant' regime from a 'neo-colonialist'. In Nigeria, the earliest political arguments centred on the more obvious signs of a lingering British presence. First came the 'Stallard Must Go' campaign against the Prime Minister's British secretary; then a storm broke over the Anglo-Nigerian defence agreement. In the end Nigeria remained 'moderate' but not 'neo-colonialist'. Stallard went and the defence agreement was abrogated.

British civil servants were still numerous. They had held two-thirds of the 'grade A' and 'superscale' posts in the Western Region in 1956; by 1960 they still held two-fifths, while their numbers in the lower scales had actually risen. As many 'established' officers left, others came on contract or as experts. No one could rationally object to this, but against the Prime Minister's secretary, who was also head of the civil service, there developed what

Balewa called 'an organised campaign' which he attributed sadly to 'the colonial mentality'. The campaign gathered momentum and the following year Stallard was replaced by Stanley Wey, a Yoruba who had risen through the civil service ranks; he was to hold the post until the second military coup of 1966.

THE DEFENCE AGREEMENT

The first political storm of the regime broke over the defence agreement, which Awolowo denounced as 'an attempt to swindle this country out of its sovereignty'.[9] Hundreds of students from Ibadan rode to Lagos in buses and mammy-waggons, broke through a police cordon into the House of Representatives and manhandled federal ministers. Their placards read: 'No bases in Nigeria', 'Balewa betrayed us', 'Britain leave Nigeria alone'. Seen against this background, the agreement itself was something of an anti-climax. The two governments had contracted to 'afford each other such assistance as may be necessary for mutual defence and to consult together on the measures to be taken jointly or separately to ensure the fullest co-operation between them for this purpose'.[10] Britain was to give help, including personnel, in training Nigeria's army, while Nigeria was to provide overflying rights and facilities for RAF 'tropicalisation' tests. An earlier draft, submitted to the 1958 constitutional conference, had provided for a leased plot of land for eventual use as a staging base, but this clause had been dropped.

Whatever the agreement did or did not say, it clearly embarrassed the new government. Equally embarrassed were the agreement's principal critics when it was revealed in the House that not only Balewa had initialled the revised agreement during the 1960 conference in London: so had each of the other three leaders who might have become prime minister after independence—Awolowo, Azikiwe and the Sardauna of Sokoto. Challenged on this, Awolowo explained that Britain had used 'barefaced, unabashed and undue influence. The four of us were bundled to No. 10 Downing Street

117

and were asked to initial this document on the understanding that unless the document was initialled, it would not be possible for Her Majesty's Government to make a declaration fixing the date for our independence.'[11]

For this, Balewa called Awolowo a liar, denying that the signatures had been a precondition for independence. The incident appeared permanently to undermine Balewa's confidence in Awolowo and may later have been a barrier to efforts at compromise during the bitter conflicts that were to follow. In fact, the defence agreement was innocuous enough. Not only was there no provision for a base, but even the overflying rights were to be subject to prior consultation. Malaya had a much more elaborate agreement; Pakistan, without an agreement, was much more committed militarily to the United Kingdom through SEATO; and Egypt, even after Suez, did not formally end British overflying rights.

Emotion and factual muddles apart, the real case of the critics was that a country must not only be free but also be seen to be free. 'Now we are inviting a situation whereby Nigeria's voice will be looked upon with suspicion in the comity of African nations', said the Action Group's Chief Akin-Olugbade in the House.[12] His point was considerably reinforced from Ghana by Nkrumah, who had criticised the agreement on the grounds that mutual defence was already 'part of the general understanding of the Commonwealth'.[13] Moreover, the Ghana government had made it clear that it was not inviting Nigeria to join the proposed African High Command because of the defence agreement.

Thus the critics won and in December 1962 the defence agreement was abrogated by mutual consent. It was now agreed that each government would endeavour to afford the other 'at all times assistance and facilities in Defence matters as are appropriate between partners in the Commonwealth'.[14] In practice, military aid continued as before, and British officers, mainly in technical grades, continued to serve with the Nigerian army. Indeed the General Officer Commanding the Army was Major-General Welby-Everard until 1965, when he was replaced by Major-General

Aguyi-Ironsi. The events of the 1964–65 constitutional crisis, during which Welby-Everard was summoned daily to State House on the one hand and to the Prime Minister's house on the other for consultations about security, was probably the last occasion when a Briton played a key role in Nigerian affairs.

Touchiness about the British gradually subsided in later years. The number of British civil servants continued to decline. Only in the commercial field was the issue of 'Nigerianisation' still alive. Newspapers complained periodically that this process was too slow but there were in fact very few industries where the case could convincingly be argued. Replacing expensive expatriates with Nigerians as fast as possible was obvious commercial sense and in some firms a better founded, though less publicised, complaint was that Nigerianisation had actually gone too fast. Officially the British kept as quiet as possible. So assiduous was the British High Commission in self-effacement that one of its staff was once heard to grumble that it was in danger of 'vanishing up its backside'. Not until the military take-over of 1966 did the British High Commissioner again come into the political news, when he was summoned to attend one of the last cabinet meetings of the outgoing regime. But it was later strongly, and credibly, denied that he had played any part in the situation.

A later upsurge of suspicion against the British occurred after the anti-Ibo riots in the North during May 1966, which followed the sudden abolition by decree of the federal system by the Ironsi military regime. The decree was fiercely resented in the North as a partisan act of the 'Ibo-dominated' government. The High Commissioner, Sir Francis Cumming-Bruce, had been touring the North in the weeks before the outbreak and comments in the *West African Pilot* and the Lagos *Daily Telegraph*, both vehicles of Ibo opinion, had suggested that there might be a causal link between his visit and the riots. When the riots broke out General Ironsi, in a broadcast, cryptically accused 'certain foreign elements' of stirring up the Northerners. It was afterwards found that he meant the British. It all looked like a recrudescence of the old feeling in the

South that the British had always favoured the more conservative North.

In times of trouble, people tend to see sinister foreign influences. For Nigerians, the British are the favourite target. Many are convinced that the British deliberately sited their High Commissioner's Residence on Marina near the Prime Minister's house so that the High Commissioner could administer regular secret briefings. In reality, British influence is far less than is generally supposed, not only by Nigerians but by other foreigners in Nigeria. Britain provides less aid than the United States, only a fraction of the total aid received from all sources. Britain enjoys no commercial preferences —of which Arthur Bottomley, Secretary of State for Commonwealth Relations, was painfully reminded in 1965 when he found the Lagos streets full of French and German cars. British influence is moral rather than material; it feeds on the 'love' content in the deep 'love-hate' relationship most Nigerians have with their former masters. In the Balewa regime it owed much to the fact that the Prime Minister himself was more pro-British than most. Had Azikiwe or even Awolowo been Prime Minister, British influence might have been less than it was.

FOREIGN POLICY

The Balewa regime started its foreign policy on a very cautious note. It maintained the frank distaste for non-alignment already expressed in the election campaigns of all three major parties and made few attempts to balance its Western links with Communist ones. Six weeks after independence Balewa told his monthly press conference that Malik, the leader of the Soviet delegation to the festivities, had brought a letter from the Soviet Prime Minister 'insisting on opening an embassy forthwith'. Said Balewa: 'We will not be bullied, and I told him protocol must be followed and we would consider an application in the proper form.'[15] The following year a Soviet embassy, rationed to a small staff, was opened in Lagos and by the end of the First Republic there were also embassies from Bulgaria, Czechoslovakia, Hungary, Poland and Yugoslavia.

For all his pro-Western bias, Balewa was a nationalist who became increasingly concerned to maintain a correct posture for Nigeria on the African stage. His government took a firm line on South Africa and consistently refused to allow South Africans to work in Nigeria. When, in December 1960, despite vehement protests about the first two tests, the French exploded their third atomic bomb in the Sahara, Nigerian policy took a sudden extremist lurch. Although the protests had come from all over Africa, Nigeria alone broke off diplomatic relations with France, maintaining that the explosion had shown 'an utter disregard for the Africans, and constituted a grave insult to the Government and peoples of this country'.[16] The French ambassador and his staff were ordered out within forty-eight hours and an embargo was placed on French shipping and air traffic. This last regulation hit Nigeria's ex-French neighbours Dahomey and Togo rather than France and was later withdrawn. It was not until 1966 that General de Gaulle was prevailed upon to reopen his embassy in Lagos. The episode, in which Nigeria had been caught out as the only soldier in step, left a bitter memory. It still lingered four years later when Ian Smith declared illegal independence in Rhodesia. The foreign ministers of the Organisation of African Unity, including Nigeria, resolved to break off diplomatic relations with Britain for its failure to check Smith. This time, Nigeria was not among the countries which fulfilled the resolution.

Throughout Balewa's term of office, Nigeria's foreign policy was impeded by internal crises which left little energy for other concerns. What policy there was, though stamped by the Prime Minister's own conservatism, was rarely free from radical pressure from home. After Lumumba's murder in the Congo in February 1961, Tunji Otegbye, president of the Nigerian Youth Congress, and five others were arrested in a clash near the American embassy. The embassy's windows and doors were broken, European passers-by were injured, and cars were stoned and police used batons and tear-gas. In June that year Awolowo, in his new pan-African guise, returned from a visit to Ghana advocating that Nigeria should join the newly-formed (and, as it turned out, abortive) Ghana-Guinea-Mali union. He predicted, wrongly, that Upper Volta and Gambia would also soon join.

A new element was added later that year when Jaja Wachuku, an Ibo lawyer who had been chairman of the UN Congo Conciliation Commission, became Foreign Minister. He had already urged in Parliament that Nigeria, because of its size, should 'not abdicate the position in which God Almighty has placed us'.[17] Wachuku was to contribute a new kind of jingoism to Nigerian foreign affairs; he was constantly reminding foreign governments and delegations of their relative lack of importance. This earned no popularity for Nigeria.

For all its initial hesitations, Nigeria did not fail in its basic obligations as Africa's most populous state. In 1961, when African governments split into the radical 'Casablanca' group inspired principally by Ghana, and the moderate 'Monrovia' group, Nigeria, by virtue not only of its size but also of some patient diplomacy, fell into a leading position among the latter. A conference held in Lagos in January 1962 made a serious effort—which nearly succeeded—at uniting the two groups. In the last minute the Casablanca powers decided not to attend, but the meeting did produce the germ of the charter of the Organisation of African Unity. The habit of international leadership grew. The last major political act of Balewa's government—and of his life—was to organise the Commonwealth Prime Ministers' Conference on Rhodesia, held in Lagos (the first ever held outside London) at Balewa's initiative. But the triumph was hollow. As the delegates landed in Lagos to grapple with the problem of the Rhodesians, scores of Nigerians were dying in riots within a mile of the airport. This was January 1966. Just as the First Republic was beginning to make an impact abroad, its internal problems were to bring it to an end.

AMENDING THE CONSTITUTION

How much of what went wrong was caused by the constitutional framework, and how much by human failings, is still under discussion in Nigeria. At the time, the independence constitution, evolved after a gestation period of nearly four decades, seemed as faithful a reflection of political realities as possible, with as many built-in safeguards against abuse as it seemed possible to devise. The bi-cameral system was designed, in the Regions, to balance the political power of the lower houses with the traditional influence of the Houses of Chiefs. At the centre, the upper house—the Senate— had an equal number of appointed senators from each Region, and was thus expected to provide a safeguard against domination by any party or alliance through its majority in the House of Representatives.

The division of powers between the Federal and the regional governments was still based on the 1954 arrangements. A list of 'federal' powers, reserved for the Lagos Parliament, covered forty-four items, including foreign affairs, defence, customs, currency, higher education, postal services and trunk roads. A 'concurrent' list of powers shared between the centre and the Regions had twenty-eight subjects, including police, judiciary, labour and industrial development. All other powers were vested in the Regions. Special provisions, by spelling out procedures not specified in Britain, were designed to safeguard parliamentary democracy in a precarious environment. The Director of Public Prosecutions was specifically exempted from political control. A Judicial Service Commission, also free from political control, was to continue to appoint the judges. Public service commissions, at the centre and in the Regions, were to control all civil service appointments and promotions. The Supreme Court was to adjudicate in any dispute between federal and regional authorities. A federal Electoral Commission, with a chairman and one member for each Region plus one for Lagos, was to arrange federal elections, while regional commissions, under the chairmanship of the federal commission's chairman, was to arrange regional elections.

The constitution guaranteed freedoms of conscience, expression, association and movement in entrenched clauses that could not be altered except by a two-thirds majority of both houses at the centre and in at least two of the Regions. Nor could the boundaries of existing Regions be altered except by a two-thirds majority in each federal house and by a majority of regional legislatures.

How safe were the safeguards? In its post-1963 republican form, the constitution survived until the night of January 17, 1966, when General Ironsi announced in a broadcast that the sections dealing with the President, the Prime Minister and the federal and regional legislatures had been suspended. But in spirit it was already in ruins. In particular, several significant changes had been made—all tending to increase the power of the executive and, by implication, to weaken the democratic safeguards.

The special protection given to the Director of Public Prosecutions was removed in a bill introduced and passed in 1961. At the time of the Western Region crisis of 1962, appeals to the Judicial Committee of the Privy Council were abolished, retrospectively, to invalidate a particular judgement of that committee (see below, pp. 150–1). Some of the remaining safeguards were discarded as part of the transition to a republic in 1963.

The decision to become a republic, thus terminating the sovereignty of the British Crown, was virtually a matter of course, following the established practice among other newly independent Commonwealth countries. Its importance lay in the opportunity it afforded to review the constitution. The federal and regional politicians, who had now had two and a half years to savour power and appreciate the threats of rivals, did not miss the opportunity to close the loopholes which threatened their position. When all the regional premiers met the Federal Prime Minister in Lagos to discuss the matter in July 1963, various proposals were already in the air, some more ominous than others. The most publicised at the time was for preventive detention, a weapon which had already done long service for President Nkrumah in Ghana. All the participants at the meeting had already expressed themselves in favour. 'I think

I like it', said the Sardauna of Sokoto, when questioned about it as he landed in Lagos for the meeting. 'The introduction of such a law need not wait until the country has become a Republic. If any action warrants it tomorrow, it should be applied.' Chief Akintola, Premier of the West, described it as 'a necessary evil' and Dr Okpara, Premier of the East, held the same view.[18] At the meeting itself Balewa argued that the authorities were being constantly hampered in their activities against known subversive elements by the need to bring cases to court. He admitted that it was he who had urged the measure all along. To forestall people from planning evil, he said, the only remedy the government had was to declare a state of emergency. He was satisfied that 'outside brains' were organising against Nigeria. The Awolowo treason trial, then in progress (see chapter 6, pp. 138-49), might have made his case easier to argue. The idea was fiercely attacked in the press. Okpara also found that several of his party's leaders, including federal ministers, were against it. The Nigerian Bar Association, through its president, Chief Rotimi Williams, described it as 'a measure to starve out liberal democracy in Nigeria'. In the end the Prime Minister told the conference that, in view of known opposition, the project had been 'deferred'. Also dropped was a proposal, long mooted by Azikiwe, for an Executive President. For two years the Governor-General had been warning of the dangers of allowing too much power to devolve on the Federal Prime Minister and proposed that an Executive President-elected by a joint meeting of the House of Representatives and the Senate, should be responsible for the democratic safeguards in the constitution: the Judicial Service Commission, the Electoral Commission, the director of audit and the public service commissions. He did not include the armed forces in his scheme and it has been suggested that, in view of the events of the 1964-65 election crisis, he wrongly believed that as Commander-in-Chief he already controlled the armed forces.[19] But Azikiwe had little support and although he raised his scheme at the 1963 conference there was little serious discussion of it.

However, two major erosions of the constitutional safeguards of

1960 were adopted and duly incorporated in the republican constitution: the Judicial Service Commission was abolished and the appeals to the Judicial Committee of the Privy Council, already nullified in effect in the Western Region crisis of the previous year, were formally abolished. A communiqué issued after the premiers' conference said the Judicial Service Commission was abandoned 'in line with practically all Commonwealth and other countries'.[20] Judges would in future be appointed by the President 'on the advice of the Prime Minister who will have such consultations as he may deem fit before tendering such advice'. Judges so appointed could be removed only by a two-thirds majority in both federal houses.

These reforms came in for fierce criticism. Chief Rotimi Williams told the Bar Association later that year that the abolition of appeals to the Judicial Committee of the Privy Council was 'probably premature', adding that 'if we must be true to ourselves, we have to admit that it will take this country very many years to build up a body of men of comparable integrity, ability and knowledge, to take over the functions of that august body'. He went on to describe the abolition of the Judicial Service Commission as 'indefensible and contrary to the principle of the independence of the judiciary'.[21] However, Nigeria was not alone in dispensing with the services of the Judicial Committee of the Privy Council: India, Pakistan, South Africa, Ghana and Cyprus had all abolished the appeals to this body.

A final chapter in the progressive strengthening of executive powers was the Press Bill, passed in modified form and amid widespread opposition, in 1964. The *West African Pilot* called it the 'beginning of the end'.[22] However, as in the case of the proposed preventive detention law, there were plausible arguments in favour of it. The reverse side of Nigeria's celebrated press freedom was editorial exuberance in political lies. The new law provided that 'any person who authorises for publication, publishes, reproduces, or circulates for sale in a newspaper any statement, rumour or report, knowing or having reason to believe that such statement, rumour or report is false, shall be guilty of an offence and liable on conviction to a fine of £200 or to imprisonment for a term of one year'. The sting of the new law was in the further provision that 'it shall be no defence to a charge under this section that he did not know or did not have reason to believe that the statement, rumour or report was false unless he proves that, prior to publication, he took reasonable measures to verify the accuracy of such statement, rumour or report'.[23]

The implications of this clause for practical journalists are wide. Although prosecutions under it have been few, it provided a remarkably effective sword of Damocles over Nigerian pressmen in the political storms that followed.

6. Hazards of Opposition

The domestic policy of Nigeria will be framed on the assumption that Nigeria shall continue to be a parliamentary democracy. . . . The Government should recognise the existence of an Opposition as an essential ingredient of democracy, and vote a salary in its budget for payment to the Leader of the Opposition.

—Dr Nnamdi Azikiwe, 1959.[1]

I have told people all along that we are not ripe for a system of government in which there is a fully fledged opposition. In Nigeria, no party can agree to be in opposition for long.

—Sir Abubakar Tafawa Balewa, 1966.[2]

THE CURTAIN HAD RISEN on Nigeria's first regime in October 1960. It fell just over five years later, in January 1966, to the sound of bullets that killed the Prime Minister, Sir Abubakar Tafawa Balewa, himself. In the intervening drama, Act One was the crisis of the Western Region. Being left out in the game of musical chairs at the federal centre proved too much for the Region's ruling party, Chief Awolowo's Action Group. The Act opened with the Action Group splitting into two factions, a memorable uproar in the regional Parliament and the imposition of a state of emergency. The party's fortunes sank deeper as a federal commission inquired into the seamier sides of its administration, and finally reached their nadir during the celebrated trial of Chief Awolowo for treason. The trial was the central political event of the Balewa regime and Awolowo's conviction marked the end of effective constitutional opposition. The Act closed with the 'Establishment'—consisting of the Northern party in alliance with the Eastern party and the small 'rump' of the Western party—firmly in power.

In Act Two this Establishment suffered some rude shocks. The action began with the general strike of 1964 in which, for a brief moment, the workers saw their privations in political terms and were able to agree on joint action. Then came the census controversy—a bitter tribal argument which wrecked the alliance of the Northern and Eastern parties. A new line-up, with both the popular parties of the South now ranged against the Northern Establishment, emerged for the 1964 federal election. The crisis that followed the election almost broke the Federation apart, but the Establishment survived. Act Three opened with the Western Region election of 1965—the final, desperate attempt of the Southern alliance to win power by constitutional means. Its failure, amid the bitterness of a rigged election, produced the spreading chaos in the West that led directly to the coup.

GOVERNMENT AND OPPOSITION

The audience is left to draw its own moral. To the more perceptive, it was clear from the start that the sophisticated constitutional mechanism which was supposed to keep three great tribal nations in harmony contained elements of instability and imbalance. One Region, the North, was bigger, and therefore commanded more seats in the Federal House, than the other Regions put together. If the North was big, it was never quite big enough to rule alone. The game of musical chairs, in which two of the three big regionally and tribally based parties shared federal power while the third was left out, proved increasingly unplayable. Perhaps, as Balewa said on the last day of his life, the country was 'not ripe' for a system which depended on an opposition in the Westminster sense. Was it the fault of the constitution, or of the politicians who failed to make it work? Perhaps it was neither of these, but simply the thinness of the spread of national resources, which made tribal rivalries too strenuous for the system to bear.

The West was by no means alone in concealing elements of opposition behind the facade of political unity under a ruling party.

Against the NPC in the North were ranged a Hausa opposition party in Alhaji Aminu Kano's Northern Elements Progressive Union, and also the Middle Belt Congress, representing a minority group in a traditionally disgruntled area. Opposing the NCNC in the East were the non-Ibo elements in the Delta region as well as splinter groups which emerged from time to time within the party. In the West opposition to the Action Group centred on the non-Yoruba peoples, later to have their own Mid-West Region and championed by the NCNC.

But all these challenges to the various regional Establishments depended on the ballot box. Even if they had been numerically dangerous, governments already had the electoral dice sufficiently loaded in their favour to cope with the threat. What happened in the West was unique : the ruling party itself split into two factions, with Awolowo, the leader of the opposition in the Federal House and head of the party, on one side and Chief Akintola, the regional Premier, on the other. That this happened in the West can be attributed partly to the divisive bellicosity of Yoruba history and tradition. Clannish rivalries played a part, especially the jealousy aroused by the more sophisticated and energetic Ijebu sub-tribe, to which Awolowo belonged. The personal and temperamental differences of the two men also played a part. But the basic reason was simply the strain of being in opposition in Lagos. The strain was least bearable for Chief Awolowo himself : Nigeria's ablest politician was deprived of power. But it was felt throughout the party. Naturally, when the West split, both the North and the East tried to exploit the situation for their own advantage.

Lacking federal power meant, in Nigerian terms, fewer scholarships, factories, jobs, loans and amenities for one's Region. Such grievances were sometimes intangible and often exaggerated. Nevertheless, they effectively split the Action Group, dividing those who wanted to join the bandwaggon of federal power from those who, whether through sticking to party principle in the Westminster sense or through the simple ambition of capturing sole power later, preferred to remain in opposition. The split ranged the moderates against the radicals (Awolowo himself referred to a struggle between 'the inside left and the inside right') and the intellectuals against the businessmen and traditional chiefs.

THE ACTION GROUP SPLIT

Late in 1961 an executive meeting of the Action Group revealed the first disagreements. A set of working papers on 'democratic socialism', prepared by a group of young party leaders at the invitation of Awolowo, were dismissed by Akintola as 'the work of revolutionary babes who haven't the astuteness to gain the party a single vote'.[3] In addition to the ideological argument was the tactical one on whether or not the Action Group should participate in the formation of a national government in Lagos—a plan known to be favoured by Balewa. Akintola, arguing on behalf of the businessmen and elders of the party, maintained that there was no point in spending more money on elections in the North and East when such expenditure had proved fruitless in the past.

How far Awolowo, a successful lawyer, could be regarded as a political radical is open to argument. There is certainly no socialism in his autobiography, *Awo*, written before independence. As a politician he must have sensed the need to reflect the growing discontent among young people in all Regions, faced with apparently hopeless unemployment and a rising cost of living. His central aim was to make this appeal nation-wide, thus solving the basic political dilemma presented by the dominance of the NPC. However the Action Group, no less than the NCNC, depended on the massive support of businessmen (and women—especially the powerful 'market mammies') on the one hand, and of chiefs and obas on the other. Neither of these groups could stomach much radicalism and both tended to support the Akintola faction.

The party rift came into the open at the annual convention, held at Jos in the Northern Region in February 1962. The convention abolished Akintola's post of deputy leader and adopted Awolowo's presidential report. A meeting of the federal executive committee voted Akintola guilty of 'maladministration, anti-party activities and gross indiscipline'.[4] It was decided unanimously to remove him both from the deputy leadership and the premiership.

Akintola, a brilliant political operator, was not to be easily defeated. His next move was to ask the Governor, through the Speaker, to call a meeting of the House and dissolve it. But the Governor rejected this advice. The party's parliamentary group then held its own meeting and voted, by 120 votes to none, that the Governor should remove the Premier. A petition with sixty-six signatures was sent to the Governor and, on the strength of this, he declared that he was convinced the Premier no longer enjoyed the support of the majority of the members of the House of Assembly. He therefore dismissed Akintola and invited Alhaji Adegbenro, a former regional minister and an Awolowo loyalist, to form a government. Akintola promptly filed a High Court action challenging the Governor's right to dismiss him without a no-confidence vote on the floor of the House. He also wrote to Balewa, asking him to request the Queen to dismiss the Governor.

The House met on May 25 to debate a vote of no-confidence in Adegbenro's new government. It was a historic session. An official statement of the proceedings reads:

Chief Odebeyi (Minister of Finance and Leader of the House) was about to move the first business motion of the day when Mr E. O. Oke, Member for Ogbomosho South-West, jumped up, raised an alarm, and flung a chair across the floor of the House. Mr F. Ebubedike, Member for Badagry East, seized the Mace and smashed it on Mr Speaker's table. Mr S. A. Adeneya, Member for Oyo East, then seized the chair and hit the Minister of Trade and Industry, Mr K. S. Y. Momoh, on the head. He was rushed to hospital for treatment. At this stage members of the Akintola faction, assisted by the NCNC opposition, smashed chairs and tables. Police had to use tear-gas to disperse the scuffling. Mr Speaker then suspended the sitting for two and a half hours. The House re-assembled at 11.30 a.m.[5]

A writer who pieced together the events of the sitting from reports of policemen and civil servants who were present recorded:

At once, the Akintola faction and the NCNC opposition began to shout and bang their chairs. Chief S. A. Tinubu sat on the floor beside the Speaker's chair and continually rang a bell. Mr J. O. Adigun threatened to throw the Record Book at the Speaker. Mr Akinyemi smashed one despatch box and Mr Adedigba threw the other at Alhaji Adegbenro (it was caught by the Sergeant-at-Arms). Mr Adeneya then hit the Speaker with a chair, while the NCNC members smashed theirs or threw them at opponents. All this time the police had been begging the Speaker to let them act, and when he finally did so they again released gas and cleared the House.[6]

'EMERGENCY' IN THE WEST

It was soon clear that there was method in all this madness. Realising that the parliamentary party was against them, Akintola's supporters had sought to have the House dissolved in disorder. They had succeeded and the Federal government was now in a position to come to their aid. The Federal Parliament was summoned in emergency session and the government moved that 'in pursuance of Section 65 of the Constitution of Nigeria, it is declared that a state of emergency exists and that this resolution shall remain in force until the end of the month of December 1962'.[7] Awolowo protested in vain that 'no state of public emergency exists', and that the government motion was 'a gross misuse of power'.[8] The motion was carried by 232 votes to 44, after Awolowo himself had asked for a division. Under the emergency regulations, an Administrator was appointed with the power to prohibit public meetings and processions and to imprison for up to five years 'any person or association guilty of publishing false reports likely to cause public alarm, or prejudice the maintenance of public order'.[9] The Administrator, Dr M. Majekodunmi, Federal Minister of Health, a Yoruba and a personal friend of Balewa, was also given the power to detain persons. Restriction

133

orders were served on Adegbenro, Akintola, Awolowo and twelve others. Meanwhile, at his native Ogbomosho, Akintola formed a new party—the United Peoples' Party (UPP).

The Balewa government has been widely criticised for declaring a state of emergency when the only disorder had been a few minutes of uproar in the regional House. One contemporary comment was that this action 'may put the burden on the Government to show that its actions are intended more for the benefit of Nigeria than the NPC and the NCNC'.[10] Balewa's answer was that the real emergency consisted not in physical violence but in the fact that there were two rival premiers. (This point lost a great deal of weight retrospectively in 1965, when Balewa consistently refused to declare a state of emergency, though this time law and order had truly broken down in many parts of the Western Region. On the later occasion, the critics pointed out, it was the NPC's political ally, Chief Akintola, who was in power.)

In July 1962, Nigeria's Federal Supreme Court decided, by a three-to-one majority, that the Oni of Ife, the now suspended Governor of the West, had exceeded his constitutional powers in removing Akintola from the premiership. The court ruled that the Governor had no right to dismiss a premier without a prior vote in the House of Assembly and also upheld the validity of the emergency regulations which had restrained Adegbenro from acting as premier and restricted his movements. One dissenting voice was that of a British member of the Court, Sir Lionel Brett. 'Always assuming good faith, the Constitution does not preclude the Governor from acting on any information which he considers reliable', he held. 'It would be unwise to apply in practice unwritten conventions of the British Constitution to the provisions of Nigeria's written Constitution.'

A CORRUPTION INQUIRY

The stage was set for the next scene—the inquiry commission. In bringing a corruption inquiry down on Awolowo's head, his opponents, both inside his own party and in the Federal Coalition government, chose an ever-ready weapon which might in different political circumstances have been used against themselves. Corruption at this level is part of a system. An essential attribute of political power is the ability to finance one's party, or at least to reward one's followers. Nigeria (or any other similarly placed country) provides few means of doing this other than through the spoils of office. That the inquiry was held in the West and not in the East or the North was a political accident. Elsewhere, precisely the same conditions would have been unearthed. Awolowo himself refused to give evidence. He wrote to Judge Coker that he had 'come to the conclusion that no useful purpose could be served' by his participation.[11]

The Commission, under the Lagos High Court judge Mr Justice Coker, held ninety-two public sittings and its four-volume report provides a unique insight into the financial workings of politics against a background far removed from Westminster.[12] It inquired into the affairs of the Western Region Marketing Board and nine other government-owned or government-controlled bodies in the Region: the National Investment and Properties Company (NIPC), the Region's development corporation, housing corporation, broadcasting corporation, printing corporation, government bank and two private banks. The essence of the Commission's findings is that through the statutory corporations and public companies very large sums of money had for years been diverted from the government to the Action Group. Most but not all the money was actually used for party purposes. Of the NIPC, the commission found that the directors, who were all top Action Groupers, 'have in different ways benefited themselves from the resources of the company knowing full well, as they ought to do, that they had not contributed one penny to the shareholding of that company'.[13] However, £4 million from the NIPC alone actually went to the party. The most controversial part of the Commission's findings was that, although he was Premier of the Region, Akintola was not to blame.[14] Some critics have found this hard to imagine and have suggested that Akintola's exoneration might have owed something to the fact that he was on the side of the political angels at the time.

The Commission found that the NIPC—a private company with the ostensible object of providing credit to businessmen—was founded in 1958 'for the main purpose of providing funds for the Action Group'. The Region's Marketing Board had diverted 'well over £6½ million of its funds' to the company. Up to the end of 1959, 'monies had been raised for the Action Group through the various accounts being operated in various names with the National Bank of Nigeria'.[15] However, in 1960, not only was Awolowo no longer the Premier, but the new Banking Ordinance had also made it impossible for a bank to make loans to its own directors. The NIPC was therefore used as a way out of the difficulty. The NIPC was formed, if not actually by Awolowo, at any rate on his insistence ('the evidence certainly shows that it was at his direction that the Directors who are, in fact, all the shareholders as well, were appointed'[16]). These appointments were made at a meeting in Awolowo's house and the first loan the company raised from the Marketing Board—£750,000 —was used to settle Action Group debts. All the share contributions were in fact paid to the party. The company was also principal shareholder in Allied Newspapers Ltd, which printed Action Group papers.

The Commission's findings on the National Bank of Nigeria, which was owned by the regional government, were strongly reminiscent of the Eastern Region's African Continental Bank inquiry in 1956 (see chapter 2, p. 40). To encourage indigenous banks to give credit to Nigerians, the Western Region government and some of its agencies had deposited money with or invested in preference shares in the National Bank. In fact, as the Commission found, the Bank utilised substantial portions of the money entrusted to it

for the purpose of making loans and advances to the Directors of the Bank or to institutions in which such Directors were jointly or severally interested. . . . We know that since the deposit of £1 million with the Bank in 1955, the Bank had virtually constituted itself into a banking asylum for the Action Group. Almost all the many accounts of the Action Group were kept in almost all the branches of the Bank and the various statements of account produced before us show that considerable over-draft facilities were granted in respect of these accounts.[17]

Loans to the party were 'operated in various names and not secured in any shape or form'.[18] To conceal the name of the party, the Bank also operated a suspense account and a sundry persons account.

Of the Marketing Board, the body responsible for buying and marketing the Region's lucrative cocoa crop, the Commission found that at its inception in 1959 it received almost £18 million from its federal predecessor but that by 1962 its net current assets were down to £1·5 million. Many of the industrial and agricultural projects in which it had invested struck the Commission as having been 'recklessly entered into without any regard whatever for the safety of the monies that were being invested'.[19] Of sixteen industrial projects invested in, none had made a profit and almost all were badly conceived. Moreover, the Board was run as a 'one man show' by Alfred Rewane, who was also political secretary of the party.

The Finance Corporation also appeared to have bought a number of businesses at exorbitant prices in questionable circumstances. The story was told of a plot of land in Lagos—the Moba land—which was originally bought in 1958 by Dr Maja, an Action Group veteran, and Chief Doherty for £11,000. Six weeks later it was sold to a Mr R. A. Allison for £150,000. Eight months after that the same land was sold to the NIPC for £178,000. Then, at the request of the Housing Corporation, the regional Ministry of Lands and Housing decided to acquire the land. A British firm of estate agents valued it at £850,000 on certain conditions. Without seeing that those conditions were satisfied, the regional government paid this amount to the NIPC. Within a few days of its receipt by the NIPC, the whole of the money was paid over to Chief Lanlehin, the Western Region treasurer of the Action Group.[20]

In its conclusion, the Commission found consolation in 'evidence of prudent and considered management and investment of public funds', as well as 'reckless and indeed atrocious and criminal mismanagement and diversion of public funds', and also in 'some bold and courageous civil servants who stuck to their guns with remarkable fortitude in the face of circumstances of a most trying order'.[21]

THE TREASON TRIAL

Balewa was in London, attending the 1962 Commonwealth Prime Ministers' Conference, when he was told that Awolowo and thirty others were to be charged with plotting to overthrow his government by force. 'I couldn't believe it', he related afterwards. 'I thought it would make us a laughing stock and told them to release him. But they assured me it was true. I just couldn't believe Awolowo would be so foolish.'[22] Just how foolish, or even how guilty, Awolowo really was is still being hotly debated in Nigeria. Like the Coker Commission, the treason trial was conducted with every show of propriety, following British procedures (except that the treason trial had no jury but only a single judge). However, the political background of both inquiries made them appear as episodes in power politics to Awolowo's followers.

The trial's background and special character made it controversial from the start. Two of the accused turned Queen's evidence and became the star witnesses. The defence could point to serious weaknesses and contradictions in much of the evidence, given in many cases by discredited witnesses. The image of justice was further blurred when the British counsel of Awolowo's choice, F. E. N. Gratien, was refused entry into Nigeria. The Lagos High Court dismissed a motion by Awolowo against this decision, but the judge acknowledged that it was 'astonishing' that Parliament, in the Immigration Act, should have conferred such wide powers on the Minister for Internal Affairs. Five months later, in a second instalment of the same trial, Chief Anthony Enahoro's

British lawyer, Dingle Foot, was also refused entry, after the chief had been repatriated from Britain. It was understood that Foot was at the time persona non grata because of previous legal engagements in Nigeria.

Awolowo was twenty-seventh in a list of thirty-one accused, facing a three-count charge of treasonable felony, conspiracy to commit felony and conspiracy to effect unlawful importation of arms. Two of the accused, Oladipo Maja, a Lagos medical practitioner, and Richard Babalola, gave evidence for the Crown and the charges against them were withdrawn. Of the remaining twenty-nine, four were out of the country—Enahoro (the publicity secretary who had gone to London via Ghana), Samuel G. Ikoku (secretary general of the party), R. O. Adebanjo (a journalist) and James Aluko, all of whom had taken refuge in Ghana. The other twenty-five included Chike Obi, head of the Dynamic Party, which opposed the ruling NCNC in the East; Joseph Tarka, head of the United Middle Belt Congress, which opposed the NPC in the North; Samuel Oredein, principal organising secretary of the Action Group; Lateef Jakande, managing director of Allied Newspapers, the Action Group newpaper organisation; Alfred Rewane, chairman of the Western Region Development Corporation and political secretary of the Action Group; and Josiah Lawanson, assistant principal organising secretary of the party.

For eight months, from early November 1962 to June 1963, the trial followed its unruffled course. It moved at a snail's pace because, in the absence of shorthand reporters, Judge Sowemimo had to take notes in longhand; for long minutes on end, the whirring of the fans in the modern-styled courtroom and the scratching of the judge's pen were the only sounds. Throughout the trial Awolowo defended himself. Looking drawn and tired, he listened attentively, taking full notes and addressing the court in tones that ranged from passionate eloquence to didactic patience and, finally, tragic resignation. He listened impassively as extracts were read out from Exhibit Q—a personal diary called *Flashes of Inspiration*. One of these read: 'Jesus said "All things whatsoever ye pray and

ask for believe that ye have received them already and ye shall
have them". I therefore believe quite firmly that I will undoubtedly become Prime Minister of the Federation of Nigeria
as a result of the forthcoming federal elections [1959]. I can even
make a picture in my mind of myself occupying the office of the
Prime Minister of the Federation of Nigeria. I thank God
Almighty in advance for granting me the object of my desire.'[23]
The *Flashes* also contained slogans designed for repetition to
himself when he was in the bath 'or at other convenient times'.
Dreams were recorded, including one in which he was trying to
set a pile of glossy papers on fire, but the matches he used were
too feeble, from which he concluded that his party organisation
was unready to defeat the NPC. In another dream he cut in two a
snake in a lake, only to find that both halves survived, just as the
Coalition members, the NPC and the NCNC, would have done.

At the end Awolowo delivered an eight-day address on which
the judge complimented him. On trial had been not merely the
thirty-one accused but a whole political way of life. The more than
eighty witnesses included politicians of all ranks, from Awolowo
himself down to doctors, lawyers, policemen, and party thugs. A
notable absentee was Akintola—whom Awolowo's supporters in
the West were accusing of having stolen their leader's rightful
place (years later they still yelled '*oleh*'—'thief'—when he passed)
and whom many believed to have been Awolowo's real accuser.

The main charge was that the accused 'between December 1960
and September 1962, in Lagos and in various other places in
Nigeria, formed an intention to levy war against our Sovereign
Lady the Queen within Nigeria in order by force or constraint to
compel our Sovereign Lady the Queen to change her measures and
counsels and manifested such intention by overt acts detailed
below'. Eight overt acts were listed: the recruitment of volunteers,
arrangements for their training outside Nigeria, their training in
the use of explosives and firearms, the importation of arms, and
reconnaissance visits to the power station, the airport, the government magazine and the naval base. Outlining the case for the

prosecution Basil Adedipe, Director of Public Prosecutions, claimed that Awolowo had lost faith in the ballot box after his defeat in the 1959 election. The following year the Action Group set up an Ideological Committee and a Tactical Committee, and, at a meeting of the latter in December 1960, plans were laid to overthrow the government by force. An intensive programme of training in Ghana followed, including the use of explosives and weapons. A 'considerable quantity' of arms was imported from Ghana and concealed around Ijebu and Ikenne, both in the home area of Awolowo. Fifty cases of explosives were also bought at nearby Abeokuta. Members of the Tactical Committee visited the Lagos power station, Lagos airport and the naval base, as preliminary reconnaissance for their plan. 'D-Day' was to be 2 A.M. on September 23, 1962. After plunging Lagos into darkness, the Governor-General, the Prime Minister and principal ministers were to be arrested, without violence unless they resisted. Three key expatriates were to be placed under restriction: Major-General Welby-Everard, GOC of the army, J. E. Hodge, Inspector-General of Police, and the commodore of the navy. Awolowo was then to broadcast, announcing he had taken over as Prime Minister.

The principal prosecution witness was Oladipo Maja, who had originally headed the list of accused—a prosperous doctor who had just built himself a £28,000 nursing home in Lagos and also had a business in Ghana. His wife was Ghanaian. Presenting himself as a man very much to the left of Awolowo, he claimed to have gone to Ghana at Awolowo's request 'to find out the programme which the Convention Peoples Party had'. Maja quoted Awolowo as saying to him that at the 1959 elections 'our boys at the post were maltreated by the Native Authority police [in the North] and the Northern boys [NPC stalwarts] and also that they were taking Action Group money without playing any part'. It was then suggested that before the next elections party organisers should be toughened by training in Ghana. Such training should include ju-jitsu and the use of arms. In cross-examination Maja admitted that when he was arrested he was 'very anxious' to get back to his surgery: 'I told Mr Lynn [the British police officer in charge of the inquiries] that I had operated on some patients that day and was anxious to get away. He then told me that the only way I could get out was to say all that I knew and petition the Prime Minister and the Administrator.'

As second witness, Lynn himself testified that during a nocturnal search of the houses of two of the accused at Ijebu-Ode he found two machine guns, twenty-four tear-gas pistols, several revolvers with some 3,000 rounds of ammunition and twenty gas and automatic pistols. Buried in the garden of Awolowo's house at Ikenne he found four spent cartridges.

The third witness was Sanya Onabamiro, a lecturer at the University of Ife and Minister of Education in Akintola's new UPP government. He said he was invited by Awolowo in 1960 to be a member of the Tactical Committee, of which the other members were Ikoku and Enahoro. At a meeting of that Committee, assignments were given out. Ikoku was to look into the military installations. Enahoro was to recruit 200 boys for training, while Onabamiro himself was to contact two senior police officers with a view to winning over the police. Cross-examined by Awolowo, Onabamiro admitted that he had been a member first of the NCNC, then of the Action Group and had lately joined Akintola's new UPP, thus identifying himself with a group that was bitterly opposed to Awolowo.

Next came a Northerner, Alhaji Ibrahim Imam, leader of the Bornu Youth Movement and leader of the opposition in the Northern House of Assembly. He said Maja had offered arms and money both to him and to Tarka, leader of the United Middle Belt Congress. They had agreed to accept money but not arms. He added that 'Awolowo had warned me seriously not to have anything to do with Maja'. However, Awolowo later told Imam that he had lost faith in the ballot box and that he proposed to 'go to a place like the Tiv Division, provided it is mountainous enough to give him cover to fight the Government'. Cross-examined by Awolowo, Imam confirmed that the latter had told him to steer clear of Maja. 'You said that the Action Group was planning along a similar line and that we should steer clear of Dr Maja. You told us that it was a bad business blowing up parliament and important buildings and bridges. You told us that it might even be that Maja was being used as a police agent.' Awolowo's cross examination also showed that Imam suffered financially through his break with the Action Group, from which Imam admitted having at one time received £1,600 a year for expenses.

The fifth witness, Patrick Dokotri, General Secretary of Tarka's United Middle Belt Congress, confirmed Imam's story that Awolowo had planned to go to the Tiv country to fight. He said he was selected for training in Ghana, where Sam Ikoku was in charge of the programme. Henry Oleari, described simply as 'a politician', confirmed the evidence about training in Ghana. Oleari himself was selected to take charge of the Ikeja and Mushin areas near Lagos on 'D-Day' and was to survey the police barracks 'to see how to blow them up at the appropriate time'. He claimed that Awolowo had told him there were 'other nations coming to help and all that was needed was to start at midnight'. Anthony Oboh, an organising secretary of the Action Group, said he had also been on training in Ghana. The training lasted about three weeks and included the use of the rifle and automatic weapons. Oboh's evidence of the assignments for 'D-Day' differed from that of Oleari in several respects. The prosecution closed its case after calling fifty-three witnesses.

In a 'no-case' submission, Awolowo claimed the prosecution had not proved the essential components of the first count: the forming of an intention. Nor had they proved the manifestation of such intention by overt acts. The fact that four spent cartridges were found at his residence was not evidence of possession as he was not in Ikenne at the time. Moreover, Maja, Imam and Onabamiro had all given the evidence of partial witnesses. He emphasised that some of the confessional statements were extracted 'in circumstances which detract from their weight and veracity'. Some of the prosecution witnesses had 'been thoroughly tutored before they came to give evidence', while Imam and Dokotri had been given proofs of their evidence before they came to court and had shared the same flat for a month before and during the trial.

Replying, the Director of Public Prosecutions said the evidence of Maja, Onabamiro, Imam, Dokotri and Oleari had all implicated Awolowo. He also referred to a document recovered from Awolowo's house, headed: 'Points—24.5.62'. One of the items read: 'Aim—to take over power: can we do this alone?' Another was: 'Constitution: defects and how they would be removed.' In his ruling the judge found there was a prima facie case on all three counts against all the accused except Chike Obi, who was discharged.

The defence rested mainly on the argument that political events, from the violent background of the 1959 elections to the declaration of the emergency in the West, had created an atmosphere of violence, fear and suspicion and that what had been presented as a plot was in fact only precautionary measures. The first defence witness, Michael Omisade, an Action Group Federal MP and one of those alleged to have gone to Ghana for training, said that after the declaration of the emergency 'there were all sorts of speculations as to what the Federal government was going to do with the Action Group; there were rumours that Action Group members were to be detained in Kaduna'. He therefore decided to go 'on holiday' to Ghana. Omisade added that he had made his statements to the police in order to be released from detention: 'There was a state of emergency then and there were threats to shoot people, especially me in particular. I was told by Dr Majekodunmi (the West Administrator) that I would be shot and there would be no report in the papers and that a law to that effect had just been passed.'

Awolowo opened his own defence by denying that he had been especially embittered by his failure in the 1959 elections. He had then prepared vigorously for elections due in the West in 1960. However, he referred to 'information received by my colleagues

a. *Sir Abubakar Tafawa Balewa*

b. *Dr Nnamdi Azikiwe*

c. *Chief Obafemi Awolowo*

d. *Sir Ahmadu Bello, Sardauna of Sokoto*

PLATE I

a. Dr Michael Okpara

b. Major-General Yakubu Gowon

c. Chief Samuel Akintola

PLATE II

d. Colonel Odumegwu Ojukwu

and myself that after independence the Action Group-controlled Government of the Western Region would be dissolved and a caretaker government installed . . . in order to tackle this problem of the West it was decided that a Tactical Committee should be appointed'. This Committee was set up by Awolowo, Akintola, Enahoro and Rosiji with the object that the party might 'place its field organisation in a state of constant preparedness to counter effectively any move on the part of the NCNC to incite acts of lawlessness with a view to bringing about a breakdown of law and order in the Western Region'. Another object was to organise publicity 'so as to put the Federal Government absolutely in the wrong should they attempt to seize control of the Western Region Government from the Action Group by means other than electoral'.

A third objective was to make 'tactful overtures' to the NCNC as 'a combination of the two parties might take over power at the federal level'. These overtures, made in 1961, were made 'sometimes directly and sometimes through agencies'. Awolowo made special contact with the Zikist National Vanguard, the militant wing of the NCNC, and also personal overtures to Azikiwe. A fourth objective of the Tactical Committee was to develop election campaigns in the North and East. 'During the years 1960 and 1961 the Action Group spent an average of £300,000 per annum by way of recurrent expenditure on field organisation. . . . I led the campaign for the Northern Region election which was held on 4th May, 1961. That election alone must have cost the Action Group £100,000.'

After the Action Group split, 'I became satisfied that Chief Akintola had been misrepresenting the functions of the Tactical Committee to other leaders and members of the Party. I decided to have nothing more to do with the Committee.' When he first heard about Maja's plans, he had told Dokotri that Maja 'must be mad' and dissociated himself from the plan. 'Indeed, I added that Maja must have been a police agent—trying to lead the Action Group into a trap so that the NPC might achieve its ambition by destroying the party.' Commenting on Maja's evidence, defence

145

lawyer M. A. Odesanya, appearing for Tarka and two others, said Maja was 'the arch enemy of the Action Group and a self-confessed felon. He has given evidence of plans which he himself has conceived and was in the process of perfecting. One has to consider the anxiety he might feel to avoid prosecution.'

In his judgement Sowemimo admitted that 'there were some contradictions and conflicts in the evidence of some of the witnesses', but held that the defence had not shown these to be material. Dismissing the claim that three prosecution witnesses were biased against the Action Group because they were now members of Akintola's UPP, he uttered a monumental example of judicial ignorance of facts not specifically adduced in court—an utterance which was to be one of the grounds of appeal. He said: 'I must confess, however, that I do not know what the alphabet "UPP" stands for. It does seem to me that it is a faction of the Action Group led by Chief Akintola and which has acquired a name of its own to distinguish it.' Of the training in Ghana, he recalled that five witnesses had testified to it. He acknowledged that both Oboh and Oleari had charges pending against them in another court—of forgery and stealing in the case of Oboh—but concluded that as witnesses they were competent.

After the eight-hour judgement, Awolowo addressed the court for ten minutes before sentence was passed. He said it was an irony that he, as one of the architects of Nigeria's independence, had had to spend half of the first three years of independence under restriction. 'The twilight of democracy and the rule of law in Nigeria is changing into darkness.' Passing sentence, the Judge said: 'I would have said it was enough for you to have undergone such a trial. . . . I do not see the purpose of sentencing you to prison. But the law obliges me to do so. My hands are tied.' Awolowo was sentenced to ten years on the first count, five years on the second and two years on the third, the sentences to be concurrent. Tarka and two others of the accused were acquitted on all counts and discharged. Omisade was sentenced to seven years. After the sentences, crowds outside the courtroom demonstrated noisily and police used tear gas to disperse them. For days strict security measures had been in force, both in Ibadan and Lagos.

What had emerged most strikingly from the searchlight the trial had thrown on Nigerian politics was the role of money and of violence. Indeed, the very foundation of the prosecution's case had been that, as a result of what had happened to his party's sympathisers in the North, Awolowo had lost faith in the ballot box. The emphasis of the defence was that violence—or at least preparations for it—was to some extent necessary to combat violence. This applied not only to the actual violence of paid party thugs but also to what was seen as the ever-present threat that the Federal government would 'take over' the Region—an event the Action Group had foreseen long before it actually happened. In his judgement, Sowemimo remarked that 'there is no doubt that there was much free money in the Party . . . and to deprive any of these party officials of this monetary inducement may lead to some bitterness against the party'. He added with admirable understatement: 'There is again not the slightest doubt that the indulgence in the advance of money to party members reached such a stage that it is difficult to see whether members were attracted and convinced of the political philosophy of the party or in the monetary gain which they received.'

Whatever its merits the trial did little to strengthen popular faith in Nigerian justice. The acknowledged contradictions and weaknesses in the evidence, the dubiousness of the motives of several key prosecution witnesses, and above all the inherent implausibility of a plot to capture Lagos with a few pistols, rifles and torches, with apparently no arrangements for winning power in the Regions, strengthened a widespread belief that Awolowo had somehow been betrayed, if not actually framed. A more moderate version of this belief is that Awolowo must have known about a plot—and that he did not reveal it to the police itself makes him guilty of a crime—but that he may well not have been as deeply implicated as the prosecution claimed. In any case, the background of violence and bribery in politics made his precise degree of guilt or innocence seem largely academic to many Nigerians—just as it had been to the people of Eastern Nigeria after their hero, Azikiwe, had been admonished for bad financial conduct by the African Continental Bank tribunal of 1956.

The appeal was filed in September 1963 and judgement announced in July 1964. The verdict was upheld, but Awolowo's sentence was reduced to seven years. The appeals in respect of three of the accused were allowed and they were discharged. The Chief Justice, Sir Adetokunboh Ademola, said in a 2¾-hour judgement that there was overwhelming evidence that there had been a plot to overthrow the government by force of arms and that as leader of the party Awolowo must have known about it. There was evidence that he had become frustrated when he failed to achieve his ambition of becoming Nigeria's first Prime Minister.[24]

A week before the Awolowo sentence was announced the party's publicity secretary, Enahoro, had been sentenced to fifteen years (later reduced to ten on appeal) for his part in the same plot. Enahoro's trial had been separate because he had managed to slip across the Dahomey border, sixty miles from Lagos, and had found his way, via Ghana and Eire, to England. He was eventually repatriated under the Fugitive Offenders Act after his case had been through the courts, right up to the House of Lords, had been debated in the Commons and had become a *cause célèbre* in Britain. 'My parting thought was a renewed regard for the British system, even though, in this instance, it had produced the wrong answer', Enahoro reflected in *Fugitive Offender*,[25] the autobiography he later wrote in prison, after that system had played cat and mouse with him for six months before finally sending him back to Nigeria. His tenacious faith provides only half of the irony in his urbane and tolerant account. He goes on to depict his subsequent trial, and that of Awolowo, as the culmination of a plot by the Federal government against his party merely because it was in opposition. In his account of the background, he maintains that it was Maja who had plotted to overthrow the government and had tried unsuccessfully to implicate the Action Group leaders. He admits that both he and Awolowo knew about Maja's plot but does not explain why neither went to the police. Salient points in Enahoro's trial were notes on a BOAC scribbling pad which he had made and which were found in his car when he crossed the frontier. These referred to 'D-Day' and 'flight arms'. The judge rejected his defence that they were notes of what Maja had told him about the plot. His defence that a quantity of high performance torches which he bought in Italy were for use in political campaigns in the Mid-West was also rejected. The Enahoro episode was much less important in Nigerian eyes than Awolowo's, and the deep offence caused in Britain by the Nigerian government's failure to admit his British lawyer in breach of a promise made to the British government passed almost unnoticed. It is a tribute to the liberality of the authorities that two weeks before his sentence was announced Awolowo was allowed to prepare a by-election speech for broadcasting, in which he bewailed what he called the 'progressive erosion' of liberty in Nigeria. The sentences on Awolowo and Enahoro were announced within a week of each other. The newspapers refrained from comment. However, the *Daily Times*'s beat-style columnist, 'Sad Sam', slipped in a remark about the state of the nation which must have found wide echo, at least in Yorubaland : 'You gotta laugh to keep from crying.'

RISE OF AKINTOLA

Akintola now consolidated his victory. Armed with the Supreme Court's decision that Adegbenro's appointment as Premier had after all been illegal, he was sworn in as the head of the reinstated government. His new cabinet was a Coalition government between his new UPP and the NCNC members in the Region. He had dismissed fourteen of the old cabinet; they remained Action Group supporters and became the nucleus of a new opposition. The Action Group purged itself and tightened its belt for the conflict ahead. Twenty-five senior members were dismissed and fourteen others were asked to explain their behaviour during the crisis. Now solidly in opposition both in the West and in Lagos, the party could for the first time claim to be radical.

The Federal House was now without a leader of the opposition. Balewa claimed that Nigeria could do without this British refinement. 'A handful of twenty people cannot provide an alternative government.'[26] The opposition received momentary encouragement from London. In May 1963 the Judicial Committee of the Privy Council reversed the Supreme Court decision and, in effect, declared Akintola's government to be illegal. Ruling that the dismissal of Akintola by the then Governor had been valid, Lord Radcliffe confirmed the right of a Governor to remove a Premier from office if it appeared to him that the Premier no longer commanded the support of the majority in the House, whether or not there had been a vote to this effect in the House. He considered that a letter signed by 66 out of 124 members had constituted evidence for this. The news from London sent the Action Group supporters dancing in the streets in dozens of towns and villages of the West and in Lagos. Some of the joy was naive. 'Now we are in power!' shouted some. 'Akintola is out and Adegbenro is in.'

But the joy was short-lived. Hard on the news from London came the news from Ibadan. Anticipating the Judicial Committee's decision by one hour, the regional government introduced and passed a bill amending the constitution retrospectively, to deny the Governor the power in question, thereby defeating the purpose of the Judicial Committee's decision. Akintola told the House that 'the British are out to bring confusion into Nigeria and to deceive our sons and daughters'. There was an obscure dispute about the voting. The relevant copy of the regional *Hansard*, which should have showed the division lists, was withheld from publication. (It has never been published.) However, it was announced that the amendment was carried by eighty-three votes to nil, after thirty-eight Action Group members had walked out. The following week the Federal House, meeting in emergency session, ratified the decision. The issue was taken to its ultimate stage a year later, when the new republican constitution abolished appeals to the Judicial Committee of the Privy Council. Speaking on the motion at the time, Balewa said: 'The opinion of the Judicial Committee is, if we may say so without disrespect, quite out of touch with the realities of the situation in Western Nigeria and unsound in principle.' Referring to a recent act of the British colonial government in Gambia, where a court decision had been over-ruled, he concluded that if anyone should accuse the Nigerian government of disregarding the rule of law, 'our answer is the same as that of Mr Sandys:* "There is nothing wrong in legislating to avoid political chaos." '[27]

The final stage in the process of dismantling the Action Group empire was the carving up of the Western Region territory by creating the Mid-West Region. Such a move had originally been supported by the Action Group, on the understanding that similar new regions would be carved out of the North and East as well, but the support was later withdrawn. The necessary amendment to the constitution duly passed the Western and also the Federal Houses and the requisite referendum in the Region was held. In political terms, the main beneficiary of the move was the NCNC, which easily gained control of the new Mid-West government. It thus became the only party to control two Regions.

The state of the parties in the West was now: UPP 41, NCNC 44, Action Group 33. The whole process of polarisation was completed later in the year when Akintola formed a new party—the Nigerian National Democratic Party (NNDP), to which most of the NCNC members crossed. This became the governing party and remained in office until Akintola's violent death and the suspension of parliamentary government on the night of January 14–15, 1966.

* Duncan Sandys, Commonwealth and Colonial Secretary in the British government at that time.

7. Towards the Coup

I believe that the problem of Nigeria cannot be solved until that of Northern Nigeria has been solved. I hold it as a fact that the Northern Region in its present state constitutes a gradual but sure brake on the fast-moving South, a lack of incentive to the Northerners to accelerate their rate of progress in order to catch up with their Southern brothers, and a dead weight on the country as a whole. . . . If the Action Group and the NCNC, both of which have a monopoly of political following in the South, and at least one third of the political followership in the North, could come together, then they would serve as a catalyst to the political situation in the North, ensure the creation of more States, particularly in the North, entrench liberal democracy in the country and infinitely increase the tempo of progress in the Federation as a whole. I hold it as a fact that such a combination is sure to win a landslide victory at a subsequent election.

—Chief Awolowo, 1963.[1]

As things stand in the present constitution, the North has half the seats in the House of Representatives. My party might manage to capture these, but it is not very likely for the present to get any others; on the other hand a sudden grouping of the Eastern and Western parties (with a few members from the North opposed to our party) might take power and so endanger the North. This would, of course, be utterly disastrous.

—The Sardauna of Sokoto, 1959.[2]

THE DOWNFALL OF AWOLOWO left power at the federal centre to an apparently impregnable 'Establishment'. The NPC was virtually unchallenged in the North, its Federal Coalition partner, the NCNC, was in power both in the East and in the newly-created Mid-West, while the NPC's new political ally, Akintola's NNDP, controlled the

152

West. The Action Group diehards, though still popular in the West and in Lagos, were firmly cut off from the financial rewards of regional power and consequently suffered massive desertions, both at regional and federal levels.

The purged, chastened and depleted Action Group had become the first major political party in independent Nigeria to be identified with the under-dog. Its continued popularity was shown in its victory in the Lagos Town Council election of October 1962. But to be liked by the tribally-mixed, proletarian population of Lagos was something that could be shrugged off in the calculations of politicians thinking on a national level. As for its popularity as an opposition party in the West—that could be taken care of by methods that were already passing into accepted practice: intimidation of opponents, diversion of public funds to party use, packing of local authorities with government party supporters, and the manipulation of elections.

However, the apparent impregnability of the Establishment was achieved against a background of growing popular disillusion. Tangible benefits of independence long promised by politicians— more jobs, more and cheaper food, electricity, approach roads and piped water in villages—had all failed to materialise. Development on all fronts was visibly bedevilled by the tribal and regional bickerings of politicians, by corruption and nepotism. While the people seemed to be getting poorer, the politicians in power were getting more ostentatiously rich—as well as more efficient and ruthless at clinging to power. Government was becoming an instrument for wielding power, instead of for conciliation and just administration.

Potential threats to this Establishment were few, but none the less dangerous. One was the break-up of the Federal Coalition, which would open the way for the grouping of Southern parties against the NPC which the Sardauna of Sokoto had long feared. A new population census might threaten the North's preponderance by revealing that it had been relatively over-counted in the previous census. An election in the West might bring the Action Group back into power there. Industrial or general unrest might threaten law and order. In the event, all these threats (except the Action Group victory in the West) materialised to some extent. Some of the ensuing crises not only rocked the Establishment but threatened the survival of the Federation itself. In the end, none of these crises resulted in the overthrow of the regime; they merely prepared the way for the *deus ex machina* from the barracks.

THE 1964 GENERAL STRIKE

A general strike on a massive scale, such as occurred in 1964, was a rarity in Nigerian politics. Trade unions, like football teams, suffered from too much fragmentation to be effective (see chapter 2, pp. 26–7). They were mostly 'house' organisations, grouping workers in a particular firm, corporation or government department. There were more than seven hundred registered unions in 1965, grouping about 1·2 million organised workers. In its early days, unionism had been in the forefront of the nationalist movement, drawing from the struggle its unity of purpose and momentum. A general strike declared by seventeen unions in 1945 had brought out 30,000 workers for thirty-seven days and won from the British authorities the promise of an inquiry into the cost of living. Such a victory was not to be repeated for nineteen years. Despite several attempts to recapture its old unity the union movement became—and has remained—chronically split. The divisions were over personalities and tactics rather than ideology. However, as has happened in similar labour splits all over Africa, one group sought support from the International Confederation of Free Trade Unions (ICFTU), based in Brussels, and the other group maintained links with either, or both, the World Federation of Free Trade Unions (WFFTU), based in Prague, and the All African Trade Union Federation, based in Accra until Nkrumah's downfall. The latter group comes broadly into the 'radical' camp; its centre was the Nigerian Trade Union Congress, which in 1965 claimed some twenty affiliated unions with a combined membership of about 140,000.

The 'moderate' group, affiliated to the ICFTU, called itself the United Labour Congress, which claims about a hundred affiliated unions. In 1965 a third group, in an unsuccessful bid to spearhead a truly united labour movement, broke away to form the Labour Unity Front. This radically-minded group claimed the support of the powerful railwaymen, post office workers and electricity workers among its thirty affiliated unions.

The 1964 strike was a struggle over the wage recommendations of the Morgan Commission (see chapter 2, pp. 24–6)—at first over the government's slowness in publishing them, and later over its unwillingness to implement them. A Joint Action Committee (JAC), led by the fifty-eight-year-old veteran labour leader, Michael Imoudou, effectively united all warring groups for action. While the protest began over wages, it quickly broadened into an attack on the Establishment as a whole—its corruption, its tactless ostentation and its flagrant inefficiency. One obvious target was the off-hand way the government was accustomed to dealing with labour matters. When the long-awaited Morgan Report was at last published, under the threat of a strike, the Federal Minister of Labour, Chief J. M. Johnson, was abroad on a goodwill tour and Balewa was on holiday at his farm in the North. Even the outbreak of the strike failed to produce a sense of urgency on the government side. Balewa returned to Lagos, but his approach was disastrously high-handed. In a broadcast he warned that the government would not negotiate while the strike was on and issued an ultimatum to the workers to return to work within forty-eight hours or face dismissal. 'We cannot tolerate this situation any longer', he concluded. The ultimatum was ignored. Within a week four federal ministers were negotiating far into the night with the strike leaders—sometimes by candlelight because the electricity workers were out too. And the negotiations were not on the basis of the government's compromise proposals but of the Morgan Commission's figures.

'No Morgan—No Work', Imoudou's men had chanted the whole week. At the outset, the police had been rash enough to try and stop a strikers' procession as it tried to cross Carter bridge on to Lagos island and in the ensuing scuffle both Imoudou and the United Labour Congress leader, Alhaji Adebola, were injured. Imoudou now wore his arm in a sling—a useful addition to the already bizarre effect of the red track suit he called his 'battle dress'. Imoudou, a Mid-Westerner, had had only a primary education and had worked in the railways since he was twenty-one. As founder of the first railway union he had achieved the unprecedented feat of accumulating £1,500 worth of union dues, thus earning a rare reputation for incorruptability. He had been dismissed and rusticated by the British authorities for his union activity. With characteristic flamboyance, he had returned from rustication to Lagos riding a white horse, waving to triumphant crowds of his supporters.

The strike began at midnight on May 31. First to come out were the railwaymen and dockers—and both ports and railways were effectively paralysed by the next morning. In the Eastern Region, especially at Port Harcourt, strike action was as prompt and effective as in Lagos. Indeed, the East, which had its own subsidiary Joint Action Committee, proved the most militant Region and the most reluctant to return to work. The North, on the other hand, was understandably more half-hearted; after intense pressure from the Northern government, the leaders of the JAC in the North called off their strike several days before Lagos. After June 1 the strike spread day by day: the postal workers came out gradually, as did electricity and bus workers. Some essential services were partially maintained by senior staff, including expatriates. The sit-down strike (JAC leaders had ordered workers to turn up for work but stay idle) spread to non-government workers. In all, some 800,000 were out by the end of the first week. A second government ultimatum, expiring on June 10, threatening dismissals, was largely ignored. However, a similar ultimatum, expiring three days later, issued by the Employers' Consultative Association, was more effective. One of the big Lagos department stores, the Swiss-owned Union Trading-Company, had actually dismissed a thousand workers; police had to be called to control the crowds of 'applicants' who arrived to take their places. The big companies felt they had been dragged into a quarrel which was not their concern, as most of them were already paying rates in excess of the Morgan minima. The strike officially ended on June 13, the day the private employers' ultimatum expired. By that time, its essential objectives had been won.

In the end the government accepted a wage level well in excess of its original proposals, though still short of the Morgan level. The settlement was immediately followed by a rise in prices—market women raised their food prices even before the settlement was announced—which more than offset the benefits. Many small firms with semi-redundant staff dismissed surplus workers, thus further aggravating unemployment. However, a massive protest had been made; the unions had tasted unity and power for the first time and, though they were never again to erupt during the First Republic, they could now be expected to seek to translate their power into political terms.

THE CENSUS CONTROVERSY

One February morning in 1964, Nigerians woke up to find that there were now officially 55·6 million of them, making Nigeria the tenth most populous country in the world.* The last time they had been counted, in 1952–53, there had been only 30·4 million. Such an increase—amounting to over 6 per cent per year, seemed to break all records. It made Nigerians appear to be multiplying faster than the Chinese, the Indians or the Egyptians.

It was not the overall figure which upset people but that, out of 55·6 million, almost 30 million were now claimed to be living in the Northern Region. As seats in the Federal House were allocated according to population, this seemed to dash the longstanding Southern hopes that a new count would end the North's numerical predominance and, indirectly, Northern political control. For years, Southern politicians—and their public—had been convinced that there were not really half as many Northerners as was claimed.

* After China, India, the Soviet Union, the United States, Indonesia, Japan, Pakistan, Brazil and West Germany.

'Why, you have only to travel in the North and you see nothing but desert for most of the day', they often repeated. There was a feeling that the British, preferring the conservative North to the volatile South, had somehow managed to swell the Northern figures. For years they had waited for the census to put the matter right.

The November 1963 count, on which the new figures were based, was the second attempt within two years. The 1962 census, which had cost £1·5 million, had been cancelled after fierce behind-the-scenes disputes over the genuineness of the figures. A second count was held, at a further cost of £2·2 million. Its results were equally controversial, and two months of muted speculation and recrimination ensued before they were published in February 1964. The government had attributed this final delay to 'the need to make detailed calculations and analyses of many thousands of figures'. In fact, the figure first returned by the officials was the altogether incredible one of 60·5 million. Further 'tests and checks'—which appeared to the cynical Nigerian public as a political compromise between the parties—brought it down to 55·6 million. A political row followed publication of the new figures, which gave the North almost as great a preponderance over the three Southern Regions as before. The figures were 'rejected outright' by Okpara, Premier of the East and leader of the NPC's Coalition partner, the NCNC.

The 1962 count was the first comprehensive census ever held in Nigeria. The previous one, in 1952–53, had been a 'group count', in which only the names of the head of each family or 'compound' were noted, together with a statement of the estimated size of each group. In 1962 a physical head-count of the whole population was undertaken by a team of 45,000 enumerators, under a British retired civil servant, J. J. Warren. From the outset, the operation was submerged in politics, with politicians and tribal leaders out to 'win'. While previous counts had been associated in the popular mind with tax collecting, the politicians now emphasised that the purpose of the exercise was the correct distribution of such coveted amenities as approach roads, running water and electricity, hospitals and industries.

Their campaign was only too successful. Despite official warnings against special migrations, thousands of people living away from their home villages returned en masse to do their duty. It was reported that one clan union in Enugu, the Eastern capital, finding its members unwilling or unable to return home, sent a union official back to the home village with a list of members, which was duly copied by the local enumerator. When the 'campaign' opened an administrative officer in the East triumphantly announced the discovery of a village of 20,000 people 'which has neither been registered for parliamentary elections, nor represented in any of the Nigerian legislatures'.[3] This was not the only newly 'discovered' village.

The 1962 totals were never published. It is understood that the first results achieved the old ambition of Southern politicians by giving the South a bigger population than the North. The North had gone up just over 33 per cent to 22·5 million, while the combined South (East, West and Lagos) had gone up more than 70 per cent to 23 million. These figures gave Nigeria a total population of 45·5 million. Warren himself dismissed the Southern figures of 1962, particularly those of the Eastern Region, as 'false and inflated'. He specified in his report that 'the figures for the five divisions of Awka, Brass, Degema, Eket and Opobo, which have recorded increases of over 100 and 120 per cent, can certainly be rejected out of hand'.[4] The Northern figures appeared to be reasonable, recording an annual increase of about 2 per cent, plus a 5 per cent increase in efficiency of enumeration over the previous count. Among the more obvious discrepancies in the Southern figures were the presence of three or sometimes four times as many adult males as appeared on the tax registers, and of many more children under five than all the women of childbearing age could have produced if they had all been pregnant continuously for the previous five years. Warren, whose contract had now expired, was dispensed with and Balewa took personal control of the matter. Verifications were carried out. The Northern government now appeared to carry out its broad political policy: to do what the

South does—only better. In the revised figures, while the South stayed substantially the same, the North claimed to have missed out all of 8·5 million people, presenting a new total of 31 million. Balewa decided to abandon the whole exercise and start again.

The new census was conducted on a grander scale. Instead of an expatriate official, the Prime Minister was in charge, at the head of a census board. In place of 45,000 enumerators, there were now 180,000. Counting by sight was to be compulsory—even for children. There was an immediate controversy about the position of women in purdah in the North. To solve the problem, some 6,000 inspectors, both men and women, were to be sent into each Region by citizens of other Regions. An advertisement in the East requested 'about 2,000 trained, educated and mature women inspectors for service in the North to help count women in purdah'. To minimise the notorious 'census migrations', the counting period was compressed from two weeks to four days.

Despite these precautions, the new count was held in much the same atmosphere as the old. Some of the Eastern inspectors in the North must have enjoyed an instructive new first sight of parts of their country, but they met with mysterious mishaps: trains were held up and even derailed and road transport was misdirected. Finally, when the new figures were made known, it was clear that the North had now fully caught up with the South in demographic arts. The North, with 29·8 million, was now claiming to have increased 77 per cent since the 1952–53 count, while the East, with 12·4 million, claimed a 72 per cent increase. The West, together with the new Mid-West Region, claimed to have more than doubled itself. The techniques of inflation have not been revealed. That the operation in the North was carefully planned is suggested by the fact that the 77 per cent increase seemed calculated just to top the increase claimed by the East in the 1962 count; also, the increase over the 1962 figure is very much the same in the various provinces of the North. Overlapping of census districts—a device not easily spotted by visiting inspectors—and double-counts were probably among the methods.

PLATE III *a. Ibadan Market*
       b. Self-Service Store, Lagos

PLATE IV *a. Street Scene, Lagos*
          b. Street Scene, Kano

Within days of the announcement of the new figures, Okpara said 'the inflations disclosed are of such astronomical proportions that the figures obtained, taken as a whole, are worse than useless. We therefore reject them completely.'[5] Okpara alleged that some of the areas selected for checking by inspectors had been disclosed to the Northern authorities before the event. Among irregularities which had been reported to him by his Region's inspectors were: the counting of the inspectors themselves; double-counting; counting of travellers and 'passers-by' without staining their thumbs; the posting of inspectors after the counting had already begun; the counting of designated sample areas without the presence of an inspector; counting in market places; refusal of entry into purdah; merging of enumeration books from two different areas, one of which was not covered by an inspector; removal of the regulation 'counted' notices from houses facilitating double counting of those households; and the continuation of counting after the close of the census. The Sardauna of Sokoto, Premier of the North, officially accepted the census in the North as 'fair and reasonably conducted', and counter-attacked with charges of inflation in the East, laying particular stress on the reports of 'newly-discovered villages' there.

A crisis had now arisen which imposed the first serious strain on the unity of the Federation. True to its NCNC political alignment, the government of the new Mid-West Region joined Okpara in rejecting the census. The West was in a dilemma as it was under a Coalition government including both Akintola's new UPP and the NCNC. Akintola, who owed his political life to the Federal government and the NPC in particular, accepted the figures, while his NCNC ministers rejected them. This strain broke the Coalition and Akintola formed his new Nigerian National Democratic Party (NNDP), which took office leaving the NCNC members in opposition. For Okpara, the census battle was now virtually lost. As a last resort his government filed a suit in the Federal Supreme Court, but it was dismissed.

What is the real population of Nigeria? No precise calculation is possible on the extent to which undercounting in the 1952–53 census contributed to the apparently staggering increase recorded by the 1963 count. After the earlier count, the government statistician estimated that the enumeration in most of the North had been accurate to 97 per cent, but that there might have been an undercount of some 20 per cent, or about 100,000 people, in Ilorin province. However, it has been argued that 'in view of the difficulties encountered in enumerating the population in some provinces, like Bornu, Adamawa, Niger and Sokoto, the returns for these provinces are no better than informed estimates of the population'.[6]

The government statistician also claimed 97 per cent accuracy in the 1952–53 Eastern Region figures, but this, too, is open to challenge; it has been claimed by an Ibo writer that 'the magnitude of the population increases recorded (in 1962–63) are to be accounted for more by undercounting in 1953 than by overstatements in 1962'.[7] At the time of the 1953 count there had been political upheavals, and there is evidence of a strong local association in people's minds between the census and tax collection. Similarly, the 95 per cent accuracy claimed for the Western Region count in 1953 might have been optimistic: whole villages were found to have been omitted from the census returns, and there was at the time considerable local opposition to the census.

Various administrative estimates were made between the two counts. Ministry of Health figures, arrived at by projecting the 1953 population at a 2 per cent per annum increase in the Regions and 4 per cent in Lagos, put the 1962 population at 36·5 million— and the 1967 total at 41 million. Medical evidence has since suggested that the birth rate could yield an increase higher than 2 per cent per annum. An estimate made by the Centre of Population Studies at Ibadan University puts the 1962 figure at 45·3 million, based on an overall rise of 2·8 per cent per annum—which would put the 1967 population at 52 million.[8] The Ibadan survey considers that the undercounting in 1952–53 was much severer in the South than in the North—especially in the East. It gives the South as a whole a slightly higher population than the North. However, in the absence of definite evidence, the survey might be held to lean too far in favour of the South.

If we accept that the South rather than the North was under-counted in 1952–53—and the evidence points that way—then a not unreasonable guess might add 10 per cent to the 1952–53 figures for the East, West, Mid-West and Lagos, and 5 per cent to those for the North. To this it would be reasonable to add a natural increase of 2·5 per cent per annum in all Regions—a rate accepted by the Federal government after the coup of January 1966[9]—and 4 per cent in Lagos. Finally, a very conservative estimate of the net effect of the population movements that followed the tribal upheavals of 1966 would subtract 0·8 million from the North, adding that amount to the East. This would give us our own ten-tative estimate of the 1967 population as 47·4 million—24·8 million in the North, 12·3 million in the East, 7·3 million in the West, 2·4 million in the Mid-West and 0·6 million in Lagos. This estimate would still leave the North with a lead of 2·2 million over the South.

POPULATION FIGURES (millions)

	1952–53 Census	1962 Census	1962 Revised	1963 Revised	1967: Author's Estimate
North	16·8	22·5	31·0	29·8	24·8
East	7·2	12·4	12·3	12·4	12·3
West	4·6	7·8	7·8	10·3	7·3
Mid-West	1·5	2·2	2·2	2·5	2·4
Lagos	0·3	0·7	0·7	0·7	0·6
Total	30·4	45·6	54·0	55·7	47·4

When the census dashed one major hope of the Southern politicians —of challenging Northern hegemony by redressing the population imbalance—their aspirations once again centred on elections. Federal elections were due in 1964 and a regional election in the crucial Western Region (the only Region where the opposition stood a real chance of ousting the government) was due the following year. In the event, both elections produced crises that nearly broke the Federation apart—and both ended in disappointment for the

Southern parties. The 1962 Western crisis and the census controversy had already indicated that the North was not going to yield power readily. The course of the election controversies of 1964 and 1965 was to confirm this to the full.

The 1964–65 Federal Election Crisis

No one gave the signal for the federal election campaign to start. It began of its own momentum in July 1964—a full five months before the election took place. It began with a major shift in party alliances. The five-year-old Federal Coalition between the NPC and the NCNC had been increasingly strained, and was now openly discarded. The NCNC made no effort to hide its bitterness over the census, while NPC leaders accused their Southern partners of fickleness and unreliability, pointing to such issues as the 1964 general strike, when NCNC leaders had agreed in private to the government's proposals, only to denounce them in their own Region. At the end of July the Sardauna stated categorically that 'even if my party fails to get the required majority in the next federal elections, it will definitely not enter into any agreement or coalition with the NCNC. . . . The Ibos have never been true friends of the North and never will be.'

Having discarded the Ibo, the Sardauna was ready to put on a formal basis his alliance with the Yoruba—or rather the anti-Awolowo faction of the Yoruba who, thanks to Federal government support, were in power in the West. Accordingly, the NPC and Akintola's NNDP formed the Nigerian National Alliance to fight the election. In accordance with the already established political pattern, the National Alliance immediately attracted opposition parties in the Eastern Region—the Niger Delta Congress (NDC) which was agitating for a separate state (though the National Alliance was so unpopular in the East that this move split the NDC), and the Dynamic Party, led by the brilliant and eccentric mathematician, Dr Chike Obi.

On the other side, the way was now open for an alliance between the two old-established popular parties of the South—the NCNC and the Action Group. The marriage was duly solemnised under the re-sounding title of the United Progressive Grand Alliance (UPGA). To complete the pattern, the Progressive Alliance took under its wing the Northern opposition parties—Aminu Kano's Northern Ele-ments Progressive Union and Joseph Tarka's United Middle Belt Congress—which themselves fused for the election into the Northern Progressive Front.

That two nationwide alliances were now competing for power—each with its own separate appeal to the electors, embodied in a manifesto—gave the election campaign an almost British look. The explicit appeal of the National Alliance was to progressive conserva-tism. Its manifesto insisted, as conservatives do everywhere, on 'responsible government by men of proved ability', warning against parties who 'want Nigeria to take a leap into the dark, flying on the wings of dangerous doctrines which have never been tried in the African atmosphere'. The National Alliance's implicit appeal was its offer of the advantages of power, of adhesion to the group that dominated and seemed likely to continue to dominate federal politics. The Progressive Alliance offered, explicitly, a programme of moderate reform on mildly Socialist lines. It advocated more forceful pan-Africanism abroad and more purposeful planning (though nothing which would scare off investors) at home. Its most radical proposal was to split Nigeria into a score of small states, along the lines of the old colonial provinces, on the assumption that this would strengthen rather than weaken the Federal government. Its most popular plank was a promise to free political prisoners, above all Awolowo. In prison, Awolowo still remained the titular leader of the Action Group: his portrait appeared prominently in the Alliance manifesto and, in his cell at Calabar, he was receiving a stream of important visitors. Implicitly, the appeal of the Pro-gressive Alliance was that it would rid Nigeria of domination by the Northerners.

'If it's a fair election UPGA must win.' This was a popular belief in the South during the five months of the campaign. The key areas would clearly be the North and West, where the governments were controlled by the National Alliance. The new census figures had reduced the number of Northern seats in the Federal House from 174 to 167, and increased those of the West (where Progressive Alliance chances were greater) from 47 to 57. Assuming that the Progressive Alliance could capture all or virtually all the 87 seats in the East, the Mid-West and Lagos, and all but half a dozen seats in the West (a Region apparently not enamoured of Akintola's regime), then it needed to capture less than 20 Northern seats to secure a majority. Okpara predicted with a show of confidence that his Alliance would get 30 to 40 Northern seats. He was able to point to the 1959 elections in which the Action Group and the NCNC, with its Northern allies, had won 33 Northern seats with over 30 per cent of the Northern votes cast.

However, much of this optimism turned out to be false. Even given conditions of free campaigning, the NPC had learned a lot about party organisation since 1959. As the plight of former Northern opposition leaders like Ibrahim Imam showed (see chapter 6, pp. 142–3), the Northern opposition had become progressively dispirited and had suffered massive desertions to the governing party. Moreover, Okpara's appeal to the Northerners lacked political acumen: it looked like an attack on Northern nationalism. Nor was Akintola idle in the West. His new NNDP established its image as the militant champion of the Yoruba against the threat of 'Ibo domination', an image calculated to undermine the unity of the Progressive Alliance. 'UPGA-ism—the Truth Unexpurgated', was the title of one of its election pamphlets. Under photographs of prosperous Ibo shops in Lagos was the caption: 'Lagos women sell their wares in the gutters. The UPGA Ibos sell in shops.' Explaining the NCNC's motives in withdrawing from the Coalition government, it concluded: 'Now that the Ibo NCNC feels there is the barest chance for an Ibo man to become Prime Minister of the Federation or Executive President, the Ibo NCNC finds the NPC stairway has served its purpose. The Northerners have served their purpose. They can now be discarded.' The pamphlet dwelt in detail on the tribalist excesses of the Ibo ministers while in power.

The campaign was fought mostly by abuse, which was reported with reasonable impartiality in the newspapers. Few words were wasted on political issues; most of the discussion centred on the crescendo of complaints from the UPGA that the NPC in the North and the NNDP in the West were preparing to 'rig' the elections. The National Alliance in turn accused the Progressive Alliance leaders of inventing excuses for an inevitable defeat. The first hint of crisis came in November, when President Azikiwe warned in a broadcast that in the coming conflict Nigeria might disintegrate 'or face troubles worse than the Congo'. He said the atmosphere 'reeks of mutual antagonisms, bitter recriminations and tribal discrimination'. The Sardauna, the National Alliance leader, reminded his opponents that the Nigerian Federal constitution had no provision for the secession of any part, while Okpara denied thinking of secession and warned in turn that if the election were 'rigged', 'the Progressive Alliance will allow no one to assume power'.

The task of handling the electoral arrangements fell to Eyo Esua, an ex-schoolmaster and secretary of the Teachers' Union, who was chairman of the Federal Electoral Commission. He presided over five members, one for each Region and one for Lagos. He introduced some last-minute reforms resulting from all-party agreements. One was that the local government police in the Regions should, for the purposes of the election, be placed under the direct command of the Nigeria police. This reflected a widespread feeling that the local police forces could become a most effective weapon in the hands of regional governments in intimidating the opposition. The arrangement was not liked and in practice largely ignored by the Northern authorities. Esua supervised the erection of polling booths, flew around the country in a helicopter and sent teams of inspectors into all Regions to ensure arrangements for the secrecy of voting and the proper publication of the voters' registers.

The Federal Parliament was dissolved in December and the date of the election announced at last for December 30. In a broadcast at dawn, a traditional chiefly hour for a grim message, Azikiwe said he had received 'hundreds of telegrams and letters' from different parts of the country pleading that he should use his good offices to ensure free and fair elections. These had complained of false imprisonment, malicious prosecution, denial of bail for trifling offences, refusal of permits to hold meetings and the beating up of political opponents. Azikiwe ended with a warning that if politicians had decided to destroy national unity, 'then they should summon a round table conference to decide how our national assets should be divided before they seal their doom by satisfying their lust for office'.

The crisis deepened after the close of nominations, when it was announced that 78 candidates would be returned unopposed—sixty-one NPC members in the North, fifteen NCNC members in the East and two NNDP members in the West. In this context, the 'unopposed' return of a government party candidate meant only one thing to the opposition: that his would-be opponents had been effectively silenced. The NCNC rejected the 'unopposed' returns in the North, complaining that voters lists had not been made available to the public until two days before the close of nominations. In its turn the Action Group declared that the two unopposed seats in the West were in fact being contested by their candidates. 'These two candidates have paid their election deposits, have been duly nominated, have duly submitted their nomination papers, properly filled, and have been issued with Certificates of Validity by the lawful representatives of the Electoral Commission.'

Azikiwe himself now became the centre of controversy. His warning about malpractices, delivered in an apparently impartial, father-of-the-nation spirit, were felt by both sides to have been specially directed against the North. President or not, 'Zik' was still an Ibo and was universally assumed to be still an NCNC sympathiser. In any case, whether or not the Northern authorities were more skilled than the Eastern in the arts of election management, it was the North (and the West) which really mattered, as these were the power bases of the Balewa administration. Northern fears that Azikiwe might attempt to take the law into his own hands seemed reflected in the Sardauna's statement that he was sure the President 'would never go contrary to the Nigerian Constitution. He can only appoint as Prime Minister any MP who appears to him to command the support of a majority of the House.' The Progressive Alliance promptly replied by quoting a section in the constitution empowering a president in certain circumstances to appoint a prime minister in accordance with 'his own deliberate judgement'. It began to look as if the Progressive Alliance leaders might already have smelled defeat and be looking around for ways to circumvent the result. Tension mounted further when Esua admitted in a broadcast, six days before the election, that there had been irregularities. In some constituencies, opposition candidates had been nominated 'yet names of [government] candidates had been announced as unopposed'. He said that in certain constituencies where candidates had been announced 'unopposed', elections would nevertheless be held. He added that the Commission was still on a federal tour and would report its findings. In fact, it never did.

Three days before the poll, the UPGA held a press conference which was also attended by grim-faced labour leaders, including Michael Imoudou (still in his track suit 'battledress') representing his newly-formed Labour Party. Reporters were handed copies of sworn affidavits detailing malpractices in sixty-five Northern constituencies. Okpara declared the election had become 'a colossal farce—a daylight fraud'. One of the constituencies announced as 'unopposed' was Bauchi South-West, that of Balewa himself. According to the affidavit, three abortive attempts to nominate an opposition candidate had been made there. The first time the nominators were arrested; the second time thugs carried away the nominators; the third time the nominators were kidnapped and held until the lists closed. An affidavit referring to another constituency said: 'Native authority police refused candidate entry into the town; candidate subsequently killed.' The Northern opposition leader, Aminu Kano, told the press conference that his Northern Progressive Front had actually paid deposits for candidates in all of the North's 167 constituencies.

The same evening—December 27—it was announced from State House that the President and Prime Minister, after conferring for one hour and forty-five minutes, had 'disagreed in the question of holding the federal election'. It had been decided that the President would summon all the regional governors and premiers for noon the following day 'to resolve the issues'. Meanwhile, a protest march, about 2,000-strong, organised by UPGA, carried through Lagos such banners as 'Abubakar—No government by fraud'. Later in the evening, the UPGA announced through the NCNC's general secretary that it had decided to boycott the election.

> It is the view of the UPGA that we have now reached a stage when further compromise is impossible and that the last-ditch battle for safeguarding the individual liberty and the fundamental rights of Nigerian citizens must be fought. We therefore call upon all progressive forces throughout the length and breadth of the country to rally round UPGA so that we might save this nation from the forces of tyranny, despotism, feudalism, and from those who now seek to come to power at all costs and to impose totalitarianism upon the people of this country.

Two days later—election eve—Imoudou's Labour Party called on all workers 'to respond to the call of their foremost leader, Michael Imoudou, their own party, the Nigerian Labour Party, their supreme industrial organisation, the Joint Action Committee, for a general strike to secure the postponement of the federal election'. Only the railwaymen and the ports workers actually went on strike. Meanwhile, UPGA vans were touring Lagos suburbs with loud-speakers, urging the people not to vote. Balewa called in the heads of the armed services, including Major-General Welby-Everard, the GOC of the army. At seven o'clock on election eve, Nigerians were still uncertain whether the election would really proceed. Azikiwe's summons to a State House meeting had been boycotted by the premiers and governors of the North and West. Declining the invitation, the Sardauna remarked that the meeting had been called 'to organise secession from the Federation'. Balewa, showing himself the master in the battle of nerves that had now developed, did not wait for the outcome of Azikiwe's meeting with the premiers and governors of the East and Mid-West. He issued a statement, which was promptly broadcast, that he had had a meeting with the service chiefs and discussed arrangements 'for the election which will be held tomorrow'. After the broadcast, the Prime Minister attended the State House meeting. Later a State House message 'regretted the absence' of the Northern and Western premiers and governors from the meeting and added: 'The conference drew the attention of the Federal Electoral Commission to the strict adherence to the provisions of the Electoral Act, 1962, in the light of allegations of irregularities made by the Chairman of the Electoral Commission in his broadcast of December 22nd.' The reference was clearly to the Commission's powers to postpone the election if it so desired.

A meeting of the Electoral Commission lasted late into the night and ended in deadlock. Two of its members—those for the East and the Mid-West—were in favour of postponing the election while a third, the member for Lagos, was in favour of 'partial' postponement: that is, postponement only in constituencies where there had been irregularities. The members for the North and West were for proceeding as planned. While his colleagues were still arguing, Esua, their chairman, settled the matter by broadcasting a statement that the election would proceed.

Against this unpromising background, Nigeria went through the strange motions of an election. Scores of polling booths had been destroyed, the boycott was in force, and in the East there was no election at all. The Eastern electoral officers—civil servants of the Region just like those elsewhere—had received orders to sabotage the poll. In some places they simply did not turn up with the voting papers. In others they reported for duty but, according to an official source, 'went home when no one turned up to vote'. In Lagos, even the booths which had remained intact—or had been hastily repaired during the night under police protection—were virtually ignored as a result of the UPGA boycott. In the West, voting did take

171

place in most constituencies, but the results later showed that the boycott had been largely effective in all but the remotest areas. In the Mid-West the boycott was observed in the morning, but at noon the NCNC Premier, Chief Osadebay, had second thoughts. Fearing that his opponents might win by default, he suddenly ordered the poll to proceed, and his supporters to vote. The peculiarities of Mid-West politics had all along made its government a half-hearted UPGA partner, and Osadebay was possibly shrewder than Okpara in foreseeing that a boycott might hand power on a plate to his party's opponents. In the North, voting proceeded smoothly.

As was now inevitable, the National Alliance won a resounding victory—even if, in places where the boycott had been effective, it was only a paper victory. Far from winning thirty seats in the North, the Progressive Alliance won only four—all in the Tiv minority area. In the Mid-West the NCNC, thanks to Osadebay's second thoughts, won all fourteen seats except one (where the election had to be cancelled after the Landrover carrying the ballot papers was set on fire). In the West the Progressive Alliance won six seats in spite of its own boycott, leaving the remaining thirty-six to the NNDP, and one to an independent.

The next constitutional step was for the President to summon Balewa, as the man likely to command a majority in the House, to form a government. Or was it? The crisis now hinged on this point. Azikiwe later published his own version of the crisis—the 'State House Diary'—in which he implied that, well before the election, members of a Progressive Alliance delegation headed by Okpara had sought to advise him that the constitution gave him power in certain circumstances to take over executive powers. There is little doubt that Azikiwe believed he had reserve powers, partly as Commander-in-Chief of the armed forces and partly in his constitutional duty of appointing a Prime Minister. According to Section 84 of the constitution, 'the executive authority of the Federation shall be vested in the President and, subject to the provisions of this Constitution, may be exercised by him either directly or through the officers subordinate to him'. Section 85 said that such authority should 'extend to the execution and maintenance of this Constitution and to all matters with respect to which Parliament has for the time being power to make laws'. Furthermore, Section 87 (II) gave him power to appoint a Prime Minister when that office was vacant. However, during the crisis the office was not vacant: Balewa was still Prime Minister. And the law also clearly gave the Prime Minister, and not the President, power to dispose of the armed forces. Azikiwe had actually summoned the service chiefs before the elections and reminded them that they owed allegiance to him as their commander. But they had come armed with legal advice and told him of the real position. In the three days that followed Azikiwe was gradually, and painfully, convinced that he had no power whatsoever.

After the election Azikiwe, knowing that he could neither appoint a provisional government to hold a fresh election nor take over executive powers, decided to do nothing. He recorded a broadcast in which he said he would 'rather resign' than follow what he admitted was the clear constitutional duty imposed on him: i.e. to summon Balewa to form the government.[10] The speech was to be broadcast at 7 P.M. that evening, January 1. But, as Azikiwe records in his diary, 'an official emissary pleaded with the President that in view of attempts to effect a compromise it was advisable that the broadcast be postponed'.[11]

Balewa had also recorded a broadcast the same day; it too never went on the air, though its text was published the following day. It was characteristic of him. Telling the story of the crisis with no direct reference to the electoral malpractices with which virtually every voter in Nigeria was by now familiar, he recalled that when he met the President on December 28 'the President told me he wanted both of us to agree that the general elections, which were to be held on 30th December, that is, in two days time, should be postponed. I asked him why, and he said it was because there were many irregularities in the methods of nomination of candidates and in the way the election campaigns had been conducted. I told the President that the question of holding or postponing the elections was neither my responsiblity nor his and that I could not agree to the suggestions he had made.'[12] As for the complaints about the election, he said: 'We have our Constitution and our Laws and the law courts are there to interpret them.' He proposed that, 'to avoid bloodshed, a conference of all governments should be held so as to decide among ourselves what the future of our country should be'.

Two days of intense negotiations followed. The Chief Justice, several federal ministers and regional judges visited Azikiwe. All advised him that to summon Balewa was the only course which the law and the reality of power left open to him. At one o'clock in the morning on January 6, 1965, Azikiwe's press secretary carried to the newspapers a handout which must, for its timing, have been unique in constitutional history. 'It is announced from State House by the visiting physician to State House, Dr H. I. Idehen, that His Excellency, Dr Nnamdi Azikiwe, President of the Federal Republic of Nigeria, who was recently indisposed, is now quite fit and fully recovered and capable of fulfilling all his engagements both inside and outside State House.' This was clearly intended to forestall a possible recourse to Section 39 of the constitution, which provided for the President's functions to be exercised by the President of the Senate or the Speaker of the House of Representatives in the event of the President's illness. Azikiwe had spent several months of the previous year in virtual retirement at the University of Nigeria, Nsukka, on gounds of ill health.

More forceful plans to circumvent the presidential obstacle were widely believed to have been made at the time. One was a military coup;[13] another was Azikiwe's physical removal on board a navy frigate to a place outside territorial waters. The nocturnal health bulletin may well have stopped such a plan, but in any case, Azikiwe's firmness was now wavering and the same evening the crisis was resolved. With his famous wide smile bravely unimpaired, the President announced in a broadcast that the crisis was over: the constitution left him no alternative but to call on Balewa to form a government. He himself was 'prepared to subordinate my personal feelings to the Constitution'; the Prime Minister and he had now agreed that 'the validity of elections can be questioned only by due process of law . . . to do otherwise is to invite chaos and disorder'. He promised, however, that Balewa's government would be a 'broadly-based national government'.[14] His broadcast was immediately followed by one from Balewa, who spoke in similar terms. However, keen listeners noticed that instead of a 'broadly-based national government', Balewa merely referred to a 'broadly-based government'.[15]

Later accounts of the crisis by its principal actors all stressed how near Nigeria had come to chaos and disintegration. Balewa later recalled in private:

> I think I can say with truth that I was the only Nigerian leader not in favour of force and bloodshed at that moment. I sat in that chair over there [in the cabinet room] and heard day after day people urging me to call out the police, the army, the navy: to arrest the President and so on. I said to them I had been Prime Minister for seven years and they might feel the time had come for me to go because I couldn't see things the way they did [presumably a reference to NPC leaders]. I told them I would not mind seeing millions of Nigerian lives lost if I felt it was for a good reason. But what was that reason? Just because some people wanted to get power for their own selfish reasons, we were plunged into this crisis. I was not willing to see lives lost for this. There are numerous Northerners, men, women and children, living in the South and millions of Southerners living in the North. Who could say how many of them would die once fighting broke out? It could not be controlled.[16]

According to Balewa, the Progressive Alliance strategy that the President should assume some kind of executive power was not spontaneously evolved, but a long-standing plan. 'As early as November, the President appeared ill at ease when discussing the future with me. Then, three days before the elections were due to be held, he came to me and asked for postponement; I said "why", and he said because law and order had broken down. I had just then returned from the North and of course could see perfectly well that there was law and order there. I told him neither he nor I had power to stop the election.'[17]

However, confirmation that there was a drastic plan to deal with the recalcitrant President came from another of the actors in the drama. 'The whole cabinet was in session and everyone was prepared for action: the Prime Minister, the NPC, the service chiefs. It was suggested that Elias [the Attorney-General] should go and make a final effort to persuade Azikiwe to yield. Everyone was doubtful. Balewa said: "Look, we have had no sleep for the last seven days and everything is now ready. Why do you think he will change his mind at this stage?" ' According to this account,[18] it was Welby-Everard who persuaded Balewa to allow one final effort to persuade Azikiwe. The army chief wanted to make absolutely sure that the plan—to remove the President on grounds of his incapacity as evidenced by his refusal to act according to the constitution—was watertight. The President had, of course, made a mistake in announcing that he had been unwell: this laid him open to his removal. 'Elias, Ademola [the Chief Justice] and Mbanefo [Chief Justice of the East] then went to see Zik. He did not yield. The three returned to the cabinet room and asked for another few hours and were given until four o'clock. The three returned to State House and found Azikiwe with Okpara. Okpara left and, after a final discussion about terms, Azikiwe agreed to the compromise of a national government.'[19]

In his *Diary*, Azikiwe claims that Okpara had threatened as early as December 26 that the East would secede. After the election, the Federal and Eastern chief justices had presented Zik with a six-point plan for solving the crisis: reaffirmation of the unity of the Federation; strict observance of the constitution until its amendment by due processes; a broad-based national government; legality of the election to be determined by the courts, and fresh voting to take place in certain constituencies where polling had been so low as 'to make a mockery of democracy'; arrangements 'within six months' for a review of the constitution and the machinery for elections by a committee of nine, of whom one was to be appointed by the President, two by the Prime Minister and two by each regional premier; dissolution of the Western House to enable elections to be held.[20] According to Azikiwe, Balewa accepted the points, except the last one, as he felt the Western House should be dissolved within two months.

The 'compromise' solution, which was clearly a resounding defeat for the Progressive Alliance, caused widespread despondency among reform-minded and politically-conscious people in the South. Calling off the six-day-old strike in the Eastern Region, Wilson Mornu, general secretary of the regional Joint Action Committee, declared: 'The State House agreement has broken the back of the progressive forces. We have failed Nigeria and the world. The workers have not capitulated to the forces of reaction but we have gone on recess.' The threatened general strike had come to nothing. The United Labour Congress, 'moderate' wing of the movement, had dissociated itself from it on the grounds that its constitution forbade it from participating in politics. Disappointment among radicals was especially vocal in the Zikist Movement, the radical wing of the NCNC; its vice-chairman, Okafor, resigned from the Movement because he was 'convinced Zikists have been wasting their time in trying to sustain an ideology which no longer exists'. This was a scarcely-veiled attack on Azikiwe himself—a feeling widely shared in the East, where his popularity has to this day not recovered from the events of January 1965. Reactions to the solution were varied. Those with a prime interest in stability were relieved that chaos had been averted. Others were indignant that democracy had been violated. Perhaps the most characteristically Nigerian reaction was one of cynicism: what can you expect of politicians, after all?

What protest there was proved ineffective. The Students' Union at the University of Nigeria, Nsukka, filed an action in the High Court calling for the nullification of the election, which it claimed was 'unconstitutional, illegal and void', and seeking to restrain Balewa from acting as Prime Minister. The action was dismissed. Of dozens of election petitions, almost all were

177

defeated. Dismissing the petition of the would-be Progressive Alliance candidate in Balewa's own constituency (where Balewa was declared elected 'unopposed') the judge commented that politics inflamed passion and the local police were 'bound to intervene from time to time to maintain order'. He added that even if it were true that the petitioner's witness had been arrested while trying to file nomination papers, there seemed no reason why someone else could not have filed them in his place.

Six weeks after the election, the Federal House met to pass the Invalidating Act to legalise the holding of elections in the Eastern Region, where no polling had taken place. In this election, the NCNC predictably swept the board. The state of the parties in the Federal House was then: National Alliance 197, Progressive Alliance 108, Independents 5. Balewa's promised 'broadly-based' government included most of the old NCNC ministers and some from Akintola's NNDP. But it was not, after all, a national government in that no member of the Action Group was invited to take part. Balewa's conception of 'broadly-based' was to include ministers from each of the parties in power in the Regions.

THE WESTERN REGION ELECTION, NOVEMBER 1965

Election fever, with its complaints and counter-complaints, its threats and counter-threats, its thugs and counter-thugs, was not long in returning to Nigeria. The Western Region government of Akintola was to finish its term in October. The ensuing regional election proved, literally as well as metaphorically as far as the First Republic was concerned, an election to end all elections. The UPGA rightly called the campaign 'operation do or die'. It was, indeed, the last desperate attempt of the two old-established parties of the South to challenge the hegemony of the NPC. By winning control of the West—a real possibility in view of the evident unpopularity of the Akintola regime—they could control all three Southern Regions as well as Lagos. Although this would not dislodge the built-in NPC majority in the Federal House of

Representatives, it would give them a commanding majority in the Senate and thus a potential stranglehold over legislation.

The United Progressive Grand Alliance, formed to fight the federal election, now proved useful again. It was an imperfect alliance. It contained groups—especially the Northern opposition parties—which radical opinion throughout the country could regard as progressive. However, most Nigerians interpreted the alliance at the level of power politics, seeing it as a device that gave the NCNC a chance to use its old enemy, the Action Group, as a ladder for climbing to federal power. The Action Group had been purged by its misfortunes of some of its more opportunistic elements, while the NCNC was still its old, full-blooded, comprehensive self, containing ministers and parliamentarians who could not by any stretch of the imagination be called progressive. The Action Group, out of power in its home Region for three years, was also the impecunious junior partner. The imperfections of the marriage were all too evident in the pre-election scuffles over nominations. Under the Alliance agreement, thirty-two seats were for the NCNC to contest, while the remaining sixty-two were for the Action Group. In the event, the vote was split by the presence of candidates of both parties in no less than thirteen constituencies.

The NNDP once again championed the Yoruba cause against the threat of 'Ibo domination'. It could indeed claim to have given the West a share in federal power for the first time since independence. It claimed to have turned this advantage to good use in such things as the sharing of federal scholarships and jobs on federal corporations. Indeed, after it had won the election, the vice-chancellorship of Lagos University was actually taken from an Ibo and given to a Yoruba. 'Since 1944 the people of Western Region have been feeling as if they did not belong to the Federation of Nigeria', said the NNDP manifesto. 'They have not been in a position to participate in the government of the Federation, they have not been in a position to share the amenities and fruits of labour emanating from the Federal Government and which other parts of the country share and openly flaunt before their eyes.' The manifesto claimed the young people of the Region had previously 'roamed the streets of Lagos for jobs which they could not get, while the youngsters from other Regions, without any effort, were placed in lucrative jobs'.

The Progressive Alliance staked its claim to support on the misfortunes and injustices suffered by Westerners at the hands of Akintola's NNDP. 'People are victimised for no just cause; thugs are let loose on innocent women and children; schools are closed down as a political vendetta on individuals and even professors and lecturers of universities are sacked on the flimsiest excuse. Produce buyers, liquor sellers, goldsmiths, have their licences withdrawn and market women have been deprived of their stalls for failing to team up with the NNDP.' The Progressive Alliance manifesto promised, 'as its first and most immediate duty', to take steps to effect the release of Awolowo. It promised to cut down drastically the swollen cabinet of the Region, in which Akintola had rewarded his followers by making almost every member of parliament a minister or a junior minister. It also promised to reorganise the public corporations 'with a view to reducing the number of parasitic appendages now parading themselves as executive directors'. A trump card of the Progressive Alliance was that it could hark back to the prosperous days of Awolowo's pre-independence government, days of high cocoa prices and consequent high revenues, contrasting it with the obvious signs of penury and business stagnation associated with the present. Not many electors were sophisticated enough to know that, while Akintola could hardly be blamed for the fall in the world cocoa price, the widespread waste and corruption under the old Action Group regime revealed by the Coker Tribunal (see chapter 6, pp. 134–8) had helped to create the present slump.

As the poll approached, it became clear that the techniques used by government parties to stay in power had been progressively perfected at each previous election in Nigeria. The electoral game had now become a macabre battle of wits in which each side knew the other's tactics in advance, and was ready with countermeasures. On the last day's sitting of the old House, the government passed a series of 'special electoral regulations'. Public meetings were banned for two months. A remarkable section provided that if any candidate declared elected 'unopposed' were murdered, he could be replaced in office without further election. Another regulation fixed the closure of the poll at 4 P.M. instead of the customary 6 P.M., thus apparentiy ensuring that employers, among whom the government itself was by far the largest, could prevent employees from voting at all.

The first stage of ritual battle was over nominations. Knowing that the government would declare a number of seats 'unopposed', the opposition took the precaution of publishing names of its candidates for all ninety-four constituencies as soon as the House was dissolved. Not content with this, it paid all their deposits and, to make doubly sure, made them all swear affidavits before magistrates that they intended to stand and that no letter of withdrawal purporting to come from them should be considered valid without oral reference to them. The UPGA was anticipating the old trick whereby electoral officers who either supported or feared the government party were persuaded to accept the nomination of the government candidate—and then made themselves scarce until the close of nominations. The opposition candidate could therefore not file his papers, and the government candidate would be declared elected 'unopposed'. Sure enough, within two days of the start of nominations, complaints resounded through the land that electoral officers had gone into hiding. At the end of nominations, sixteen government candidates—including Premier Akintola himself—were duly declared 'returned unopposed'. The opposition at once claimed that the Premier's would-be opponent had 'not willingly withdrawn' and that the other 'unopposed' candidates were all in fact opposed. In these bizarre electoral circumstances, the opposition actually regarded itself as having won the first round, on the assumption that the government must have planned many more than sixteen 'unopposed' returns. Indeed in some places the opposition got its man nominated only after what

looked like an organised manhunt for the missing electoral officer.
They were reported to have caught up with one fugitive officer in
Lagos, about to board a plane for London.

The unenviable Esua, chairman of the Federal Electoral
Commission and *ex officio* chairman of the regional commission,
now repeated his performance during the federal election. He
admitted in a broadcast that there had been irregularities but
proved unable to do anything about them. 'Electoral officers
appointed by this commission in some cases have had their lives
threatened and some of them have been kidnapped and prevented
from discharging their duties to the commission', he reported.
Travelling round the Region with the other commission members,
Esua replaced some of the offending officers. However, in some
cases validity certificates issued to the candidates by the new
officers were not recognised by the government. At Egba East II
constituency, the Esua commission sacked the electoral officer for
absenteeism and appointed a substitute, but fourteen hours later
a local government officer and the chief electoral officer for the
division sacked the substitute and reappointed the original officer.

The UPGA decided to go to the courts over the nomination issue.
The Action Group administrative secretary filed a motion in
Ibadan High Court seeking a court order not to declare any
candidate elected in constituencies where the electoral officers
had not discharged their functions. At the same time, five UPGA
candidates filed an action in Oshogbu High Court against the
'unopposed' return of NNDP candidates in their own constituencies.
Both actions failed. Before the Ibadan High Court, Chief Rotimi
Williams, for the defendants, argued that such actions should
have been filed in the constituencies and not centrally and that in
any case the motion was too late as the candidates concerned had
already been declared unopposed before the day of the hearing.

After the nominations, the next phase of the battle was the
polling itself. The main idea at this stage was to try to prevent the
official polling agents of the opposition from being present in the
booths, while enabling the government party agents to stay on.

All accredited agents had to be issued with special identity discs. At the last moment, however, it was decreed that these discs had to be countersigned on the reverse side by an electoral officer. When polling day dawned, the government party agents had theirs duly countersigned, while those of the opposition found theirs were not. Needless to say the electoral officers were nowhere to be found. These were only the more obvious devices. Behind the scenes, large numbers of ballot papers mysteriously disappeared from police custody, presumably to find their way into the government party boxes. A number of supporters of both sides were arrested in possession of illegally-obtained ballot papers, but prosecutions were quashed. On the eve of the poll, an electoral officer was shot dead in the office of the electoral commission at Ibadan. On polling day, two electoral officers and two party polling agents were also shot dead.

After the polling came the third stage of the battle: the counting. The technique here was to try to keep the opposition's polling agents and candidates away from the count. In Ibadan and the major cities, a curfew was imposed which took effect before the counting was due to start. One opposition candidate later complained that he was forced, under cover of the guns of the local government police, to sit on a chair several yards away from the table where the counting was going on. 'When I tried to leave in disgust, I was forced to remain.'[21]

When all else failed and the opposition candidate was elected, a last resort was to reverse the result. In several well-attested cases, the UPGA candidate was declared elected by the returning officer and even given a certificate to that effect, only to hear his opponent declared elected over the radio. Special instructions had been issued that results were to be channelled through the Premier's office before being broadcast, instead of being announced in the constituencies, as the regulations provided.

As the results began coming in, a unique situation developed. The Eastern Region broadcasting station, fed by a team of reporters lodged in Chief Awolowo's house in Ibadan, broadcast one set of results as they came in, while the Western Region radio broadcast another. The federal radio in Lagos, after a 'false' start with the Eastern radio results, began broadcasting the official Western radio ones. The morning after the poll, most morning papers led with the news of Akintola's new government. But the *West African Pilot*, organ of the Progressive Alliance, led with the new government of the Action Group leader, Alhaji Adegbenro, claiming that the Alliance had won sixty-eight out of the ninety-four seats. The Eastern radio was actually listing Adegbenro's ministers while the Western radio was featuring Akintola's new cabinet. The official result was: NNDP 71; Action Group 15; NCNC 2.

A few hours after the Western radio had declared Akintola elected, Adegbenro, the UPGA leader, wrote to the Governor of the Region, Sir Joseph Fadahunsi, complaining of 'open rigging' in the election and asking him not to call on Akintola to form a government. 'In the alternative, as leader of the most popular party, I will form my own government.' That evening, Adegbenro gave a press conference in which he declared he had formed his own government. The Governor refused to receive him and duly called on Akintola to form a government. The following day Adegbenro and some of his 'cabinet' were arrested and charged with unlawfully forming 'an interim executive council'. In court Mr Justice Morgan, the Region's Chief Justice (the Morgan of the wages report—see chapter 2, pp. 24–6—but now in a different role), told the prisoners that he could not grant them bail 'until there has been a retraction of the publication relating to the circumstances of another government constituted by persons stated in the publication'. Adegbenro then gave a press conference at the police station where he was being held, declaring that the statements he was quoted as making at his earlier press conference did not mean that he had actually attempted to form a government—only that he had been 'prepared to do so' should he have been called upon. He added that his party would pursue its aims by constitutional means.

Meanwhile, Ibadan took on a wartime look, with soldiers in armoured cars patrolling the streets and riot police free with their tear gas. Within a day the crisis had become federal. 'Give us guns', chanted some of the wilder ones among hundreds of demonstrators who marched through Enugu, the Eastern capital. The 'enemy' was the government of the West and the demonstrators were marching in support of the stand taken by their Premier, Okpara, that the Western regime constituted 'an attempt to impose an illegal and undemocratic government on the people of Western Nigeria'. The unity of the Federation seemed at its lowest ebb.

Replying to criticisms that if it was dissatisfied with the election it should go to the courts, the UPGA, in a statement, said 'we consider it a waste of valuable time and money. To go to court means filing as many as 70 petitions. First, we will be lucky if half the petitions are determined within two years. Even if all the 70 petitions are finally determined within 24 months, who will order the 70 by-elections? The NNDP's Mr Speaker? In the meantime, the Western House of Assembly would have continued to pass laws which make free and fair elections impossible.' The UPGA might also have added that, by that time, most of its members in the House, in accordance with well-established practice, would have crossed to the government party.

Lest anyone should still be in doubt about the conduct of the election, six weeks after it was held Esua decided to defend his own personal role in it in an open letter to the regional Governor. The letter is a valuable document in the psephology of a developing country. Esua admitted it was 'a notorious fact that some electoral officers refused to accept nomination papers of certain candidates, or failed to report for duty. Some, in fact, after accepting nominations of the candidates of one particular party, thereafter deserted their posts before all the other candidates in their constituency had a chance of filing their nomination papers.' Esua explained that his commission had tried to help by insisting that names of unopposed candidates should first be cleared with the commission; however, 'in the event they were announced without such clearance'. Esua went on to report that the secretary of the regional electoral commission, a civil servant responsible only to the Western Region Public Service Commission, revoked the appointment of some electoral officers after they had accepted nomination papers from opposition candidates. 'It was a great surprise to me to learn that some ballot papers were discovered in the hands of unauthorised persons at some of the polling stations.' He explained that, 'in view of the many apprehensions, to be quite safe, the ballot papers were handed to the Commissioner of Police, Western Region, with instructions that they were to be released for distribution to the polling stations only on the morning of the polling day'. Notwithstanding these precautions, large numbers of papers had disappeared from police custody and were later found in unauthorised hands.

Referring to stage four of the battle—the announcement of results—Esua said that 'returning officers who refused to announce the results of the election at the polling stations clearly acted in breach of the provisions of Section 46 (1) of the Electoral Regulations. . . . Why some returning officers refused to take this stand is incomprehensible to me, and has given good cause for misgivings about the authenticity of the results.' Esua further reported that 'some persons in Local Government Police uniform had proved themselves to be nothing but thugs in their operations'.

Stressing his own impotence in the situation, Esua recalled that regional elections were the responsibility of regional commissions, governed by regional regulations and carried out—with the sole exception of himself—by regional officials. 'One does not have to be a genius to know to whom the Commission's staff manifest their loyalty.' Expressing doubts about the future of free election in Nigeria, he suggested, as possible remedies, that senior staff of the electoral commissions should be appointed by the commissions directly and not through the civil service. Commissions should have greater powers in handling the return of unopposed candidates, the postponement of elections and the announcement of results. He proposed that nomination papers should be handled centrally by the commission instead of individually in the constituencies. He suggested the adoption of 'the French system' for polling, to guard against mass dumping of ballot papers: voters should secretly place their marked paper in an envelope and then drop it into a single box in the public view. To guard against malicious prosecution of candidates he suggested that when a valid candidate was charged with a criminal offence he should be either released on bail or permitted, under police escort, to file his nomination papers.

Popular disillusionment about democracy, already far advanced after the federal elections, was now almost total. In the West, a wave of riots, arson and political murders gradually engulfed the Region. At first details were published in the newspapers; but the threat implied in the 1964 Newspaper Amendment Act (see chapter 5, pp. 126–7) progressively damped the story down. Within four weeks of the election the official death roll had reached forty-six, but most people considered this a fraction of the true figure. In the town of Isho police opened fire on a group of demonstrators, killing eleven on the spot, while a further nineteen, including four policemen, were seriously injured. In Ijebu province, Awolowo's home area, a customary court judge was driven from his house by armed men and beheaded. Many Hausa from the North were killed. The *Nigerian Tribune* (the Ibadan Action Group paper which somehow managed to keep going though it was banned, its press burned and most of its staff arrested several times) calculated in January 1966 that 567 people were by then known to have been killed and 1,000 injured. The following day's issue reported a further '36 killed in two days'. Estimates made later suggest that over 2,000 people were killed in the Region between August 1965 and January 1966.

Premier Akintola could well claim—as he repeatedly did—that hordes of hired thugs had been sent over from the Eastern Region, and that robbery and plain hooliganism played a major part in the riots. The presence of a lawless situation and a genuine popular grievance were an obvious temptation to unemployed or semi-employed youths to go out on the rampage, burning the houses of NNDP members or known supporters and looting in the process. As the riots grew in momentum, passing motorists were waylaid on the roads. In January, while delegates were arriving at Lagos airport for the Commonwealth Conference, scores were killed in riots only a mile from the airport. The riots reflected a disillusionment that went far deeper than a particular election. A young man who poured petrol on to the car of a woman teacher in the Lagos–Ibadan road and threatened to light it if she did not part with money, said: 'Akintola has had his share. Now we want ours.'

Akintola's basic political crime lay not in the ideas of his party—Yoruba chauvinist ideas that found wide echoes—but in the ruthlessness of his regime. This was a matter of degree. Few of his methods—coercing people into supporting the party by the threat of petty prosecution, the withdrawal of trading licences, the denial of privileges, the harassment of opponents at elections—were new to the West. They had been practised in the days of Action Group power—when the same Akintola had been their chief planner. Only when a regime is unpopular are such methods taken to excess; the Action Group had used them intensively only in the Mid-West, where its regime was unpopular before the new Region was created there. Now Akintola had used them throughout the Western Region.

The tension immediately following the election was enlivened by an incident in the Ibadan broadcasting station. It was the evening when Premier Akintola was scheduled to make his first broadcast since the election. As the tape of his prerecorded speech was about to go on the air after the seven o'clock news, a masked gunman appeared in the channel, seized the tape and forced the engineers to broadcast a substitute tape. Instead of Akintola's familiar high-pitched voice, listeners heard: 'This is the voice, the true voice, of the people of Western Nigeria. Akintola get out, get out and take with you your band of renegades who have lost all sense of shame.' Nigeria's leading playwright, Wole Soyinka, was later charged with the offence, but the prosecution failed to prove the gunman's identity and Soyinka was acquitted.

In the weeks after the election army units were deployed in the Region. But the presence of the soldiers—many of whose rank and file were UPGA sympathisers, only increased the tension. Eventually, at the insistance of the General Officer Commanding, Major-General Aguyi-Ironsi, the troops were withdrawn. The disorders gew steadily worse until, by mid-January, everybody was agreed that something had to happen.

There was strong pressure on Balewa to act. His critics pointed out that in 1962, when disorders were restricted to a scuffle in the House of Assembly, he had declared a state of emergency. Why not again, now that law and order had effectively broken down throughout the Region? Everywhere, tax collecting had come to a halt and customary courts were not functioning, either because their buildings had been burnt or because their judges and officials had been murdered. However, Balewa was either un-willing or unable to convince his party leadership in Kaduna that the political disadvantages that would arise from the fall of Akintola were far less serious than the general calamity which now promised to overtake the whole regime. In the last interview given by Balewa, to Miss Bridget Bloom of *West Africa* on the day of his death, he repeated that he had simply 'no power' to impose a solution on the West. 'I only wish I had. The Chief Justice, and others, have been working with me, and are still working, trying to get a solution.' The violence, he stressed was 'planned by people who are determined that there shall be no peace in the West'. He admitted that while the Action Group had accepted his mediation in the dispute, the NNDP 'had asked for more time'.[22]

But there was no more time. On January 14, Akintola flew to Kaduna, capital of the Northern Region, to see the Sardauna. They discussed warnings of an impending military coup and possible countermeasures. Balewa himself had received such warnings, but had discounted them after reassurances from the Special Branch of the police. All three men now seem to have realised that the crucial weekend had come. It is believed that they discussed a plan for a drastic new solution of the Western problem, involving emergency legislation to be introduced in the Federal Parliament the following Saturday morning. They were also reported to have planned the removal on leave of General Ironsi (who was considered to have UPGA sympathies), the disbandment of some army units considered unsafe, and the massive arrest of dissident politicians, officials, writers and journalists in the West.

On that same Friday evening Akintola returned to the Premier's Lodge at Ibadan. Meanwhile, Balewa received an UPGA delegation, led by his Trade Minister, K. O. Mbadiwe, which appealed to him once again to take the Western situation in hand by declaring a state of emergency and arranging for a fresh election. But it was too late. Within a few hours Balewa, Akintola and the Sardauna were all dead. It was the end of the First Republic.

8. Three Coups

Our purpose was to change our country and make it a place we could be proud to call our home, not to wage war. . . . We were five in number and initially we knew quite clearly what we wanted to do. . . . Tribal considerations were completely out of our minds at this stage. But we had a set-back in the execution.
—Major Chukwuma Nzeogwu, May 1967.[1]

I do submit that the only realistic form of government today—until tempers have cooled—is such that will move people slightly apart. . . . It is better that we move slightly apart and survive. It is much worse that we move close and perish in the collision.
—Lieutenant-Colonel Odumegwu Ojukwu, January 1967.[2]

We should keep up the army's oneness as much as possible. Otherwise I think what will happen is that we will start having private armies; and then you have private police, prisons, and we start dividing the country gradually that way.
—Lieutenant-Colonel Yakubu Gowon, January 1967.[3]

A REVOLUTION of some sort was widely expected in January 1966. With the Western Region in disorder and the Eastern government in open disaffection, the federal authorities under Sir Abubakar Tafawa Balewa seemed to have lost their grip.

At the time the most likely kind of coup seemed to be a move by the authorities to concentrate power more effectively in their hands. Evidence of such a plan by the Northern Region's Premier, the Sardauna of Sokoto, is largely circumstantial but by no means implausible. The subsequent military regime claimed to have captured documents of a 'master plan' which involved fomenting a revolt in the non-Ibo area of the East to provide a pretext for the declaration of a state of emergency in the Region and a 'ruthless blitz' on all opposition elements in Lagos and the West.[4] The Sardauna was known to have conferred on January 14 with his political ally Chief Akintola, the Premier of the Western Region, and Brigadier S. O. Ademulegun, commander of the First Brigade. As all three men were to die the following night, no authoritative account of their meeting is available.

An army coup seemed less likely. There had been recent precedents abroad—by mid-January soldiers had seized power in Togo, Dahomey, Central African Republic and Upper Volta—but these were small, French-speaking countries where political conditions were different. Africa had not yet seen an army coup in an ex-British colony, with British-type parliamentary institutions and, above all, a British-type army with Sandhurst-trained officers. Nigeria's army had kept scrupulously out of politics. It had distinguished itself for its discipline and decorum while serving as part of the United Nations contingent in the Congo. At home, when controlling the Tiv riots in 1964, the disaffected Tiv had welcomed the soldiers as more impartial peacemakers than the local government police. During the election crisis of 1964–65 the army had acted correctly in a delicate situation. It was then still under its last British GOC, Major-General Welby-Everard. He and his fellow commanders had taken careful legal advice and, when called on by President Azikiwe to support his stand, informed him that they could take their orders only from the Prime Minister.[5]

In February 1965 Welby-Everard was replaced by a Nigerian, Major-General Johnson Aguyi-Ironsi. He was the senior Nigerian officer, but there had also been a Northern and two Western Brigadiers to choose from. Sir Abubakar's choice of an Ibo in that tense period reflected the general confidence that the army was and would remain politically neutral.

For so big a country, it was a small army—only 8,000 strong in 1965. Federal and regional police numbered about 23,000. An embryo air force, formally launched only a month before the January coup, had about twelve Dornier trainers and a group of

West German instructors. The Nigerian navy had only a frigate and two coastal patrol vessels. The army officers, still 70 per cent British at the time of independence, had been entirely Nigerianised by 1966. In the ranks, Northerners predominated in the 'general duties' grades, while Ibo of the Eastern Region were prominent among clerical and technical grades. A high proportion of the Northerners were Tiv and other Middle Belt people. Of the officers, perhaps 75 per cent were Ibo; in 1960 there had been only six Northern officers. After independence the Federal Minister of Defence, Alhaji Ribadu (a Northerner), laid down a quota system under which half the officers were to be Northern, but this could not be effected overnight.

On the night of January 14–15 a big party was given in the Lagos home of Brigadier Maimalari, the North's senior army officer. Soon after it broke up truckloads of soldiers from Abeokuta barracks, between Lagos and Ibadan in the Western Region, moved into Lagos. A detachment led by Major Emanuel Ifeajuna arrested the Federal Prime Minister in his house. Balewa left quietly after saying his prayers. The same group also took away Chief Festus Okotie-Eboh, the wealthy and influential Minister of Finance, from his house next door. Chief Festus was reported to have struggled violently and to have been beaten. The power station, telephone exchange, cable office and broadcasting station were put under guard. The three most senior Northern officers, Brigadier Maimalari, Lieutenant-Colonel Pam (Adjutant-General) and Lieutenant-Colonel Largema (commander, Fourth Battalion), were shot dead: Maimalari and Pam in their homes, Largema at the Ikoyi Hotel where he was staying. Pam, a dashing commander in both the Congo and Tiv operations, and Maimalari had been popular officers throughout the army. There was also an Ibo casualty that night—Lieutenant-Colonel Arthur Unegbu. He was in charge of the ammunition store at Ikeja barracks and had refused to hand over the keys when asked for them. He, too, was shot dead.

It is believed that Balewa had received intelligence reports that a coup was being planned. But he was fatalistic by temperament and

193

in his five troubled years in office he must have become inured to reports of trouble brewing. Who planned the coup, and with what object, will long remain a subject of controversy. Most Northerners and many Westerners are convinced the coup was a politically inspired attempt by the Ibo to reverse the hegemony of the North. Others see it—perhaps more accurately—as a sincere attempt at a national and radical revolution, planned without thoughts of tribal advantage, but which later came to be contaminated and perverted by tribalistic considerations. At his first press conference after the event Major Chukwuma Nzeogwu, the coup leader in the North, explained that the coup had not gone according to plan in Lagos and Enugu. 'We carried out our assignment: others did not.'

The truth was certainly complex. Several coups must have been planned in several quarters and in any case the one that took place failed to bring its leaders to power. Conflicting versions agree that the coup was planned by five Ibo majors. They intended removing the politicians of all parties and all Regions. According to one version the plan was to release Chief Awolowo, the Yoruba leader imprisoned for treason in 1962, and hand over power to him.[6] But it turned out differently. The coup went off according to plan only in Kaduna and Ibadan. In Lagos it was foiled within a few hours—a failure which also caused the plan to fail in Enugu. In the Mid-West, where no soldiers were stationed, there was no coup at all.

Ironsi seemed also to have been intended to die that night. He was at the Maimalari party and later went on to another party aboard the Elder Dempster mailboat *Aureol* at Apapa. When he reached home his telephone was ringing. It was Lieutenant-Colonel Pam, who warned him that something was happening, only minutes before Pam himself was shot. Ironsi acted quickly. He drove out of Lagos to the Ikeja garrison. On the way his Landrover was stopped at a rebel checkpoint, but he mustered enough personal authority ('Get out of my way') to get through.[7] At Ikeja, Ironsi, who had risen through the ranks, made straight for the regimental sergeant-major's quarters and rallied the garrison. The coup had been foiled and the leaders, Major D. Okafor, head of the Federal Guard, and Major

Ifeajuna, fled from the town. According to another version they left
for Enugu to effect the coup there, having inadvertently failed to
leave reliable officers in charge in Lagos.[8] The bodies of the Prime
Minister and Finance Minister were found a week later in bushes
beside the Lagos-Abeokuta road.

The coup went off more dramatically in the Western and Northern
Regions. In Ibadan troops arrived soon after midnight at the house
of Chief Fani-Kayode, the Western Deputy Premier, and took
him away. His wife telephoned the Premier, Chief Akintola, to warn
him. But there was considerable personal rivalry between the
Premier and his deputy and Akintola suspected a trick. Convinced
the so-called soldiers were only hired thugs, he telephoned his other
ministerial colleagues, asking them to come to his Lodge with as
many bodyguards as they could muster. But the ministers checked
with Mrs Fani-Kayode, learned the truth, and stayed at home. At
the heavily-guarded Premier's Lodge, the soldiers met only token
resistance from the police, but inside they met a hail of automatic
rifle fire from Akintola himself. In a twenty-five minute exchange
the Premier killed several soldiers before finally being taken down
to their car, in which Fani-Kayode was lying blindfolded. Akintola
was already badly wounded and he was finished off before his body
was bundled into the car. The soldiers drove to Lagos. But the
capital by this time was in 'loyal' hands; when they reached its out-
skirts the soldiers were arrested and Fani-Kayode released. 'Loyal'
troops by this time were in control in Ibadan.

In Kaduna Major Nzeogwu, the brilliant young chief instructor
at the Nigerian Defence Academy, left the Academy early that
evening with a detachment of soldiers, mostly Hausa, on 'routine
exercises'. Nzeogwu was an Ibo, from the Mid-West, but he had
lived most of his life in the North and spoke better Hausa than Ibo.
When his troops were well outside the town, he told them of the real
assignment. 'They were armed and I was not', he explained later.
'They could have shot me if they wished.'[9] At the Premier's Lodge
three security guards were shot dead and one of the attacking soldiers
was killed before the group could enter the grounds. The house was

shelled with mortar fire and to get inside Nzeogwu blew the door open with a grenade, injuring his hand. The Sardauna was shot dead, together with one of his wives and two house servants. Meanwhile another group had entered the house of Brigadier Ademulegun, the Yoruba commander of the First Brigade, and shot both him and his wife in their bed. Colonel Shodeinde, second-in-command at the Defence Academy, also a Yoruba, was shot too; his wife escaped by feigning death at his side.

The North was the only Region where the coup went off as planned. On the afternoon of January 15, Nzeogwu broadcast a proclamation 'in the name of the Supreme Council of the Revolution', declaring martial law over an area designated for the first time as the 'Northern Provinces of Nigeria'. Nzeogwu announced that the constitution was suspended, the regional government and assembly were dissolved, and departments were to be run by their permanent secretaries for the time being. In ten proclamations the death penalty was prescribed for looting, arson, homosexuality and rape, embezzlement, bribery or corruption, obstructing of the revolution, sabotage, subversion, false alarm and assistance to foreign invaders. Nzeogwu went on: 'Our enemies are the political profiteers, swindlers, the men in high and low places that seek bribes and demand ten per cent, those that seek to keep the country permanently divided so that they can remain in office as Ministers and VIPs of waste, the tribalists, the nepotists, those that make the country look big for nothing before international circles.' He ended: 'Thank you very much and good-bye for now.'

In Enugu the revolt was short-lived. Soldiers surrounded the Premier's Lodge at 2 A.M. They invested the radio station and the Governor's Lodge, where Archbishop Makarios of Cyprus was staying the night on the last leg of a tour of the Federation. Early listeners to Radio Enugu heard the voice of a studio engineer at 6.30 A.M.: 'This is Effiong Etu. The Army are here with us in the studio and they have ordered us to tune in to NBC Lagos.' At 10 A.M., the Premier, Michael Okpara, and the Governor, Sir Francis Ibiam, were allowed to drive in procession to the airport with the Arch-

bishop and see him off. Soldiers formed a discreet part of the procession. However, Okpara and the other politicians were later
allowed to leave Enugu for their home towns and villages. At 2 P.M.,
on orders from Lagos, soldiers returned to barracks. The failure
of the coup in Lagos had scotched the one in Enugu. Whether the
presence of Archbishop Makarios had saved Okpara's life, or
whether Ibo soldiers had, after all, found it impossible to kill one
of their own tribesmen, is not yet clear.

In the Mid-West capital of Benin, nothing happened until 10
A.M. on January 15. Troops arrived in a detachment from Enugu
and surrounded the Premier's and Governor's houses. They were
withdrawn, on orders from Lagos, at 2 P.M.

At midday a statement broadcast from Lagos said that 'certain
sections of the army' had revolted and kidnapped the Prime
Minister and Minister of Finance, but that the 'vast majority' of
the army remained loyal and that General Ironsi was bringing the
situation under control. The General spent the morning at police
headquarters trying to live up to this promise. As he emerged a
reporter asked him how things were going. 'Very badly indeed', he
replied. The army was in a critical condition. A column of troops
under Nzeogwu was driving southwards from Kaduna, apparently
intending to join other rebel forces in a march on Lagos. They
reached Jebba, on the Niger river. Had they crossed, nothing could
have stopped them from reaching Ibadan, where troops were already
defensively dug in on the Northern approaches. Nigeria seemed
close to civil war.

The same Saturday Alhaji Dipcharima, the Federal Minister
of Transport who was the senior NPC minister in the remnants of
the cabinet, held an informal cabinet meeting; Balewa's chair was
respectfully kept vacant. Throughout the morning, encouraging
information came through. Kano, in rebel hands that morning,
was now reported loyal; so were the Eastern, Western and Mid-
West Regions. Ironsi asked the Acting President of the Republic,
Dr Nwafor Orizu (Azikiwe was abroad convalescing), to appoint
a Deputy Prime Minister who could give valid orders to the army.

Ironsi remembered the 1964–65 crisis, when the lesson had been painfully learnt that it was the Prime Minister and not the President who gave valid orders. Orizu wanted to appoint his fellow Easterner, Dr Mbadiwe, Minister of Trade, but it was soon impressed on him that the consensus of the cabinet demanded another NPC man to replace Balewa. It was now Sunday. Ironsi had asked that the whole cabinet should meet. Only half, including most of the NPC members, were assembled, but the Progressive Alliance ministers, meeting separately in Mbadiwe's house, insisted on a military escort. This was provided and they finally arrived, with the exception of one minister who was so disconcerted by the sight of armed soldiers that he slipped out by a back door.

Ironsi now explained to the ministers that the situation had gone too far to be saved. He could not ensure the loyalty of his officers unless he himself took over power. The remnants of the cabinet, under Dipcharima's chairmanship, had no alternative but to agree. Fifteen minutes before midnight Ironsi announced in a broadcast that 'the Government of the Federation of Nigeria having ceased to function, the Nigerian Armed Forces have been invited to form an interim military government for the purpose of maintaining law and order, and of maintaining essential services. This invitation has been accepted and I, Major-General J. T. U. Aguyi-Ironsi, the General Officer Commanding the Nigerian Army, have been formally invested with authority as the head of the Federal Military Government, and Supreme Commander of the Nigerian Armed Forces.'[10] He went on to announce suspension of the provisions of the constitution which related to the offices of president, governors, prime minister, premiers, executive councils and parliaments. Military governors were appointed in each Region, directly responsible to the Federal military government.

Major Nzeogwu did not hold out. A safe-conduct agreement was reached and he returned to Lagos. However, he and the other coup leaders were detained. Ifeajuna had fled, first to Enugu and then to Ghana, but he was persuaded to come back and was also detained.

It had been a dream of a coup. 'Bang, bang, you're dead!'—a

198

satisfying infantile aggression fantasy. In a single night the Sardauna of Sokoto, symbol of Hausa-Fulani domination and of feudalistic reaction, Chief Akintola, high priest of election rigging, and Chief Okotie-Eboh, byword for luxury and ministerial corruption, had been killed. Scores of ministers, corporation chairmen and parliamentarians—all people who had occupied free houses, used up over-generous allowances and driven subsidised cars—were swept out of office.

The new order was deliriously welcomed in the South and received with cautious optimism in the North. 'Bribe? E Done Die. Chop-Chop—E No Dey' ran a joyful banner headline in the *Morning Post*. ('Bribery is dead. Corruption is not there.') Stirring rumours abounded. According to one, they were lining up traffic policemen who took bribes and shooting them by the roadside. Each of the new regional governors encouraged the new mood. In a speech accompanying his first decree, the Governor of the Eastern Region, Lieutenant-Colonel Odumegwu Ojukwu, attacked 'ten wasted years of planlessness, incompetence, inefficiency, greed, corruption, avarice and gross disregard for the interests of the common man'.

The North was widely expected to react differently. The displaced regime had been predominantly Northern; it was the North which had lost its senior army officers, while the coup leaders had been Ibo. However, the North had never been as united nor as uncritical of the Sardauna's leadership as it had seemed. The coup leaders may have been Ibo but they were not, after all, in power. There was a general readiness to let Ironsi attempt to overcome the regional bickerings of recent years. Another reassuring factor was the choice of Major Hassan Katsina as the Northern Military Governor. Katsina, son of one of the North's most powerful emirs, had presumably survived the coup because of his progressive views. Nzeogwu himself recalled at his press conference that after the attack on the Premier's house on the Saturday morning, 'I went to the home of Major Hassan. I had a gun in my hand. When I saw him standing outside I said, "What side are you on? Are you with me or are you with them?" Major Hassan replied: "Don't bother, I'm on your side." '[11]

Ironsi now found himself at the head of a revolution not of his own making. He showed few signs of political talent when he came to power, and even fewer signs of ability to learn as he went on. At his first press conference he was asked if he would still be in office when the proposed constituent assembly met. He replied promptly and with obvious sincerity: 'I hope not'. Asked whether, in the meantime, he would appoint a cabinet, he looked up at the ceiling for a full minute—and then passed without a word to the next question. Clearly, it had never occurred to him.

He had been born forty-two years earlier at Umuahia in the heart of Iboland. He enlisted in the army early and was a company sergeant-major at twenty-four. After the officers' training course at Eaton Hall in the United Kingdom he went on an infantry course at Warminster. He was appointed equerry to the Queen on her visit to Nigeria in 1956. He later led the Nigerian contingent to the UN force in the Congo. He was a convivial, hard-drinking, extrovert and entirely non-political soldier.

Ironsi's first political act was maladroit. An Ibo civil servant, Francis Nwokedi, was named as sole commissioner 'to inquire into the unification of the regional public services'. This came as a bombshell in the North, where the regional administration was prized as the main safeguard against domination by Southerners. After protests that so crucial an inquiry should not have been entrusted to one man—and an Ibo at that—a Mid-Westerner was added to the Nwokedi Commission. But the first seeds of doubt had been planted in Northern minds. They were to germinate rapidly in the months that followed.

The regime had started with impressive momentum. Ironsi had promised in his earliest statements that a return to civilian rule would be preceded by study groups, a constituent assembly and a referendum on a new constitution. Chief Rotimi Williams, the distinguished Yoruba lawyer, and Dr T. O. Elias, the former Attorney-General, were appointed to draw up the outlines for the new constitution. Another commission was to explore ways of unifying the judicial services. A commission on economic planning was entrusted to Chief Simeon Adebo, a leading Yoruba civil servant who was now Nigeria's representative at the United Nations, and Dr Pius Okigbo, the Federal Economic Adviser.

The commissions all pointed in the same direction—unification. This highly controversial idea was publicly mooted in the earliest stages of the regime. At the end of January the Mid-Western Region's Military Governor, Colonel David Ejoor, declared that the military government intended to 'reintroduce a unitary form of government'.[12] Ironsi told a press conference in February: 'It has become apparent to all Nigerians that rigid adherence to "regionalism" was the bane of the last regime and one of the main factors which contributed to its downfall. No doubt the country would welcome a clean break with the deficiencies of the system.'[13]

The unitary idea had considerable support. It was especially popular among the Ibo, the most travelled and best qualified of the major tribal groups. The Ibo felt that the federal system militated against them; it placed their traders in the North in the position of second-class citizens; it seemed to perpetuate a double standard in the appointment of public officers. The same double standard was seen in the North as an essential safeguard against being relegated to the back of the queue. Apart from these tribal and regional overtones, the unitary idea appealed to reform-minded people in all Regions—men sufficiently well-educated not to fear competition and aware of the economic and political advantages of doing away with the wasteful rivalries of the regional power blocs. The idea also appealed strongly in the army, which was itself perhaps the most Nigeria-minded group in the country.

The idea made more progress in the regime's first budget. Under a new decree the regional military governors were made members of the Federal Executive Council. In his budget broadcast Ironsi explained this was 'to underline the fact that there is now only one government in the country'.[14]

Meanwhile the regional government lost no time in dismantling the corrupt edifice of patronage and politics of the old regime. The process seemed most ruthless in the West, perhaps because the grievances were more obvious there than anywhere else. The Governor, Colonel Adekunle Fajuyi, proved able and energetic. If, as his detractors claimed, he identified himself too closely with the Action Group faction, this was only tantamount to sharing the popular distaste for the ruthless and autocratic methods of the NNDP, the former ruling party. Fajuyi promptly dismissed all the local government officials appointed by the Akintola regime. Customary courts, so long misused for political victimisation, were debarred from hearing criminal cases. Full salaries were restored to those chiefs who had had them suspended because they did not toe the Akintola line. Eleven ministers of Akintola's party, including the former Federal Minister of Education, Richard Akinjide, and the former regional Deputy Premier, Chief Fani-Kayode, were detained on suspicion of plotting against the regime.

In the other Regions also a new order made itself felt. The North began inquiries into its public corporations and into reforms in the emirs' courts. In the Mid-West Colonel Ejoor locked 150 senior civil servants out of their offices one morning for having arrived late for work. He made them parade in Benin's central square and publicly warned them that next time their fate would be worse. In the East one sour note was struck by Governor Ojukwu's appointment of his own father, Sir Odumegwu Ojukwu, to be chairman of two regional corporations. Sir Odumegwu, a wealthy transport and property tycoon, was known for his administrative ability and would have done the job well; but it was all too reminiscent of the nepotism of the old days, and even the cautiously respectful Lagos newspapers criticised the appointment. However, Sir Odumegwu fell ill soon afterwards and resigned for health reasons. In Lagos inquiries were set up into the reputedly infamous affairs of the Lagos City Council and the Railway Corporation. A Banking Amendment Ordinance gave the police powers to examine the accounts of anyone suspected of corruption for a retrospective period of six years. An Indian hemp decree prescribed the death penalty or twenty-one years imprisonment for anyone found planting or cultivating the weed.

Unfortunately, none of these reforms made life any better for the people. An ill-conceived rent decree ordered a 10 per cent cut in the rent of rooms, but without enforcement provisions it was quite ineffective. More serious was a catastrophic rise in food prices. A newspaper claimed that such basic items as gari, yam, plantain, fish, bread and meat had gone up 'by 100 per cent or in some cases by 200 per cent' in Lagos.[15] Similar rises occurred in the Regions. Rumour had it that disgruntled ex-politicians were deliberately buying up supplies to embarrass the government. The real cause was probably the rural disruption in the West the previous year. Crude and frightening publicity given by the new regime to punishments in store for 'profiteers' must have made the situation worse. Fearing depressed prices, producers held back supplies.

The young radicals among the Yoruba and the Ibo soon found that the more things changed the more they stayed the same. 'Peter Pan', the popular *Daily Times* columnist, reviewing the regime's first hundred days, complained of the 'palatial edifices' into which the new military rulers had moved, and the large cars they drove about in. The new regional governors, 'Peter Pan' found, represented much the same tribal pressure groups as the old premiers. He suggested that they should be rotated.[16]

Disillusion was of much more serious proportions in the North. 'The impression one gets in the North is that the intelligentsia is slowly rising in hostility', 'Peter Pan' was bold enough to report.[17] Hausa language newspapers in the North were beginning to discuss such awkward questions as why the coup leaders, although branded 'mutineers' and guilty of the murder of their superior officers, had not been brought to trial. It was even reported, correctly, that they were still drawing their pay while in prison. What to do about the imprisoned majors was the most awkward of all the regime's dilemmas. The Northern demand that they should be tried was balanced by the Southern demand, especially in the East and among radicals in the West, that they be freed as national heroes. The North was also restive about the conduct of some of the inquiry commissions. Particular offence was taken to Nwokedi, whose all-important inquiry into the unification of the public services had taken him on tour in the North. Northern civil servants and emirs complained bitterly that Nwokedi listened to their points of view without seeming to hear them. Their fears seemed confirmed when it was learned that he had handed Ironsi a one-man interim report, drawn up in apparent disregard of their views.

Ironsi was clearly being pushed in opposite directions. He made heroic attempts to stay impartial, trying above all to avoid any impression that his was an Ibo regime. He appointed Lieutenant-Colonel Yakubu Gowon, the most senior surviving Northern officer (who probably owed his life to the fact that he had been abroad in January) as Chief of Staff (Army). He appointed a young relative of the Sardauna of Sokoto, Mallam Hamsad Amadu, as his secretary. He even depended on Northern soldiers for his personal protection—which may later have cost him his life. However, his regime increasingly displeased the hard-liners on both sides. Northerners were outraged when a series of army and diplomatic promotions and postings seemed to favour the Ibo: they were quite unmoved by the argument that these were fields in which Ibo happened to be the best qualified. The Easterners and the Yoruba reformists, convinced that discontent in the North was deliberately stirred up by disgruntled ex-politicians, urged Ironsi to 'take the bull by the horns' and unify the country before it was too late. Which group really influenced the general cannot be finally established. He was known to have been on friendly terms with ex-President Azikiwe. He was also widely believed to have been under the influence of a closely-knit group of senior Ibo officials in Lagos—Nwokedi, Tim Eneli, a permanent secretary, Pius Okigbo, the Economic Adviser, and Gabriel Onyiuke, the Attorney-General.

Whatever propelled him, Ironsi finally stopped dithering. On May 24 he broadcast news of a new Constitution (Suspension and Modification) decree. Explaining its provisions, he dropped a bombshell that was to reverberate for years to come. 'The former Regions are abolished, and Nigeria grouped into a number of territorial areas called provinces. Nigeria ceases to be what is described as a federation. It now becomes simply the Republic of Nigeria.'[18] The regional governors would henceforth be assigned to groups of provinces. Ironsi added that 'in order to avoid any major dislocation of the present administrative machinery, the grouping of the provinces has been made to coincide with the former regional boundaries. This is entirely a transitional measure and must be understood as such.' The public services were to be unified under a single Public Service Commission, but provincial commissions would continue to appoint all but senior officers. 'Every civil servant is now called upon to see his function in any part of Nigeria in which he is serving in the context of the whole country.' In a somewhat illogical attempt to disarm opposition, Ironsi added that the new arrangements were 'without prejudice' to the activities of the Williams Commission then working on the new constitution. This inquiry had been specifically charged with examining the relative respective merits of unitary and federal systems: Ironsi had jumped the gun.

In practice Decree No. 34 changed little but names. What had been Regions became 'groups of provinces'—under the same governors and the same constitutions. What counted, as always in Nigerian politics, was the matter of appointments. The provincial public service commissions were to continue to appoint all officers with salaries of less than £2,292—that is, all but the most senior.[19] While sophisticated officials appreciated that, for the moment, the new decree made little difference, reaction in the North was swift and violent.

May 24 was a Tuesday. By the weekend hundreds of Ibo had been killed in pogroms throughout the North. The killings began in Kano with a students' demonstration and spread to Kaduna, Zaria and other towns. The pogroms were both organised and spontaneous. They were stage-managed by disgruntled civil servants, ex-politicians, local government officials and businessmen whom the change of regime had deprived of lucrative contracts. At the same time there was massive popular feeling that the Ibo regime had at last come out into the open: its aim was to take over the country, exploiting and colonising the backward North. 'Let there be secession!' said placards of demonstrating civil servants in Kaduna. 'No unitary government without referendum.' 'Down with Ironsi.' In Kano the riots followed a pattern similar to those of 1953: a peaceful demonstration escalated into a massacre. Waves of armed thugs crossed the no-man's-land between the old city and the *sabon gari*—the 'strangers quarter'—where the Ibo lived. Houses were sacked, rows of Ibo market stalls burned out, Ibo garages and hotels razed to the ground. Events in other towns followed the same pattern.

Ironsi at this point showed signs of losing control. In a broadcast he claimed the killings had been organised 'in collusion with certain foreign elements. . . . The Government sincerely hopes that these foreign elements are not being backed by their respective governments.'[20] This cryptic reference was to the British. Spurious 'intelligence' reports from Ibo in the North had apparently reached the government in Lagos, claiming that British staff in the Ahmadu Bello University, Zaria, and elsewhere, had helped organise the killings. In fact, some expatriate as well as Nigerian members of the staff risked their lives to shelter Ibo where possible.

Lieutenant-Colonel Katsina, the North's Military Governor, acted firmly. He called a meeting in the Kaduna parliament building of all the Northern emirs. But many arrived with clear 'mandates' from their people to insist on immediate secession of the North from Nigeria. As he left his palace the Emir of Zaria was virtually mobbed by crowds begging him to demand secession. After their meeting the emirs presented the government with a secret memorandum which was in effect an ultimatum: Decree No. 34 must be abrogated or the North would inist on secession. The Sultan of Sokoto, spokesman for the emirs, publicly appealed for calm, 'to give the Government a chance to consider our recommendations'.[21]

The four regional governors and Ironsi conferred in Lagos. They appointed a Commission of Inquiry into the killings, and resolved to improve information media 'to ensure that the policy of the Government is properly interpreted to the public'.[22] This information exercise involved some sharp back-tracking by the government. The governors' statement went on to 'reassure the entire nation that this decree (No. 34) was designed to meet the demands of the Military Government under a unified command and to enable it to carry on its day to day administration. It has in no way affected the territorial divisions of the country.' In Kaduna the emirs met a second time to receive the government's reply to their memorandum. The Sultan of Sokoto announced that they were 'satisfied'; they were now 'in no doubt that no permanent pattern of government will be imposed on the country without the consent of the people, to be ascertained by a freely conducted referendum'.[23] Colonel Ojukwu, the Eastern Governor, broadcast an appeal to Ibo who had fled from the North to return to their homes, 'as the situation is now under control'. He was later bitterly to regret this appeal; his feelings of guilt for having sent thousands to face a second massacre played a part in his later reactions.

The government in Lagos continued to grope for remedies to the rising tension. It was announced that the military governors would be rotated from region to region, as the *Daily Times*'s 'Peter Pan' had suggested two months earlier. The curious announcement was made that this rotation would be effective 'after the expiry of their first six months in office'; the six months had already elapsed but no move was made to implement the decision. Nigerians in all regions grimly speculated what might be the fate of, say, Colonel Ojukwu as he descended the steps of his aircraft after landing in Kaduna. In what seemed a desperate attempt to do something, Ironsi started a tour of the Regions. He was never to return.

A counter-coup was now widely expected. Ironsi's regime had spectacularly failed to solve its basic dilemmas, satisfying neither 'side'. The January coup leaders, though detained, had not been brought to trial and were being paid. There was an increasingly audible demand for revenge, not so much for the death of the Sardauna of Sokoto, Balewa and other politicians, but for the murder of the Northern officers. A coup was also half-expected from the other direction—those who expressed reformist sentiments (mainly, but not exclusively, Ibo) and who had been thwarted by the failure of the January coup. A Southern coup might also have been in the offing simply to forestall a Northern one. The absence of Ironsi from his secure home base might have offered a tempting target for either side.

Like the January coup, the July one started at the Abeokuta barracks. Conflicting versions later published by both 'sides' agree that it began with the shooting of three Ibo officers by their Northern colleagues. The pro-North version, later published by the Federal government, says there were 'widely circulating rumours that the "uncompleted" job of January 15th was to be finished by eliminating the remaining officers of non-Eastern origin. . . . There were also rumours of a counter-coup planned by some Northern elements in the Army with the assistance of civilians.'[24] This version says the Ibo officers had armed themselves as a precaution and Northern officers acted first as a counter-precaution. An Eastern version describes the killing of the three officers as a 'pre-arranged' signal for the 'massacre' of Eastern and Mid-Western officers and men.[25]

Ironsi was staying with Colonel Fajuyi, the West's Military Governor, at Government Lodge, Ibadan. At 5 A.M. on July 29, a detachment of Northern soldiers arrived at the house. They met no resistance from the guards, who were Northerners already prepared for the action. According to the Eastern version, 'Major Danjuma took some of his men upstairs, confronted and questioned the Supreme Commander, saluted him, and ordered his arrest'.[26] According to the well-established and credible legend that has grown up, Fajuyi protested vehemently that such a thing should have happened while Ironsi was his guest, insisting that he, too, should be taken away. The Eastern version, based on the account of the air force aide-de-camp to Ironsi, says Ironsi and Fajuyi were both stripped, had their hands tied behind their backs, 'were flogged, tortured and then put into separate police vans'.[27] They were driven to a spot ten miles from Ibadan where they were led away from the road. After all three had been so badly beaten that they could hardly walk, one of the captives—the air force aide-de-camp—escaped into thick bush. Ironsi and Fajuyi were separately finished off with a few rounds of machine-gun fire. It was not until six months later that their deaths were to be officially announced.

The revolt spread to the Ikeja barracks, near Lagos, where the rebels took control of the international airport. A BOAC airliner captain, bound for London, was ordered first to take a plane load of Northern soldiers' families to Kano before being allowed to proceed. This was the first news to the outside world that it had been a Northern-led coup. Brigadier Ogundipe, the Yoruba Chief of Staff and the senior officer in Lagos, sent a detachment of troops from Lagos to quell the mutiny. They were ambushed with heavy losses. Northern garrisons quickly supported the new regime but there was no coup in the East. Nigeria was now under two autonomous commands. Ogundipe had no alternative but to negotiate with the rebels.

From Enugu, Colonel Ojukwu telephoned Ogundipe and asked him, as the senior officer, to take over as Supreme Commander. Ojukwu later recalled that he gave Ogundipe a firm promise that if he went on the air to say he had taken over, Ojukwu himself would 'within 30 minutes' announce from Enugu that he was in agreement.[28] Ogundipe was apparently not optimistic about his chances. He had already had 'an ordinary sergeant' refuse to take an order from him without first consulting his own (Northern) captain.[29] Senior Northern civil servants now attempted negotiations with the rebels. The rebels apparently declared that they were under strong pressure from the Northern rank and file to secede from Nigeria. A correspondent of the magazine *West Africa* reported that there appeared to be support in Lagos for a proposal that the North and West, including Lagos, should secede together.[30] 'There followed frenzied attempts to stop this happening from many quarters.' After 'a day of complete vacuum, with no one willing to take a lead', it appears that Lieutenant-Colonel Yakubu Gowon, the Chief of Staff (Army) was sent to negotiate. He was at first taken prisoner by the rebels, but later agreed to take over as Supreme Commander.

15—N

Gowon, aged only thirty-one, found himself in an even less enviable political position than Ironsi had been in January. Like Ironsi, he has been accused of having been a party to the coup. He may well have had some fore-knowledge; if so, he would have had every excuse, for it was obvious to all that a counter-coup was in the offing. The difficulty of his new position was that the coup had taken place only in a part of the country. The North had seized effective power in Lagos, the West and the Mid-West, but not in the East. In January the coup leaders' plans had been carefully laid on a national basis but were upset at the last moment: this time there was no last-minute hitch. There had simply not been any plan to take power in the Federation as a whole. The rebels' idea was, first, revenge for the murdered Northern officers, and second, for the North to secede. For the North, secession was an irrational proposition. It would have cut the Region off from the sea and from Nigeria's promising new oil wealth and, not surprisingly, Northern leaders soon had second thoughts. But in July and August secession, first proclaimed in banners the previous May and embodied in the emirs' memorandum in June, was still the popular Northern demand.

In the disputes that followed, Eastern leaders often quoted against Gowon a remark in his first broadcast: 'the basis for unity is not there'. He was able to reply that he had not meant the Federation but the unitary system of government set up by Ironsi. However, the tone and wording of the broadcast strongly suggest that its vital passages had been rewritten at the last moment: that it had originally heralded a more drastic change than merely a return to the federal system. The way he led up to his point suggests that he had been intending to announce secession. After reviewing the 'fateful years' which had seen 'two grave and serious situations in the country', he went on:

I now come to the most difficult but most important part of this statement. I am doing it conscious of the great disappointment and heartbreak it will cause all true and sincere lovers of Nigeria and of Nigerian unity, both at home and abroad, especially our brothers in the Commonwealth. As a result of the recent events and of the other previous similar ones, I have come to strongly believe that we cannot honestly and sincerely continue in this wise, as the basis for trust and confidence in our unitary system of government has been unable to stand the test of time. I have already remarked on the issue in question. Suffice it to say that putting all considerations to the test, political, economic, as well as social, the base for unity is not there, or is so badly rocked not only once but several times. I therefore feel that we should review the issue of our national standing and see if we can help stop the country from drifting away into utter destruction.[31]

If the July coup was intended primarily for revenge, it was singularly successful. The published Eastern version gives the names and ranks of forty-three officers and 171 other ranks who were murdered, with details in each case of how, where and by whom they were killed. After the shooting of the three officers at Abeokuta at 11 P.M. on July 28, two sections of Northern troops 'besieged the barracks'.

> Northern troops disarmed the Southern soldiers among the guards, broke into the armoury and magazine, distributed arms and ammunition to more Northern troops, and sounded an alarm for action. Many soldiers in answer to the alarm assembled, but Southern soldiers among them were arrested and detained. . . . Troops of Northern origin then went from door to door in the barracks in search of troops of Southern origin who did not answer them. Some of those caught were manhandled and pushed into the guardrooms while others were shot at sight. Others were got at in some civilians' houses near the barracks. A vehicle was parked near one of the unoccupied married officers' quarters, and into this vehicle were dumped the bodies of the Southern officers and men as they were killed. By daybreak most of the Southern senior non-commissioned officers were brought out of the guardrooms and shot in the open and their bodies dumped in the storage vehicle.[32]

It was much the same routine at Ikeja and in the various garrisons of the North. In listing the episodes, the Eastern account records 'one bright spot' when a Captain Mumadu of the First Brigade Signal troops allowed his Ibo officers and men to escape.[33] The killings in the barracks went on throughout August. During the whole of that time, according to the Eastern version, the secessionist flag of the North—'red, yellow, black, green and khaki—the Republic of the North'—flew outside the Ikeja headquarters of the Second Battalion, where Gowon had his temporary headquarters.[34]

Lieutenant-Colonel Gowon, the new Supreme Commander, gave a striking impression of sincerity, of modesty amounting to shyness (he spoke softly and haltingly) and of genuine reluctance to hold political office. He is a Christian, a Middle-belt Northerner from a tiny tribe in the Pankshin division of Plateau province. His father was a mission-trained evangelist. After attending mission and grammar schools he joined the army at nineteen. He trained at Eaton Hall, Sandhurst, Hythe and Warminster, and became the first Nigerian Adjutant; later, like Ironsi, he joined the Nigerian contingent in the Congo. During the January coup he was in the United Kingdom at the Joint Services Staff College. On taking office, he harped continuously—and more convincingly than most soldiers in power—on the need for an early return to civilian rule. Within a week he had announced a three-stage plan for this: first, return to the federal structure abolished on May 24; second, a meeting of an all-Region advisory committee of 'responsible and independent citizens'; and third, a constitutional review assembly. The plan was put into immediate operation.

However, the new regime had first to face three urgent unsolved problems. The killings inside the army had to be stopped; a supreme commander acceptable to all had to be found; and an acceptable basis of association among the newly created regional military power blocs had to be agreed. Only on the first point was some progress made. At a meeting of regional representatives on August 9 it was agreed that soldiers would immediately be posted 'to barracks within their respective Regions of origin'.[35] Security in

Lagos was to be arranged by the Supreme Commander in consultation with the regional governors. This agreement enabled Northern troops in the East to be repatriated and Easterners still at large to be sent back to safety. But the problem remained of Northern troops stationed in the West. There were virtually no Yoruba troops that could replace them. They stayed, looking to the Yoruba very much like an army of occupation—and, in some cases, behaving like one.[36]

On the other two issues failure to agree was to lead, after a year of brinkmanship and tortuous negotiations, to the breakup of the Federation and civil war. 'Militarily Gowon is not my superior and the question of acknowledging him does not arise', said Ojukwu flatly.[37] Finding an acceptable basis for association between the Regions proved equally difficult. Not only the East but the North and West as well initially favoured a much looser arrangement than before. Later, when the East showed itself determined to make a clean, formal and even permanent break, the North changed its mind. The West, deeply divided within itself, continued to oscillate between the two positions.

Meetings of 'leaders of thought' in each Region prepared positions for the Ad Hoc Constitutional Review Conference which opened in Lagos on September 12. Gowon opened the Lagos talks by submitting four alternative arrangements for Nigeria: a federal system with a strong central government; a federal system with a weak central government; a confederation; or 'an entirely new arrangement which may be peculiar to Nigeria and which has not yet found its way into any political dictionary'.[38] Each Region was represented by three senior civilian delegates. The East and the North both began by proposing a loose association amounting, in effect, to a confederation. To emphasise its mood of separateness, the North appended to its proposals a detailed memorandum about the East African Common Services Organisation, which it offered as a model. The Northern memorandum also insisted that any member state in the proposed union of autonomous states should reserve the right to secede unilaterally. Each state should have its own army, air force and police but there should (for obvious geographical reasons) be a joint navy.

The West proposed the creation of more states according to linguistic and ethnic boundaries or, failing that, a 'commonwealth of Nigeria' in which existing Regions would be sovereign and Lagos would be part of the West. In the second alternative a Council of States would be responsible for assuring common services. The East proposed a loose association of the existing Regions. Only the Mid-West proposed to maintain the existing Federation, with the proviso that more states should be created within it.

Soon after the various memoranda had been submitted, there appeared to be a crisis within the Northern delegation. There was an adjournment of several days, during which Colonel Hassan Katsina arrived in Lagos from Kaduna and some of the delegates flew North for consultations. The North now presented a new and significantly different set of proposals. It insisted that there should be an effective central government, immediate agreement 'in principle' on the creation of more states, and abandonment of the idea that secession should be written into the constitution as a basic right. The Eastern interpretation of this sensational volte face was that the Middle Belt elements—Gowon's own people, who were especially influential within the army—had forcefully exerted their influence.[39] The Middle Belt had long led the demand for more states. This seemed the first appearance of a new power situation in Nigeria, in which the minorities were to hold sway over the three large tribal groups which had hitherto disputed power. The Middle Belt viewed with natural anxiety any proposal that would give the old Regions even greater autonomy than before; it would mean that the domination of the Hausa-Fulani, which they had found so irksome in the past, would be more firmly entrenched than ever. The East, too, had traditionally favoured more states, as a means of breaking the monolithic power of the North. Now it saw the danger of this weapon being turned against itself. It could hardly be viable as an autonomous unit if the non-Ibo minorities—the Ijaw, Efik, Ibibio, Ogoja—were carved out into separate units. The East was preparing to answer separatist demands with a new system of semi-autonomous provinces. For the moment, its delegation declared that the times were not opportune for the creation of new states.

The Ad Hoc Conference was interrupted by the outbreak of a second and much more terrible massacre of Ibo in the North. The September–October massacre was a traumatic event in Nigerian history. It destroyed the illusion that tribal rivalries could be dismissed as growing pains in a new nation and laid the foundations for the secessionist feeling that was to become an irresistible force in the East. No accurate figure for the number who died is available. The East's first claim, made at the Aburi conference three months later, was 10,000; [40] the official figure given later was 30,000. Whichever figure is more accurate, no one disputes that it was a pogrom of genocidal proportions.

The September–October massacres cannot be attributed to a single or simple cause. The socio-economic problems arising when an alien minority dominates trade and technology were not unique to Northern Nigeria. Parallels have been drawn with the Chinese in Malaya, the Indians in East Africa, the Jews in Central Europe. There were perhaps a million Ibo in the North—clerks, traders, civil servants, artisans. Envy and resentment against them increased steadily, as their numbers grew and as successive generations of Northerners came out of school to find that the best jobs were already filled by Ibo. Some Ibo characteristics also played a part: they were inclined to arrogance, clannishness and excessive nepotism. In the tense days of the Ironsi regime, there were complaints that Ibo used to display provocatively pictures of Major Nzeogwu, the January coup leader who had killed the Sardauna of Sokoto.[41]

This resentment needed a spark to ignite it. In May the spark had been the unification decree, with its implied threat of Ibo domination of the North. Now, the July countercoup had at last dislodged the Ironsi regime, but had failed to establish itself throughout Nigeria. The idea behind the organisers of the killings was to drive the Easterners out of the North—perhaps out of Nigeria. As in May, ex-politicians, civil servants, local government officials and former party stalwarts stage-managed the pogroms. The main difference was that this time the army joined in. If one of its aims was to drive the Ibo out of Nigeria, the operation succeeded. Ironically, the North was quickly to change its mind and was to go to war to keep the Ibo in Nigeria.

A contributory cause of the outbreak were reports broadcast by Radio Dahomey, rebroadcast from Kaduna, that Northerners were being killed in the East. The pro-North version, published by the Federal government, says that these killings started 'around September 23rd'—that is, some five days after they started in the North.[42] This report says that Northerners in Enugu, Onitsha, Port Harcourt and Abakaliki 'had been attacked by the Ibos, some of the Northerners killed and their houses looted and set on fire'. A more outspoken Northern account speaks of a 'well organised onslaught launched by Ibos in August against Northerners resident in Abakaliki, Enugu, Owerri and Aba. 1,000 Northerners are known to have been killed.'[43] Little documentary evidence of these killings has been produced; whatever happened may have been deliberately exaggerated to provide an excuse for what happened in the North.

The killings began sporadically throughout the North, significantly coinciding with the start of the Lagos constitutional talks. Between September 18 and 24 they occurred in Makurdi, Minna, Gboko, Gombe, Jos, Sokoto and Kaduna.[44] As before, *agents provocateurs* were seen encouraging the mob, driving from town to town carrying the news. Small units of the Fourth Battalion in Kaduna got out of barracks and acted in combination with local thugs. Colonel Hassan issued a stern warning but with no effect. The climax of the holocaust was reached on September 29, as the Lagos talks were about to adjourn. At Kano airport a crowd of Ibo refugees waiting to board a BOAC airliner for Lagos was set upon by mutinous soldiers of the Fourth Battalion. Scores were shot. Some were dragged out of the plane. This mutiny was later put down personally by Hassan. But no details of courts martial or sentences were published.

The role of social and economic envy came out clearly in some of the incidents. Looting was universal. According to the official Eastern version 'a number of student survivors from institutions of learning in Northern Nigeria were captured and all the fingers of their hands chopped off before they were released. That would help in curtailing, they were told, the educational lead of Eastern Nigeria over the North.'[45] The refugees pouring into Enugu told their story, with their wounds as evidence. After a fortnight, 'the scene in the Eastern Region continues to be reminiscent of the in-gathering of the exiles into Israel after the end of the last war', a British writer observed.[46] The Enugu authorities took pains to document the accounts of the survivors.[47]

A clerk in Kano had hidden for three days in a gutter after his house had been looted. He saw streets 'lined with bodies'. At the railway station he saw refugees being killed while waiting for a train back to the East. A Jos trader's wife saw her husband hacked to death inside their store. A Kaduna postal worker saw 'a man drenched with petrol and burnt alive at the Ahmadu Bello Way. As I turned into Yoruba Road I saw an Easterner abandon his Honda motor cycle while he was hotly pursued by the mob. As the man was about to run into a police station I saw the policeman push him out. He was killed by the pursuing mob right in front of the police station.' The postman succeeded in getting aboard an East-bound train but his troubles were not over. At Oturkpo, armed soldiers attacked the passengers. 'They killed three girls from Kano who stepped out of the train, wounded several passengers and also killed one man, cutting away his head and dumping his headless body into the train.' This body duly arrived in Enugu and was photographed by the publicity services. 'Armed soldiers went from house to house and shot everyone they saw', recalled an airline clerk in Kano, who had escaped after sheltering in a Yoruba house-hold. 'After the soldiers had finished the killing, armed bands of civilians moved in. They went from house to house taking away everything they liked but in addition to looting property, the armed mob killed off anyone who escaped the slaughter of the soldiers.' Easterners were killed indiscriminately, whether they were Ibo,

Ibibio, Efik or Ijaw: this was later to be a factor in promoting a greater sense of unity among the peoples of the East. Ibo and other Easterners lacked the tribal markings that distinguish the Yoruba. A fireman at Kano said he was on duty when eight armed soldiers arrived at the station in a Landrover.

> One of them who was a sergeant ordered that all Easterners should raise up their hands. . . . The sergeant asked us whether we could remember what happened on the 15th of January when the Prime Minister and the Premier of the North lost their lives and the Ibos were all very happy. We said, 'No, Sergeant'. Paying no heed to that he asked us to give our names and addresses and send any messages we have for our people because we were going to die. . . . They drove us five miles away to the Katsina road, brought us down and started shooting us. I felt my leg shattered and I fell down. . . . I managed to crawl into a bush.

How widely shared was the guilt for the massacres? A Northern account claims, plausibly, that by no means everyone approved, and that efforts were made to stop the killings and make good the damage. 'Curfews were imposed and in some places unruly elements had to be shot down. . . . Tens of thousands of Ibos were given food, shelter and protection in Kaduna, Zaria, Jos, Kano and all other affected towns for several days by the Northern Nigerian Government and people, while evacuation was carried out by air, rail, and road. In Kaduna alone, the Regional Government has spent the sum of £19,000 to transport these people to Enugu by air.'[48]

An immense movement of populations followed the massacres. More than a million Ibo poured into the East. For their own safety, Colonel Ojukwu ordered that all non-Easterners should leave the Region. Ibo refugees also arrived from the West, the Mid-West and Lagos. As the constitutional crisis worsened and the possibility of a complete break became imminent, the refugees from Lagos came to include senior civil servants of the Federal government. These were to constitute a powerful pressure group behind Ojukwu, urging him to secede from the Federation. They in turn were to accuse the remaining federal officers of having a 'vested interest' in maintaining the Federation intact. In the North the exodus of Ibo seriously disrupted business and public services. The Jos tin mines lost two-thirds of their labour force, telephones were scarcely manned, petrol stations closed and trains stopped running. But the dislocation did not last long. Northerners themselves took over with an ease which was in itself a commentary on the massacres.

In the East the demand for secession now became overwhelming and Ojukwu, seen outside as an Ibo firebrand, was in fact a moderating influence. His father Sir Odumegwu, had recently died, leaving him an immense fortune, most of which was in the form of property in Lagos. The fact that he personally stood to lose by political separatism lent weight to the sincerity of his policies. Chukwuemeka Odumegwu Ojukwu was thirty-three. He was born at Zungeru, in Northern Nigeria. He went to King's College, Nigeria's foremost 'public' school, and graduated at Lincoln College, Oxford, before joining the army in 1957, at the age of twenty-four. Intellectually he was considerably ahead of his present colleagues and opponents —a factor which might well have increased his unwillingness to recognise Gowon as his superior officer. In the months leading to secession and war, he was to become a highly controversial figure, seen by the Ibo as their saviour and by his opponents as an ambitious and reckless fanatic.

After the massacres, Ojukwu refused to attend further instalments of the constitutional talks or meetings of the Supreme Council unless his own safety could be assured. He also refused to send delegates to constitutional talks until an agenda had been agreed and memoranda circulated by all delegations. He insisted that Northern troops must first leave the West, and that the police, not the army, should be in charge of security in Lagos. Meeting without Ojukwu, the military governors decided to bring civilians into the government forthwith. Immediately after the July coup Chief Awolowo and Chief Enahoro, the Action Group politicians who had been imprisoned in 1963 for conspiracy, had been released.

Gowon had explained that this decision had been taken during the previous regime, but nevertheless the action gave his regime a much needed boost of popularity in the West and Mid-West Regions.

Tension between the East and Lagos increased day by day throughout November and December. A DC-4 aircraft laden with arms crashed near Garoua in Northern Cameroon, apparently bound for Port Harcourt in the East. It was now clear to both sides that an arms race was in progress. The telephone line linking Ojukwu in Enugu with Gowon in Lagos was still open, but it was scarcely used. Each side was on a different wavelength. As the East refused to attend, Gowon now dismissed the Ad Hoc Constitutional Conference —an act which Ojukwu denounced as 'dictatorial'. Gowon announced that a committee would draft a new constitution, for submission to a constituent assembly, based on an increase in the number of states to between eight and fourteen. He added that a temporary confederation, on the lines Ojukwu was demanding, was 'unworkable'. In Enugu, Ojukwu told his Consultative Assembly that Gowon was 'still living in a world of unreality as regards the present situation'. He was 'advised by a group of civil servants in Lagos who, because of their vested interests . . . still believed that a strong central federal government is feasible in this country in the near future'.[49] A pressing problem for Ojukwu was the host of refugees, including hundreds of civil servants. Early in December he confided to a foreign reporter: 'I cannot wait indefinitely for Lagos, so I have to make other arrangements.'[50] Gowon, meanwhile, gave his first clear hint that force might have to be used. 'If circumstances compel me to preserve the integrity of Nigeria by force, I will do my duty.'[51]

There was now increasing popular pressure that the military leaders should find a way of meeting, inside or outside Nigeria, to get back on speaking terms. Nigeria had a long tradition of political brinkmanship and compromise and, even now, most Nigerians felt that if only the colonels could meet a showdown could be averted. General Ankrah, head of Ghana's military government, had been

taking an avuncular interest in the disputes of the colonels. He had
sent emissaries and had received short visits both from Gowon and
from Ojukwu, and was in touch with both sides by radio. Finally,
it was arranged that a meeting of the Supreme Council should take
place in Ghana in January 1967.

The meeting was held at Aburi, in ex-President Nkrumah's
luxurious country seat in the hills overlooking Accra. The two-day
meeting seemed the last hope that Nigeria might stay together. It is
among the best documented conferences in history. Ankrah, aware
that it was a crucial meeting that might later give rise to conflicting
versions and interpretations, proposed that it be tape-recorded and
that each participant should later be handed a copy of the tape. He
was right; there was immediate disagreement on what had been
decided—and Ojukwu promptly issued the entire tape as a set of
six long-playing records.

Gowon went to Aburi with the firm idea that Nigeria was somehow to remain one. But he had no other preconceptions. He and
the others, with the single exception of Ojukwu, regarded the
meeting as a friendly get-together of officers, to get back on speaking terms and sort things out. Ojukwu, on the other hand, came
fully prepared for serious business—with a team of advisers,
secretaries and a sheaf of papers. He got his way with little effort,
by being the cleverest. He was the only one who understood the
real issues. Step by step, the others came to acquiesce in the logic
of Ojuwku's basic thesis—that to stay together at all the Regions
had first to 'draw apart'. Only Ojukwu understood that this meant,
in effect, a sovereign Biafra and the end of the Federation.

Though there was an agenda, the talks followed an immutable
logic of their own. In his measured, sepulchral voice, Ojukwu first
brought up the question of the arms race. 'I have accused the
Federal Government of purchasing arms. I have been accused of
purchasing arms.'[52] He claimed to have captured a document
showing that a Major Apollo had bought 'vast quantities' of arms
in Rome. Gowon explained these were routine purchases—and
countered with a reference to the plane that had crashed in

Cameroon. It was agreed, in vague terms, that each Region should count and declare its weapons.

Ojukwu now brought up the next of his preoccupations—the disposition of troops. He reminded Gowon of his promise on August 9 that all troops should return to their own Regions—and that despite this Northern troops still 'occupied' the West. Gowon said he had intended this agreement to apply only to the repatriation of Northerners in the East and of Easterners outside their own Region. He had to keep Northern troops in the West because there were no Yoruba troops. This brought a mild protest from Colonel Adebayo, the West's Military Governor, 'because I am the one who is really hit at the moment'.[53] While delivering this protest, Adebayo incautiously referred to the 'Supreme Commander'—and incurred a sharp rebuke from Ojukwu for using so controversial a phrase.

This led inexorably to the next issue, formulated by Major Johnson, the Administrator of Lagos. 'Is there a government in Nigeria today? Is there a central government?'[54] Ojukwu said there was not. After the July coup the country 'resolved itself into three areas—the Lagos, West, North area; the Mid-West area; and the East area'.[55] No one disagreed. Gowon admitted that he had thought it 'expedient' not to announce Ironsi's death at the time. It was now agreed that this must be done at once. In the meantime, the meeting retired delicately out of microphone range while the gruesome details of Ironsi's death were related.

Next came the reorganisation of the army. Here Gowon was firm. He was against splitting the army up on regional lines more than was absolutely necessary.

We ourselves were built up as a family over one hundred years ago, and I think we have grown over the years. Although unfortunately last year that basis was badly shaken, and it continued to be shaken in July, August and September, it is my strong feeling that in our case it would probably be wrong for us now to decide to start going back at this stage, whilst a lot of people have started to build up into one whole. I think we should try to keep what we have got, with realistic modifications where necessary. We should keep the army's oneness as much as possible.[56]

With relentless logic, Ojukwu observed that before one could talk about how to arrange the army one needed to know what sort of government one had. He suggested a council of state with a chairman —as in Ghana. This idea led to a good deal of floundering.

Gowon (to Ojukwu): Are we not a federation; are you not part of the federation?
Ojukwu: Are you the federation?
Gowon: I am part of the federation.
Ojukwu: All I say is I must be consulted before that sort of thing that is likely to affect the East is promulgated....
Hassan: Let us try to be honest. If the East does not recognise the federation I think you better secede and let the three of us join together. Please let us be honest.
Adebayo: That is not what he is saying.
Hassan: That is what he is saying.[57]

Ojukwu now brought out his big guns, arguing with feeling and eloquence that what had happened in the army and in the country made a 'drawing apart' of the Regions unavoidable.

As long as this situation exists, men from Eastern Nigeria would find it utterly impossible to stay in the same barracks, feed in the same mess, fight from the same trenches as men in the army from Northern Nigeria. . . . Each Commanding Officer will never be sure when his day will come. You wake up in the morning, you go down the barracks square and you find four or five dead bodies, nobody will know and nobody will be able to say who killed them and this will continue on and on and on. For these basic reasons, the separation of forces, the separation of the population is, in all sincerity, in order to avoid further friction and further killing.[58]

Hassan agreed, adding that there had even been dissension within the North and West. 'Therefore we had better try to keep the big groups together [i.e. the Regions] at the moment and then gradually get the various groups slowed down.' He was agreeing with Ojukwu, but without understanding the implications. Adebayo was in much the same predicament.

Who was to be in command of what remained of the centre? Ojukwu's proposal was clear, if somewhat amateurishly expressed. 'If we are not going to get ourselves into another friction, then, I think this must really be spelt out, so that what I envisage is that whoever is at the top is a constitutional chap—constitutional within the context of the military government. That is, he is titular head, but he would only act where, say, when we have met and taken a decision.'[59] On this proposal each of the colonels returned home to sleep.

On the second day agreement was reached on a new formula—again at the suggestion of Ojukwu. There was to be neither chairman nor Supreme Commander but a 'commander-in-chief and head of the Federal Military Government'. Each Region was to have an 'area command' with responsibility for internal matters. The concurrence of all was to be necessary for any decision affecting a Region or the country as a whole. To satisfy the West, it was agreed that massive recruitment of Yoruba should begin at once. It was also agreed that Ibo civil servants who had fled from Lagos would continue to be paid from federal funds up to March 31, the end of the financial year.

Nigerians were vastly relieved that their leaders were still on speaking terms and had apparently managed to reach agreement to settle their differences peacefully. But the relief was short-lived. While Ojukwu triumphantly published the Aburi decisions, the Federal government issued only a summary which omitted the main points. The reason was that Gowon's government had second thoughts. Seen in the cold light of government offices in Lagos it was apparent that the agreements, if fully carried out, would have meant the end of the Federation—and perhaps of Nigeria.

All the Federal permanent secretaries met on January 20 to consider the Aburi agreements. In a secret report, later captured by Eastern agents and released to the press, the civil servants demolished the Aburi agreements point by point. The title 'Commander-in-Chief', they felt, 'would be a subtle way of either abolishing the post of Supreme Commander or declaring it vacant'. The transferance of executive authority to a Supreme Military Council implied that 'the Commander-in-Chief would have no powers of control or dismissal over the Military Governors—a situation which is incompatible with military administration'. The report concluded bluntly that the arrangements 'amount to a confederation'. Another Aburi proposal that senior military, administrative and diplomatic appointments should be approved by all 'would tend to paralyse the functions of the federal public and police service commissions'. The loyalty of regionally-appointed federal officers would be to the Regions—'meaning in effect that there will be no federal public service'.

'On Aburi we stand' was now the Eastern slogan. Ojukwu refused to attend further meetings unless the Aburi decisions were first implemented. In a dawn broadcast at the end of February he issued an ultimatum that 'if the Aburi agreements are not fully implemented by March 31, I shall have no alternative but to feel free to take whatever measures may be necessary to give effect in this Region to those agreements'. March 31 was the end of the financial year. When the Eastern government invited thirty European and American journalists to Enugu, at its expense, an announcement of secession was widely expected. Instead, the journalists saw civil defence posters on Enugu walls, showing an armed soldier, with the caption: 'This is your Region. This man is ready. Are you?' Ojukwu told the journalists that he would secede only if the East were attacked or blockaded.[60]

The Federal government made what seemed a last desperate effort to meet Ojukwu's demands. It issued a decree which gave formal effect to the Aburi decisions and all but turned Nigeria into a confederation. Legislative and executive powers were vested in a Supreme Military Council, which could take decisions on vital

225

matters only with the concurrence of all military governors. Ignoring the jaundiced comments of the permanent secretaries, it also implemented the Aburi proposal that all senior appointments had to be approved by all Regions. Within their own Regions, the military governors were to be virtually autonomous.

But Decree No. 8 still failed to satisfy Ojukwu. He lost no time in pointing out its deficiencies. One of its clauses laid down that governors could not exercise the powers they had been given 'so as to impede or prejudice the authority of the Federation or endanger the continuance of federal government'. No sanction was prescribed, but another section enabled the Federal government to take over the functions of a regional government which was 'endangering the continuance of the federal government' or attempting to secede. Worse, it provided that a state of emergency could be declared in any Region with the consent of only three out of the four governors. This last arrangement was ominously reminiscent of the pre-1966 situation—in particular the Balewa government's high-handed action in declaring a state of emergency in the West in 1962. Ojukwu rejected the decree out of hand.

March 31, expected to be the East's 'D-Day', was an anticlimax. Instead of seceding, Ojukwu issued a Revenue edict, merely appropriating all federal revenues collected in the East. He gave as a reason the failure to implement the Aburi decision to pay absent civil servants up to March 31, and the need to make provision for the massive influx of refugees. This decree did not affect oil revenues, as these were collected in Lagos.

Gowon's government now faced a serious threat from another quarter—the Western Region. Relations with Chief Awolowo and the other Yoruba leaders had long been strained. Awolowo's following was mainly in the proletariat and the reformist wing of the intelligentsia, who resented the presence of an 'occupation force' of Northern troops. The promise that Yoruba would be recruited to make the withdrawal of Northern troops possible did little to allay these feelings. It would take time to create a Yoruba army. The West's bombshell was dropped at a 'Leaders of Thought' meeting in Ibadan, which met late in April to prepare the ground for a re-sumed session of the Ad Hoc constitutional talks. Awolowo announced his resignation as Yoruba delegate to the talks—and added that if the East seceded the West would now feel free to follow suit. In his letter of resignation he explained: 'It is my con-sidered view that whilst some of the demands of the East are ex-cessive, within the context of a Nigerian union most of such de-mands are not only well founded, but are designed for smooth and healthy association among the various national units of Nigeria.'[61] Centrifugal sentiments were contagious. Colonel Ejoor, the Mid-West's Governor, now joined in the revolt against Lagos. The Mid-West, with its large Ibo minority, considered itself a buffer zone and wished to avoid becoming a theatre of war. Ejoor called for a 'demilitarised zone' in his Region.

Faced with the threat of disintegration in its own ranks, the Federal government obtained a new lease of life from the North. At their own 'Leaders of Thought' meeting, the Northern emirs decided that the North 'should be irrevocably committed to the creation of states—whether or not they are created elsewhere—as the basis of stability in the North and also in the entire federation, and urges the federal government to take immediate steps to set in motion the machinery for the creation of these states'.[62] This de-cision was revolutionary. The creation of more states had been a perennial demand of the East—and it had been fiercely resisted by the North. Northern leaders now saw it as the only way to keep the Federation together. The decision was also spurred on by the increasing restiveness within the army of the Tiv and other Middle Belt people—always the most forceful advocates of a strong centre with many states.

This revolution rallied the federal side. Awolowo had himself long been an advocate of more states, drawn as far as possible on ethnic lines. Throughout his career, his stumbling block had been the monolithic North. The new proposals now won him round. He agreed to become Commissioner for Finance and Deputy Chairman of the Supreme Council in a new, mixed government of soldiers and

227

civilians. It was the nearest he had ever been to becoming Prime Minister of Nigeria. Chief Enahoro and other former 'opposition' leaders were also appointed commissioners in charge of ministries.

Now that his ranks were solid again, Gowon was prepared for a showdown with the East. Early in May, the Federal Government blocked all postal and postal order services to the East, in retaliation against the Revenue Ordinance. Ojukwu confided to Reuters: 'I think we are now rolling downhill—and it will take a great deal to halt the momentum. We are very close, very, very close.'

There was to be one final peace move—a last-ditch attempt to revive the old Nigerian brinkmanship. The Federal Chief Justice, Sir Adetokunboh Ademola, and the Nigerian Institute of International Affairs convened a National Reconciliation Committee. Together with Awolowo, its members visited Ojukwu in Enugu on May 7. Ojukwu snubbed the mission, calling it an 'ill-conceived child' because it included Okoi Arikpo, a non-Ibo Easterner who did not support Ojukwu's stand. However, he gave the Commission his point of view. It accepted all his demands, and called on the Federal government to implement them. The Federal government was to end its economic sanctions, while the East was to revoke its revenue edict; troops should be posted to their Regions of origin, while security in Lagos was to be left to the Commander-in-Chief in consultation with his colleagues. On May 20, Gowon, still anxious to avoid a showdown, accepted all the recommendations. The Federal government announced that its ban on the flight of Nigeria Airways planes to Enugu was lifted, together with other sanctions. Colonel Hassan flew from Kaduna to Ibadan to break the news to the Northern troops that they were to be moved.

But hopes of an eleventh-hour reconciliation were illusory. The East's Director of Information, Cyprian Ekwensi, declared that the revocation of sanctions had been received in the East with 'contempt, levity and apathy'. He had some justification in not taking Lagos too seriously. The Director of Nigeria Airways quietly admitted that no specific order had, after all, been received to resume flights to the East. One of his aircraft had already been hi-jacked by

Easterners and he clearly had no desire to risk others going the same way. As for the Northern troops in the West, it was solemnly announced that they would be moved to Ilorin and Jebba—which was only just across the Northern border. The implication was that they would be ready to come back at a moment's notice.

Ojukwu now faced irresistible pressure to secede. On May 26, addressing his Consultative Assembly of some 300 selected provincial representatives, he declared, in answer to federal threats to use force, that 'there is no power in this country, or in black Africa, to subdue us by force'. He suggested it was for the Assembly to choose between various courses of action: '(*a*) accepting the terms of the North and Gowon and thereby submit to domination from the North, or (*b*) continuing the present stalemate and drift, or (*c*) ensuring the survival of our people by asserting our autonomy.'[63]

The Consultative Assembly took the hint. It passed a resolution mandating the Military Governor to declare 'at an early practicable date, Eastern Nigeria as a free, sovereign and independent state by the name and title of the Republic of Biafra'. This was not yet secession, but the Federal government immediately activated its contingency plan. The same evening Gowon broadcast, declaring a state of emergency. He announced that he had assumed full powers 'for the short period necessary to carry out the measures which are now urgently required'. He announced a decree dividing Nigeria into twelve states: North West, Kano, North East, Plateau-Benue, West Central, North Central, Lagos, West, East Central, Rivers, South East and Mid-West. He announced the reimposition of the blockade against the East and the abrogation of Decree No 8.

At 2 A.M. on May 30 diplomats and journalists in Enugu were summoned to State House to hear Ojukwu make a solemnly-worded announcement.

Fellow countrymen and women. You, the people of Eastern Nigeria, conscious of the supreme authority of Almighty God over all mankind, of your duty to yourselves and posterity; aware that you can no longer be protected in your lives and in your

property by any government based outside Eastern Nigeria . . .
unwilling to be unfree partners in any association of a political or
economic nature; . . . now, therefore, I, Lieutenant-Colonel
Chukwuemeka Odumegwu Ojukwu, by virtue of your authority
and pursuant to the principles recited above, do hereby solemnly
proclaim that the territory and Region known as Eastern Nigeria,
together with her continental shelves and territorial waters, shall
henceforth be an independent sovereign state of the name and
title The Republic of Biafra.

War was now inevitable. Radio Biafra declared that 'neither the so-
called state of emergency that Gowon has declared nor the decree
purporting to create states can apply to this Region'. It called
Gowon's moves a 'one-man coup d'etat'. This was not very far from
the truth. May 30 had been, in a real sense, the third coup—the coup
of the minorities. It was the profoundest revolution of all. Nigeria
was no longer to be disputed between the big groups—the Hausa-
Fulani, the Yoruba and the Ibo. Now it was the Nigeria of the Tiv,
the Ejaw, the Benin, the Kanuri, the Ibibio. To the East, the
arbitrary division of its territory into three, leaving even Port
Harcourt—a predominantly Ibo city—outside the Ibo state, was an
open challenge to secede. But by that time the die was already cast.
    Foreign reaction was to be crucial. Long before secession Eastern
spokesmen had been touring world capitals, with special emphasis
on the African ones, explaining the Eastern case. They had enlisted
much sympathy and when they seceded they calculated that they
could count on British and American neutrality and recognition by
some at least of the African governments. On the first day of the new
regime, Radio Biafra announced that Ghana, Israel, Ethiopia,
Gambia and Togo had already recognised the new state. This was
promptly denied by all the states named. Federal counter-diplomacy
had by now had its effect and this was enhanced by the increasing
firmness of purpose that emanated from the Federal government.
An initial statement from President Nyerere of Tanzania expressed
much of Africa's anxieties about the danger of moving from the

negotiating table to the battlefield. He 'deeply regretted' the break-up of Nigeria and reaffirmed his faith in the territorial integrity of African states. 'But we also firmly believe that such unity can be achieved only by agreement and not by conquest or coercion. Let us, by all means, encourage the people of Nigeria to maintain their unity, but under no circumstances should we encourage a civil war in Nigeria. Eastern Nigeria is not Katanga.'

Britain attempted, with little success, to stay neutral. Herbert Bowden, then Commonwealth Secretary, told the Commons that, while there was some diplomatic contact with Enugu, 'at this stage there can be no recognition of the Eastern Region by ourselves, and nor has any other country recognised it'. But Britain was to become increasingly involved, whether it wished to or not. Most British companies observed the federal blockade against Biafran ports. Shipping companies, and the big trading concerns, generally had more at stake on the federal than the Biafran side. However, the opposite was true of the oil companies. Their dilemma was at its height when Ojukwu insisted that oil royalties were now payable to his exchequer. Some £7 million advance royalties were due in July—and Ojukwu demanded a token payment at once. The companies, with the concurrence of the British government, which itself has a substantial shareholding in Shell-BP, felt they had to accede to this demand. The Federal government retaliated by extending its blockade to cover oil shipments from the terminal at Bonny. The intended payment to Ojukwu was never made, with the result that Britain—and the oil companies—managed to incur the profound displeasure of both sides. The situation was not improved by the British stand over the shipment of arms. While expediting regular supplies of small arms, the British government refused to supply jet planes, or even seaward defence boats. In the classic manner, the Nigerians turned to the Russians for their jets, effecting an overnight transformation in Nigerian foreign policy.

On July 6, federal troops advanced into Biafra on two fronts, at Nsukka and at Ogoja. After three coups and two massacres, Nigeria was at war with itself.

9. The New North

In the past we have tended to wait for everything to be done for us. This attitude of idleness and fatalism has, let us face it, made our people backward and weak. We all now realise this is a competitive world and unless we stand on our own feet squarely we shall find ourselves even further behind than we do now. . . . It will be sad indeed if the impression gains ground that in these provinces we have only enthusiasm for destroying what hardworking people have built.
—Lieutenant-Colonel Hassan Katsina, Military Governor, Northern Provinces, 1966.[1]

I would rather be called Sultan of Sokoto than President of Nigeria.—Sir Ahmadu Bello, Sardauna of Sokoto, 1965.[2]

On the night of January 14–15, 1966, an army major leading a small group of soldiers shot dead the Premier of the North. When the Sardauna of Sokoto died so, perhaps, did the traditional concept, held both inside and outside Nigeria, of 'The North'. Whatever the real 'North' had or had not been, it was never to be the same again. The imperious, militantly Moslem leader had been more than a symbol: he had been the last leader of a regime which, in its essence, had antedated the six decades of British rule. The January coup eliminated not only the Sardauna's regime in a Region, but also that of the Northern-dominated Federal government in Lagos. At a stroke, it had abolished the hegemony of the North in Nigerian politics.

In the North itself, the aftermath of the coup was to do much more than change a regime. For decades, Northern politics had turned on the efforts of Northerners to catch up with the South in education, and thus compete on an equal footing with the Ibo and the Yoruba. In May and October of 1966, the massacres of the Ibo in the North caused a mass exodus of Southerners—and among them were most of the Region's clerks and technicians and a high proportion of its businessmen and industrial workers. Six years after Independence the North was only beginning to adapt itself to the departure of the British civil servants. Now, overnight, the Ibo had left too. As if this challenge was not enough, the following year was to bring an even more radical revolution. On May 27, 1967, the regime of General Gowon issued a decree splitting the North into six separate states. This single decree achieved what Southern politicians had been trying for decades to do—and what the Sardauna had so fiercely resisted. It ended an administration that had been unified since the Holy War of Othman Dan Fodio in 1817.

Ironically, after he had been killed, few Northerners missed the Sardauna. The widely expected 'reaction' did not come. The end of the Ramadan feast, which could have been the occasion for violence, passed peacefully and even in Sokoto the Sultan appealed for co-operation with the new military government. It became clear to the outside world, which in this context includes Southern Nigeria, that the image of the North had been wrong all the time.

According to the image, the North is an empty, desert land, supporting a monolithic, feudal, static and reactionary society. The feudal image impresses itself on visitors because of the social atmosphere: emirs, chiefs, ministers and other magnates seem surrounded by obsequious retainers, both in their homes and on their travels. The image was further strengthened by the postures and attitudes of the Sardauna himself. He spoke and acted like a Fulani chieftain. For foreigners, the image is sustained by the medieval overtones of an agrarian society in which the horse is still an everyday means of transport. In the immense countryside, peopled by illiterate but devoutly-Moslem peasants, the emirs in their palaces and courts are islands of wealth and authority. Yet the emirs seem to have an intimate, personal relationship with their subjects, reminiscent of the English barons in their heyday. The North seems monolithic because of the authoritarian nature of its

predominant religion and its society, and because of the heavy
accent on tradition and respect for elders. The apparent emptiness
of the land was an image that rankled in the South, because of the
bitter census controversy. It certainly looks empty: one can drive,
or even fly, for hours over the countryside without seeing much
humanity. The presence of camels in the streets of Kano or Katsina
enhances the desert atmosphere, as does the dusty and barren look
of the parched ground.

Even before the 1966 revolution, the image of 'the North' had
been largely false. While the 'Moslem North'—in fact, only 70 per
cent of the Region—may be feudalistic in atmosphere, it was by no
means feudal in the technical sense. Land, the basis of feudalism,
was held not by individuals but by the state. The peasants paid
neither rents nor tribute for its use. True, they paid taxes to a local
government which was dominated by chiefs and elders, but these
derived their authority from religion, tradition and, in the last
resort, the support of the government: a more precarious basis for
authority than ownership of land. The 'emptiness' of the North is
also largely illusory. Hausa society is not urban, as Yoruba is. A
road in Yorubaland winds and curves, as it does in Britain, following
well-worn tracks connecting villages and towns. Northern roads
were drawn in straight lines connecting distant centres, largely
ignoring the lie of the human geography. In other words, Northerners are not easily seen from the road. Speeding along the dusty
tarmac from Zaria to Kano, one feels as if one is driving through
desert. But a closer look reveals signs of cultivation almost all the
way; the people themselves are generally only just out of sight.

The biggest error of all about the North is that it is 'Hausa-
Moslem', monolithic and static. In fact, only about 30 per cent of
it is Hausa and only 70 per cent Moslem. If there is a 'typical
Northerner', he is to be found only in the so-called 'far North' of
the new North West State, comprising Sokoto and Katsina
provinces. Even the Hausa are not monolithic. Those in Kano are
a powerful community of traders, with their own separate attitudes
and long-established Kano State Movement. As recently as 1962

the Emir of Kano felt himself—wrongly as it turned out—strong enough to challenge Kaduna. He was deposed and exiled.

Apart from the Hausa-Fulani, the North has more than a hundred tribes. In the north-east are the Kanuri, proud and pious warriors who were more than a match not only for the armed might but also for the religious fervour of Othman Dan Fodio (see chapter 3, pp. 74–6). To the Kanuri, Hausa is the language of slaves and even today they disdain to teach it in their primary schools. The Sardauna's regime was careful to keep the two million Kanuri happy; fortunately, they make especially able administrators. The Governor of the Region, Sir Kashim Ibrahim, was a Kanuri from Maiduguri; so also were a disproportionate number of federal and regional ministers and permanent secretaries.

A more conspicious contrast to the 'true North' is the pagan and Christian 'Middle Belt', a loosely defined area including Benue, parts of Bauchi, the Jos Plateau and Southern Zaria. Scores of small pagan tribes have each a rapidly growing community of Christians. The most prominent group are the million and a half Tiv of Benue province, a fiercely independent people who have provided Nigeria with its most intractable minority problem. As old and as separate as the Kanuri of Bornu are the Nupe of Niger province, whose kingdom flourished in the sixteenth century. In the same province the equally distinct Igala and Idoma number between a quarter and half a million each. In the provinces of Kabba and Ilorin are almost a million Yoruba, speaking the language of the Western Region. Separate from all these groups are the itinerant and ubiquitous Fulani herdsmen, easily distinguished by their lighter skins and delicate sensual features. Finally, until the massacres and exodus of 1966, more than one million Ibo and Yoruba lived all over the North, owning hotels, running garages and providing much of the manpower for offices and factories.

For those who look for it, the North still offers pageantry, in a milieu outwardly medieval if no longer so in spirit. The simultaneous charge of a hundred ornate Kanuri horsemen at a durbar has lost none of its splendour over the years. The ornate, cloistered palace of the Sultan of Sokoto still looks very much the same, and has much the same atmosphere, as it did in 1824, when the explorer Clapperton visited Sultan Bello, the present Sultan's great-grandfather.

> In front of it there is a large quadrangle, into which several of the principal streets of the city lead. We passed through three coozes, or guard-houses, without the least detention, and were immediately ushered into the presence of Bello, the second Sultan of the Felatahs. He was seated on a small carpet between two pillars supporting the roof of a thatched house, not unlike one of our cottages. The walls and pillars were painted blue and white, in the Moorish taste; and on the back wall was sketched a fire-screen, ornamented with a coarse painting of a flower-pot.[3]

In appearance, today's Sultan is not unlike Sultan Bello, who wore 'a white muslin turban, the shawls of which he wore over the nose and mouth in Tuarick [*sic*] fashion'.[4] The present Sultan emerged as a natural spokesman for the North after the elimination of politicians in 1966, as he had been in the days before the rise of politicians in the 1950s. He is a quiet man, with a shrewd and humorous manner. In his palace Sultan Bello and the other descendants of Othman Dan Fodio are entombed in a mausoleum of concrete; the oblong structure has been draped with a cloth of rich, red velvet, secured at the sides with zip fasteners. Well-kept lawns and flowers give the palace a serene atmosphere. Yellow-legged birds, like pelicans, perch indolently on the trees, while beggars hover around the gates.

If there is a feudalistic element in the North's social life, it has always a touch of informality. Visits of the Sardauna to Sokoto, his home town, were usually celebrated by horse races, games and jousts, including a playful form of wrestling in which combatants with bandaged hands try to make their opponents touch the ground. But the bandages keep coming undone: it was all very informal and amateurish and there was much laughter.

The clash of epochs seems especially striking in Kano, home of the North's largest emirate. A visitor seeking an appointment with the Emir first sees his 'prime minister', the Madaki. This powerful, handsome old figure, his lined face surrounded by a bright yellow turban, wears horn-rimmed glasses as he sits behind his desk. On the desk is the silver seal of the administration, wrapped in a red cloth. Officials of the urban administration coming into his office prostrate themselves, and remain crouching on the ground throughout the interview. On the wall of the office is a Japanese pin-up calendar and in the corner someone has piled some useless old chairs, where they remain, catching layers of dust. In another corner stands a refrigerator. The incongruous touches give the room something of the makeshift quality of Bedouin in their tents. The Madaki talks quietly, in an English which sounds far better than it is because of the impeccable accent that educated Northerners acquire more readily than Southerners. His small talk with a visitor might be about the progress of education, or the injustice of the fact that Kaduna has been replacing more and more Kano's former dominance in trade and industry. Then he takes up his telephone and rings the Emir, whose palace is across the square, for the appointment.

The Emir's palace is a whole village. Its big brown walls of mud conceal houses, shops and schools. Small groups of retainers and 'hangers-on' wait around endlessly outside the main gate; saddled horses are tethered there also, adding another anachronistic touch. After passing through walled courtyards the visitor is ushered into a waiting room, where he is offered last week's *Paris Match* to look at. The Emir, like Sultan Bello during Clapperton's visit, is seated on an ornate cushion. He is a young man who was a police chief and an ambassador before he was called, without warning, to the throne. He talks knowledgeably about reception conditions on various wavelengths for the BBC. He is much concerned with reform: indeed, since the military take-over of January 1966 he has been identified with 'the younger set'. But he is wise about reform. 'You have to go carefully and slowly. People don't like too much change. For example, visitors have asked me why the public in our native courts have to sit on the stone floor: why don't we provide benches for them to sit on. Well, they prefer it the way it is. A court has for so long been a place where you sit on the floor.'[5]

Northern society is shot through with contradiction. The penal code makes it an indictable offence for Moslems to drink. But the hotels are owned by Southerners and provide a discreet retreat. Even in Sokoto, right under the Sardauna's nose, as it were, one could find even senior officials of the native administration and the NPC enjoying a quiet beer. Much of the insistence on outward Moslem forms, especially on keeping wives in the seclusion of purdah, appeared to owe much to the personality of the Sardauna himself. Even when the Sardauna was alive, the Grand Kadi, judicial head of the Moslems, maintained that purdah was a social custom and not a religious one.[6] The new post-Sardauna North already looks gayer.

THE ROLE OF SIR AHMADU BELLO

For all his social conservatism, the Sardauna was a modernising politician, regarded as a dangerous radical by some of the emirs. His descent from Dan Fodio was a political asset, but in his later years he became obsessed with religion, conducting crusades at which vast numbers of 'converts' were claimed among the pagans. But the Sardauna's over-riding political aim was to preserve the identity, independence and way of life of the North from the real and imagined threats of Southern domination, until it could catch up with the South in education and technical training, and 'stand on its own feet'.

His paramount fear—not without foundation—was that the Southern parties might come to dominate federal politics and that the enterprising Southerner, especially the Ibo, would then in some way colonise the North, as well as secure most of the jobs in the Federal government and its agencies. This nightmare seemed to be coming true under the regime of General Ironsi. That was why the North reacted so violently in May 1966, and the Sardauna was posthumously reinstated as a popular hero. During his lifetime, the fierceness of the struggle, the lack of understanding of the North in other Regions, and perhaps also an inferiority complex had combined to make him seem much more reactionary than he really was.

'Others talk and shout a lot, while we here keep silent, yet no other Region has done as much as we have', he once protested. 'We have always been neglected and backward. People never realised there was money to spend in the North until the Legislative Council of 1947; there were then five schools in the whole of the North. Two-thirds of everything you see today was built in the last ten years. Education has multiplied by ten.'[7] In his later years the Sardauna was no longer prepared to 'keep silent'. He became increasingly concerned to match the propaganda of the South with his own. In its last year his regime spent £300,000 on setting up a modern daily newspaper, the *New Nigerian*, which was deliberately made into the best-produced daily in the Federation. In conversation he tended to glory in the conservatism of his views. Challenged on the North's continued denial of votes to women, he admitted that if Nigeria were ever to elect an executive president, as his Southern opponents were then demanding, he would give women the votes for that. 'That would be in the nature of a holy war to protect our religion. But after the vote we would send them back into purdah again.'[8]

MODERN POLITICS

The true origin of the Northern Peoples' Congress regime is in the Holy War of Othman Dan Fodio, which in 1817 united the Hausa kingdoms under Fulani rule. The Fulani thereafter assumed a dual role: the so-called 'town' Fulani intermarried with the Hausa, maintaining an aristocratic aura, while the 'cattle' Fulani retained their calling as nomadic herdsmen. The British took over the emirates, with their sophisticated system of local government, as going concerns. They called them, as they are still called, 'native authorities'. The system was extended—not always with happy results—to the non-Hausa areas and was progressively modernised. Today the six Northern states have seventy-one native authorities, grouped in thirteen provinces. The provincial system is superimposed on the emirates. During the period of centralised regional government, the key figure in the system was the provincial commissioner, a political officer who replaced the non-political Resident of British days. He was the direct representative of the government in Kaduna and ranks in local precedence above the emir.

The NPC was formed as a deliberate, if at first reluctant, answer to the urgent challenge of the Southern politicians over the control of the newly-independent Federation. The South was politically organised long before independence. If the North were to join a federation it had to be given a chance to 'catch up'; meanwhile it had somehow to find a way of holding the political fort. Towards the end of its rule, the NPC, despite its late and ad hoc beginnings, had become as efficient and as ruthless an instrument as the NCNC and the Action Group had become in their respective Regions.

In organisation the party followed the structure of the native administrations, with branches in every ward, village, district, division and province. Its backbone was the native administration staff and the emirs themselves. Its active agents were also drawn increasingly from the new class of Northern traders and contractors, prominent beneficiaries of party patronage and with a vested interest in the government's policy of 'Northernising' business. In its last years the NPC's able and eloquent spokesman was the Northern Region's Minister of Agriculture, Alhaji Ahman Galadima Pategi, general secretary of the party. Pategi's barbed pen, in common with everything else about the party, became visibly more practised and professional month by month. By the end, no statement from the South went without its answering press handout from the North, often within a day. At election time, the Southern parties could teach the NPC little in the way of intimidation of opponents, 'unopposed' returns and general harassment of opposition. Local justice, in which Moslem judges (alkali) held their courts, and the Moslem code itself, which held it an offence to 'insult the leaders', both helped to win elections.

As a government, the NPC was no less radical than the Southern parties. In centralising his government—at the expense of the emirs—the Sardauna went further than any of the other premiers. The main secret of the NPC's success among Northern civil servants was its policy of 'Northernisation'. This meant giving as many jobs as possible to Northerners at all levels, at the expense of Southerners. Where no Northerners were yet available, expatriates were openly preferred to the appointment of Southerners. This infuriated the South, but the Sardauna had clear ideas on the subject. 'If we cannot have a Northerner in a job we would rather an expatriate than a Southerner. Foreigners do their job and then go back home, leaving a vacancy to be filled. Southerners want to stay for ever.'[9] Northernisation received its most spectacular boost when the Ibos fled after the 1966 riots. For better or for worse, the North was now for Northerners. The NPC, no less than its Southern counterparts, was also a big bandwaggon, joined after every election by considerable numbers of the opposition. After the 1961 regional election, five out of the eleven elected opposition members crossed the carpet. However, opposition there was. It was of two kinds: regional and ideological.

THE OPPOSITION

The main ideological opposition came from Alhaji Aminu Kano's Northern Elements Progressive Union (NEPU). Aminu Kano is far from being a demagogue. An Alhaji (a Moslem who has made the pilgrimage to Mecca) and a Hausa, he was of the same stock and cultural background as the leaders of the NPC. He differed from the Sardauna in his personality and ideas. He is a nervous, cerebral man—by nature a reformer. Like Balewa, he began his career as a schoolteacher. His party took its stand on the need for better planning and greater democracy, finding all too easy targets in the deficiencies of both the regional and federal regimes. The party attracted the few real left-wingers to be found in the North. But it was not on the whole more alien to the Establishment than its leader was. Predictably, when the NPC fell from power in the military coup,

241

Aminu Kano became one of the group of political spokesmen who represented the North with little distinction of party.

Apart from NEPU, opposition in the North has been regional. In keeping with the basic pattern of Nigerian politics, the Southern parties were in alliance with the various minority groups as well as with NEPU. The Bornu Youth Movement, for example, might have developed into a strong regional opposition. But it was in alliance with the Action Group, and did not long survive the eclipse of that party in 1962. Its leader was Alhaji Ibrahim Imam, whose sufferings as an opposition politician had come so vividly to life in the Awolowo trial.

However the important territorial opposition within the North came from the Middle Belt, the largely pagan area where Christian missionary schools had produced a more educated and thrustful population than was to be found in Hausaland. The most important tribe in the Middle Belt is the Tiv. There are about a million and a half of these rather short, dark-skinned, largely pagan people, who occupy a large fertile slice of Benue province. Most of them are farmers but a higher than average (for the Region) proportion have been to school. Soldiering is one of their traditional callings and they have figured disproportionately first in the British and later in the Nigerian armies.

'Wild in look and ruder in dress, greatly tatooed and constantly carrying with them their bows and arrows, these men seem the perfect impersonification of savages', wrote Baikie, who explored the Niger and Benue in 1854. Since then more serious students have concluded that their problem was not savagery but the perennial lack of a government which understands the Tiv mentality. They are fiercely individualistic. The Tiv, who migrated originally from Bantu areas of Africa, have no traditional chiefs, let alone kings; they do not normally even live in towns and villages but in tiny compounds, with populations varying from two to a hundred, but normally about ten. They have erupted periodically, under both the British and the Northern regimes. The most serious outbreaks were in 1929, 1939, 1960 and 1964. During the latest uprising, which resulted in well over three hundred deaths, the army was sent in to police the area for several months.

There were three ways a government three hundred miles away could deal with such an area: (1) it could devise and impose a centralised administration; (2) it could try to build democratic and decentralised institutions in keeping with the Tiv mentality; (3) it could get rid of the Tiv altogether by giving them a separate state. The British tried the first course and immediately ran into trouble. In 1946 they created, against much expert advice, the Tor Tiv, the first chief with authority over the whole area. The first of a long series of riots followed. The third course was favoured as a distant objective by Lord Lugard, who was sympathetic to the idea of a Middle Belt State—a cause which has ever since been passionately championed by Tiv politicians. The Northern Government appointed a commission of inquiry into the 1964 disturbances, which in turn produced a report which was so critical of the negligent and inept administration that it was not published. The government did, however, issue a White Paper[10] summarising the commission's findings and recommending a return to representative institutions which had been in abeyance for fifteen years—a switch to policy number two.

Maladministration was at the heart of the problem. In a backward and neglected area the normal defects of Nigerian rule—its corruption, its oppresive and all-pervading politics—were at their most painful. Makurdi, the Benue provincial capital, had no telephone line to Gboko, the Tiv division capital sixty miles away. For a division of some 1·5 million people, the local authorities had provided only twenty-three primary schools, of which only eight had 'senior primary' classes. In contrast, the missionary agencies had seventy primary schools. With the advent of politics and the struggle between the NPC and the opposition United Middle Belt Congress (UMBC), matters rapidly deteriorated. The UMBC stood for a separate state for the Middle Belt and was in alliance with the Southern NCNC. But for most of the Tiv, it represented 'us' against 'them'—and the Tor Tiv was seen as an agent of Kaduna. The original Tor Tiv appointed by the British in 1946 had eventually become popular, but an unashamed NPC supporter was installed as his successor and politics began to exacerbate old animosities.

In 1964, however, the Northern government was ready to take the commission's report seriously. It decided that the council, suspended for fifteen years, was to be restored. Its members were to be indirectly elected, through district councils, and would thus indirectly reflect political loyalties. But the most popular reform, the release of hundreds of prisoners, did not come until after the military coup when Colonel Hassan Katsina, one of the army officers sent into Tivland in 1964, became the new Military Governor of the North.

Nigeria has not heard the last of the Tiv. Their predominance in the army helped to shape events in the days of military rule— especially the revolution which split Nigeria into twelve states in May, 1967. The UMBC politician, Joseph Tarka, emerged (like Aminu Kano) as a new civilian leader, first of the North and later at the federal level. Tarka, a restless, dynamic man, with a love of fast cars and (thanks to the support of the NCNC in the old days) no shortage of money, appeared to have won an assured place in the sun both for himself and for his people. He has suffered a good deal. In 1960, a local Tiv court sentenced him to six months imprisonment for seducing his sister away from her husband. The conviction was quashed by the British District Officer. After a long trial, he was acquitted of complicity in the 1960–61 riots; in 1962 he was one of the accused in the Awolowo trial and was again acquitted. In 1965 he was once more imprisoned for inciting riots and 'insulting the Premier'. He was appointed Federal Commissioner for Transport in Gowon's regime in 1967.

THE EDUCATIONAL REVOLUTION

On many government office walls in Kaduna is a map of the Region showing thirteen circles with a blacked-out segment in each. This shows the percentage of elementary-school-age children actually at school in each of the provinces. The variations are large. The lowest is in the 'true' North: Sokoto province. Only one in thirty-five children was at school there in 1962. The highest is for Kaduna Capital Territory, with one in eight. The charts, regularly renewed, are a symptom of the over-riding importance attached to education. Indeed the North devoted to education the lion's share of its development plan—35·7 per cent, a **higher** proportion than any other Region.

The educational revolution is already well under way. On average throughout the Region, less than 10 per cent of children in the 6–12 age group were at school before independence. In 1965 the percentage was up to 12 per cent. The 1968 target set by the Ashby Commission in 1959 was 25 per cent. This aim has been scaled down to 15 per cent because of rising costs and the staggering increase in the official population which occurred in 1963. The progress of secondary education has been more remarkable. The number of secondary school pupils—6,500 in 1961—had doubled in 1964 and was expected to double again by 1968, almost reaching the Ashby target of 30,000. The social revolution inherent in this explosion is at its most spectacular in female education. Girls in secondary schools, almost unknown before independence, numbered well over 2,000 in 1965.

The North has not been content merely with educating the young. The remarkably productive Public Enlightenment Campaign provides literacy classes for hundreds of thousands a year—aged from eight to forty-five. Some 8,000 classes each handle two sessions a year, with an average of twenty-three pupils in each session. The cost is shared between the regional government and local authorities—but the former is careful not to provide its grant unless the local authority can produce at least seven literacy certificates for each session.

The Ahmadu Bello University at Zaria, which opened with eight faculties in 1962, typifies the North's determination to do everything the other Regions do—at least as well. The elegantly-housed university has found it difficult to recruit sufficient qualified students of Northern origin: Southerners still constituted 42 per cent of undergraduates in 1965. But this is obviously a temporary situation; indeed, the tribal upheavals of 1966 may well have hastened 'Northernisation' here as everywhere else.

THE NEW ADMINISTRATION

For the Region's over-all progress, the most important academic department is the Institute of Administration at Zaria. In addition to its full-time courses, it provides in-service and refresher courses for judges and other native administration officials.

The North's administration is a fast-changing hybrid, part Moslem, part British, part pagan. It is being transformed from something resembling the private courts and exchequers of medieval princelings to something approaching modern local government. For the citizen, the native administration is to all intents and purposes the government. Its councillors—who often have specific portfolios—are the ministers; its numerous officials are the bureaucrats; its courts and policemen are the law. The seventy-one native authorities vary enormously in size and wealth. That of Kano has an income of more than £2 million and employs 5,000 officials, while that of United Hills in Sardauna province spends less than £15,000 and employs only forty-eight. The theoretical gradations in structure are complex, varying from 'chief-in-council' through 'chief-and-council' to councils without chiefs. The trend has been to give more power to elected councils, but in practice these can often do little to control powerful chiefs and their well-entrenched 'portfolio' councillors. But whenever an elected council fell foul of the political authorities, as often happened in the Plateau and Middle Belt area, it tended to find itself dissolved by order and replaced by official rule.

Superficially the most medieval aspect of the system is its courts, especially the traditional alkali courts where no lawyers may plead. The alkali system is controversial. Its apologists claim that it is in better accord with village realities and with the Moslem mentality than the paraphernalia of magistrates' courts. The alkali himself imparts traditional wisdom and has a more intimate knowledge of the background of cases before him than a magistrate. It is argued that there is always recourse to appeal—from the lowest alkali court right to the Federal Supreme Court in Lagos. Moreover, standards of training of alkalis and their court officials, and of government supervision of their activities, are constantly being improved. When the military regime placed all alkali courts under the jurisdiction of the Ministry of Justice in 1966, this seemed a radical reform, but in practice the Ministry had already been closely supervising these courts. The courts ranged from the emir's (Grade A) court, with powers of life and death (subject to confirmation by a minister and appeal to the High Court) down to the village (Grade D) courts, presided over by district heads, with maximum penalties of £15 or nine months imprisonment in criminal cases, and £50 in civil cases. The critics can point out that many alkalis are illiterate; very rough justice is done and, when it comes to politics, even the pretence of real justice is often dropped. At the chief alkali's (Grade B) court in Bauchi, the alkali sits cross-legged on an ornate mat, the accused on the stone floor, grovelling whenever he addresses the judge. In a case witnessed by the author,* a man owed £1,200 to the Northern Nigeria Development Corporation. After establishing that he could not pay, the court remanded him in custody while his goods were sold. It seemed fair—though possibly somewhat harsh in the light of subsequent investigations into the Region's Development Corporation, which showed how easily influential people could secure loans from the Corporation, with no more intention of repaying them than the poor defendant at Bauchi.

The military rule which displaced the politicians in 1966 was to take more radical action against the power of the emirs than the Sardauna's regime had done. In particular, it took over the native administration courts. These had long been theoretically subject to official supervision. But from April 1, 1966, the most important of the emirs' and alkalis' courts (Grade A and Grade A Limited)

* In December 1965. For another case heard on the same day, see chapter 2, pp. 44–5.

were taken over by the government, by decree. A year later the remainder of the 'native courts' were due to be taken over. However, it will take some years before this ambitious reform can effectively transform the emirs' courts.

Administration in the North relies more on expatriates than elsewhere in Nigeria. However, Northernisation has proceeded well. Today almost all District Officers are Northerners, often doing work which must seem formidable to a young man in the midst of powerful local vested interests and privileges. In the Northern civil service as a whole, there were, in 1960, about 1,500 British officers in senior posts and only 500 Northerners. Today there are well over 2,000 Northerners in senior posts and fewer than 1,000 Britons, of whom fewer than 400 are pensionable, the remainder being contract officers. Before the Ibo exodus of 1966 there were also some 350 Southerners.

MOSLEMS AND CHRISTIANS

Perhaps 70 per cent of the North is Moslem, 25 per cent pagan and 3·5 per cent Christian. In the last years of his life the Sardauna was determined to increase the proportion of Moslems. He claimed to have converted as many as a million people within a few months on a series of proselytising tours he made throughout the Region. Both Moslems and Christians were somewhat sceptical about the campaign. Large amounts of money were handed out, if not to the converts themselves then to the local emirs and chiefs, to pay for Moslem teaching. Lengths of cloth were also given away, because a Moslem must cover his body during prayer. For this campaign, the Premier had a grant of £100,000 from the Saudi Arabian government and £150,000 from the Sheikh of Kuwait. He was vice-president of the World Moslem League; the president was the Grand Mufti of Saudi Arabia and the secretary-general the Saudi Finance Minister. The Sardauna's campaign for souls alarmed the Christians, who included among their numbers a Northern minister and two permanent secretaries. They formed a

Northern Christian Association which formally protested against instances of persecution, though this in fact amounted more to over-zealousness on the part of some emirs and local officials than to persecution.

The Christians were simultaneously building up their own campaign. 'New Light for All' was modelled after the 'evangelism in depth' campaigns of South America. The pace of evangelical rivalry quickened in the last months of the Sardauna's life; in the Nupe area alhajis on motorcycles were despatched to counteract the gospel teachers' influence. There were Christian meetings of Billy Graham proportions in the stadium at Kaduna, where Howard Jones, an American Negro preacher trained by Graham, addressed 16,000 people. In one village an alhaji lined up all the Moslems on one side and the Christians on the other and invited any Christian to cross over. One intrepid Christian got up and returned the invitation. He was later jailed for incitement. However the Christians could not seriously complain of discrimination; religious toleration in the North contrasted markedly with political intolerance. 'New Light for All' was able to broadcast sermons in Hausa four times a week over the national radio station and once a month over the regional station.

ECONOMIC PROSPECTS

If Nigeria broke apart, could the North manage on its own? The question became highly relevant during the inter-regional crisis of 1966. While Colonel Yakubu Gowon, as head of state, was arguing that Nigeria must stay together as a federal unit, a powerful school of thought in the North, based more on emotion than reason, was in favour of splitting up the Federation and going it alone. This attitude was rooted in pride. 'What does money matter when it is a question of honour?' It was also based on misconceptions, popular in all Regions, about revenues. Early in 1967 a senior Northern official assured the author that not only had revenues deriving in the North kept the Federation going in the

249

past but they were still doing so today. In fact, though Northern groundnuts were once relatively more important than they are today, the North has never been a net contributor to federal revenues. Palm products made the East the first net contributor until it was overtaken by the West's cocoa, to be overtaken once more by the East's mineral oil.

The North received almost £30 million—about three-quarters of its revenue—from federal sources. How much of federal revenues derive in the North is not precisely known. The biggest item is import duties. Then comes some £3 million a year which groundnuts contribute to export taxes and about £3·5 million in royalties and rents from the tin industry. Exports of Northern origin—groundnuts, tin and columbite, cotton and cotton seed, hides and skin and benniseed—were worth about £70 million in 1965. Northern cattle also made the Region a net exporter in inter-regional trade. However, for a people of 25 million, the North has very little industry. While it would undoubtedly survive, and live at a standard no lower than that of many another landlocked African economy, life would become much harder if the Federation broke up. Apart from the revenue shortfall, the North would have to pay for such federal services as it now gets free, including the federal police, the railways, roads and defence. It might also have to pay dearly for its access to the sea.

The political cohesion of the North might also be in jeopardy if it were to become a separate country. The advent of military rule in 1966 gave the North the feeling of being under pressure—which made it more of a unity than it had ever been under the Sardauna. But if political independence were accompanied by a drastic curtailment of revenues, there would probably be more acrimonious disputes than ever about the sharing out of a reduced national cake. In the meantime, whatever the political future, the events of 1966 have been traumatic. The massive departure of the Ibo is likely to have hastened historical processes of change, while the splitting of the former Region into six new states is a revolution that will take years to digest.

10. Ibo and Other Easterners

It would appear that the God of Africa has specially created the Ibo nation to lead the children of Africa from the bondage of the ages.—Nnamdi Azikiwe, 1949.[1]

It appears there is a conspiracy and a carefully laid out plan to reduce the Ibos to second class citizens in the Federal Republic of Nigeria, if not to annihilate them.
—Chief Z. C. Obi, President, Ibo State Union, 1965.[2]

I have been thinking about the Easterners. I found it puzzling, how can they hear all these accusations of corruption made against them without apparently minding or changing their ways? I have been thinking and I have come to the conclusion that it's because those people are in the first generation, the first generation to live this sort of life, the life of politicians, of an ordered society. They simply cannot see that certain actions are wrong, so they go on doing them.—Sir Abubakar Tafawa Balewa, 1965.[3]

NOTHING ENDEARS NIGERIA more to the foreigner than the subtle contrasts between its main ethnic groups. The dignified Hausa, God-fearing and conservative; the inscrutable Yoruba, lazy and devious; the clever Ibo, go-getting and adaptable—the three stereotypes seem reassuringly complementary, like the assorted members of a family. Seen in slightly sharper focus, the stereotypes contain disturbing paradoxes. The gentle manners of the Hausa proclaim him as more civilised, yet he hails from the least educated of the Regions. For all his sophistication, the Yoruba seems furthest removed from the European mind, and in some ways least able to cope with 'modern' life. The Ibo is quickest to learn: he is at home in an office, a factory, a Rotary Club or a ballroom. Yet in the social and political arts of living with other peoples in a federation, without getting himself heartily disapproved of, he has failed totally and disastrously. However, the paradoxes are not insoluble. The Northerners may be cultured, but it is their own culture—Islamic rather than Christian. In fact they strike the European as cultured only in those aspects of culture which are universal: respect for tradition, politeness and the ability to wield power with moderation. Yoruba mix less easily with Europeans because their own culture is rich and their social relationships and obligations are so absorbing that they have less need for relationships with foreigners. If the Ibo are 'clever' it is mainly because, like the Jews, they have had to be. Their overcrowded and agriculturally poor Region has forced them to seek their fortunes abroad in large numbers. Their own individualistic culture offered no inherent obstacles to Western modernisation. Coming from a largely fragmented society, with no big towns, no empires, no strong central leadership or even important chiefs, their condition made for physical and social mobility. How much Ibo 'aggressiveness' owes to all this, and how much is native, no one can say. The careful anthropologist has recorded simply that among the Ibo 'it is the go-getter that is admired, the man who has wives and children and who bestirs himself to make money. A man who sits quiet is not respected.'[4]

In the federal context, the Ibo mentality has long been dominated by a sense of grievance. Under British rule they felt neglected. The British then left the North too big, able to dominate federal politics by its numbers; yet because of its poverty it absorbed a disproportionate share of federal revenues. As for the Yoruba, was it not they who were given the best education and, through it, the best jobs, merely because they happened to be colonised first? This sense of grievance, coupled with their distribution throughout Nigeria as well as their thirst for modernity, put the Ibo naturally in the vanguard of Nigerian nationalism. True, this modern force was seeded in Lagos and its pioneers were not Ibo; but it was Azikiwe and his early Ibo lieutenants who made it the instrument of the first national party, the National Council of

Nigeria and the Cameroons (NCNC). Although the NCNC was stopped from obtaining outright federal power, it enabled the Ibo to share power with the Northerners, leaving the Action Group of the Yoruba 'out in the cold'. However, this success was short-lived. Because of the excesses of politicians on both sides, the coalition broke up. The resultant election crisis of 1964–65 left the Ibo as the 'odd men out', now facing a new alliance between the NPC and a section of the Yoruba (the NNDP) which made 'anti-Iboism' a main plank of its policy.

The army take-over of January 1966 changed everything. For the first time in Nigerian history, the Ibo were at the apex of the power structure. But their success did not last more than six months. A fatal political blindness in General Ironsi and in his largely Ibo advisors quickly dissipated the regime's initial popularity. After the Decree of May 24, 1966, abolishing the federal system, the Northerners rioted and killed hundreds of Ibo in their midst. Then followed the Northern counter-coup and a second wave of massacres, resulting in several thousand Ibo deaths. This trauma dwarfed all previous Ibo grievances. It lead to the secession of the Eastern Region and to civil war.

The commonest reproach against the Ibo by the non-Ibo is that they are the most 'tribalistic' of Nigerians. It is a stock jibe that 'wherever two Ibo meet, they open a branch of the Ibo State Union'. In such celebrated tribal rows as those of the universities of Lagos (in 1965) and Ibadan (in 1966), the Ibo became famous for their perpetual meetings, often far into the night. However, in justice, it should be observed that the Hausa, away from their natural habitat, stick just as assiduously together; as for the Yoruba, their politics is openly centred on tribal affiliation. In reality, strong ethnic allegiances are common to all Nigerians, but the ubiquitousness and the worldly success of the Ibo made them more vulnerable to criticism.

Solidarity has its positive sides, and its good effects can be seen scattered liberally throughout Iboland and wherever Ibo live. Many a village has its post office, or maternity clinic, or approach road, or school, built by communal savings and often communal labour. Communities club together to send their abler 'sons' to university. Away from home, solidarity is even more marked. Whether in Lagos or in London, few Ibo seem to have their Sunday afternoons to themselves: there is always a clan or village meeting, with problems to solve and, inevitably, money to raise.

THE IBO STATE UNION

At the centre of Ibo corporate existence is the Ibo State Union, a body which, in non-Ibo eyes, has acquired sinister political overtones because of its early association with the NCNC. If the Ibo State Union's president, Chief Z. C. Obi, really believed, as he said in 1965, that there was 'a conspiracy' against the Ibo, he must have thought the wheel had come full circle since 1949, when Azikiwe told the Union in a farewell message that 'the Ibo giant is awakening from his stupor and is asserting his inalienable right in the scheme of things'.[5]

There is much of the Ibo story in Chief Obi's personality and career. He is a short, bespectacled man in his sixties, with a brisk and businesslike air. When in the Port Harcourt headquarters of Z. C. Obi and Sons he wears a gaily patterned overshirt, with pens and a cheque book sticking out of his pocket. He is urbane and hospitable, far from the fire-eating tribalist his published statements sometimes make him appear. His chieftancy, apparently untypical, is in fact not hereditary but was conferred on him for life. Although he is the nephew of the Obi of Nnewi, one of the few hereditary Ibo kings, he is a self-made man. His father grew yams, coco-yams and guinea corn; after his schooling up to 'Standard Six' in the local Anglican elementary school, he decided to become either a teacher or a priest. But, he recalls, 'I realised that neither a teacher nor a minister seemed to be well paid, so I decided to go into business'.[6]

He joined the United Africa Company at the age of eighteen as a junior shorthand typist and stayed thirty-one years with the company. He became a branch manager in Calabar, a non-Ibo area. 'I did not like it there; I felt isolated.' When the company declined to transfer him, he used his savings to go into business. His catering firm has its headquarters at Port Harcourt (it has Port Harcourt prison among its more lucrative customers), and he also has several houses in his native Nnewi, where he often goes at weekends. He has several wives (he declines to say how many) and 'about twenty' children.

Chief Obi emphatically denies that there is anything political about the Ibo State Union. 'Members are free to join any political party and they often do.' The Union is the headquarters of some two hundred local unions whose purpose is 'to look after our communal interest'. He emphasises the role of the Union in that most characteristic of all Ibo activities: migration. 'Whether we move from our village to a town in the Region, say Onitsha, or to another Region or to another country, our need is the same. We want to find out if any among us are bad people, and if there are any, to send them back where they came from.' He recalls his own role in the founding of the Union back in the 1940s—'when independence was on the way and tribalism made its first appearance'—and expresses its essential purpose with a favourite phrase: 'to get ourselves together'.

AN OVERCROWDED REGION

Crossing the Niger bridge from the Mid-West to the Eastern Region, one emerged from the forest into more open country. From Onitsha to Enugu the road was wide and fast (the East had the best roads in Nigeria) and the villages looked substantial and prosperous, with solid walls around family compounds. It is difficult to drive anywhere on the roads without being in sight of humanity: in contrast with the apparent emptiness of the North, there seems to be a town or a village every few hundred yards. This effect was further enhanced in 1966 by the arrival of the refugees from the North, perhaps numbering over a million. This new influx turned

255

villages into towns. It brought the population density of the East to a probable 440 per square mile, making it the most densely-settled area in Africa after the Nile valley.[7] (Nigeria's national density was about 132; that of the West is 243 and that of the North 87. That of Ghana is also 87.)*

Overcrowding in the more fertile areas made the East's un-employment problem even worse than that of the other Regions. While in all Regions—and, indeed, in all developing countries—the boy who has been to school tends to leave the village, the East faced the additional problem of serious over-cultivation. Fallows were so short that there was insufficient time for recuperation, and traditional methods of shifting cultivation were no longer possible. In the densely settled areas there was no place in agriculture for the new generation. Only a few were ready to move into virgin forest lands or swamp to develop them by modern methods; the rest moved into the towns, or went abroad.

The Eastern Region was by no means homogeneous. The Ibo constituted less than 70 per cent of a population approaching 13 million (see chapter 7, pp. 157–64). Traditionally a people of small units, the Ibo are subdivided into thirty sub-tribes, sixty-nine clans and five hundred village groups. However, Professor Dike, the Ibo historian, has pointed out that 'beneath the apparent fragmentation of authority lay deep fundamental unities, not only in the religious and cultural spheres, but also . . . in matters of politics and economics'.[8] As among the Yoruba, deities are held in common, and many clans have a more than local character. The Aro clan have a traditional pre-eminence and authority, based on their famous and lucrative oracle at Arochuku. Also prominent are the Nnewi and the Onitsha. These both have hereditary king-doms, but, for the most part, Ibo have no important hereditary chiefs. Prominent citizens 'take' titles late in life to add to their prestige; they pay money for the honour. The Ibo are perhaps Nigeria's most natural democrats.

* The Nigerian density figures have been calculated from the estimate of populations given in chapter 7 above, p. 163.

Clannishness is an important factor in Ibo politics. Azikiwe is from Onitsha; Okpara, to whom he handed over the premiership in 1957, is from Umuahia. The change of premier inevitably meant a massive transfer of patronage from Onitsha people to those of Bende division. The trend was reversed again after the 1966 coup when Colonel Ojukwu, from Nnewi, came to power.

MINORITY PROBLEMS

Minority problems have beset the East at least as much as the other Regions. More than 8 million Ibo (counting the refugees of 1966) are largely concentrated on a low plateau, bordered in the north by Nsukka, in the south by Aba, in the west by Onitsha and in the east by Abakaliki. The plateau has poorer soil and lower rainfall than the land around it. The minority areas, peopled mainly by Ibibio (1·2 million), Ijaw (0·7 million) and Efik (0·5 million) are to the east along the Cross river, to the south-east (including Calabar), and along the creeks, islands and swamps of the south. The southern swamp country belongs mainly to the Ijaw, of whom there are a further 100,000 across the Niger in the Mid-West. The Efik and Ibibio live further east, towards the mouth of the Cross river. Further to the north along the river, the Minorities Commission found 'many tribes, intermingling in a confused multitude which we shall not attempt to particularise'.[9] The Commission heard of languages spoken by no more than 50,000 people and found that there were in all '17 major languages and some 300 of lesser importance in the Region'.[10]

The 'Rivers people', as the Ijaw and Efik minorities are loosely called, have long played a part in Eastern politics. In the halcyon days before tribe became an issue, Professor Eyo Ita of Calabar, one of the outstanding nationalists of the first generation, was a close associate of Azikiwe. After the Eastern government crisis of 1953 he was expelled from the NCNC. A letter from the party, signed by the national secretary but attributed to Azikiwe,[11] contained an early hint of future discords: 'your behaviour on the question of your resignation is a shame to you and your race'. The leader of the first major party to oppose the NCNC was an Ibibio, Dr Udo Udoma. His United Independence Party (UNIP) continued to support the idea of a unitary government for Nigeria even when the NCNC had been converted to a federal system. This was characteristic of the minority attitude—fearful of domination by the predominant tribe, it placed its hopes in a strong central government in Lagos. When federalism gained the day, Udoma's UNIP merged with the new Calabar-Ogoja-Rivers State Movement (COR State Movement), agitating for a separate Region to be composed of the three provinces (except the predominantly Ibo enclaves at Abakaliki and Afikpo) of that name. The Ijaw to the south now formed their own Niger Delta Congress (NDC) advocating a state for themselves and for the Ijaw across the Niger in the Mid-West.

Minority politics in the East followed the national pattern: the national rivals of the party in power (the NCNC) lost no time in exploiting the opportunities among the regional opposition. The COR State Movement was duly supported by the Action Group, and consequently declined after the eclipse of the Action Group in 1962. The NDC developed links with the NPC as soon as that party's coalition with the NCNC broke up. Neither state movement made much headway at the polls. The minority areas themselves lacked cohesion and unity, especially among the inhospitable swamps where communication is impossible and where loyalties are strongly localised. The electoral geography also favoured the party in power. Forty-nine out of eighty-four regional seats were in the 'Ibo plateau' itself. Together with the Ibo enclaves at Ahoada and Port Harcourt the Ibo controlled fifty-four seats. Of the remaining thirty, twelve went to the NCNC in the 1957 regional election and eighteen to opposition candidates.

The Minorities Commission examined the case for separate states and found it wanting. In Ogoja province it found no dominant tribe except the Ibo themselves in their enclave within the province. In Calabar area, while the Ibibio were the most numerous, the Efik among them formed an aristocracy, having long held sway through a powerful secret society called the *Ekpe*. In the Rivers province the Commission calculated that at the time of the 1952–53 census there had been some 305,000 Ibo, 240,000 Ijaw and 156,000 Ogoni. 'To the East of the square block of the Ibo plateau lie the two provinces of Calabar and Ogoja, linked by some common use of the Efik language, by the *Ekpe* society, and by a share, diminishing as one leaves the coast, of a derived culture, linked too by a resentment of Ibo leadership, and divided by tribal differences and in part by some suspicion of the Ibibios and Efiks.'[12]

The Commission advised against creating new states—as it had done in the case of the Tiv and the Mid-Westerners—holding that the new Nigerian nationalism would eventually weaken local tribal feelings. It recommended certain safeguards: buttressing the 'human rights' clauses of the federal constitution and a strong and truly national federal police force. Both these recommendations were carried out. In the case of the Rivers province, the Commission went further in recommending that it be considered a 'special area', to be cared for by a statutory commission of the Federal government. The Niger Delta Development Board was duly set up at independence, but it was destined to make little impact. It did not hold its first meeting until March the following year and two years after that it had not got beyond assembling five expatriate experts (an agricultural officer, a soil scientist, a forestry officer, a civil engineer and a fishery expert), seven launches and eight powered dinghies.[13] Its surveys and experiments showed that the creeks could support rice growing; but the experts could hardly ignore the fact that the Rivers area was unpromising for much in the way of 'development'. The economic hopes of the area now came to centre on oil, as it has about two-thirds of the Eastern Region's oil fields. It has become a major grievance of the minorities that they have benefited so little from the revenue. 'Rivers' politics now turns on this issue.

General Ironsi's regime opened with an Ejaw 'revolution' in

Yenagoa province. Followers of Isaac Boro, a former under-graduate of the University of Nigeria, Nsukka, seized a police post, sabotaged a local oil pipeline and, with a handful of sup-porters, proclaimed a new government. Whether there was method in this apparent madness has not been authoritatively established. One unconfirmed theory is that in the tense days before the January coup the NPC, whose political allies against the NCNC were the Niger Delta Congress, had planned to foment trouble. The idea was to try to 'balance' the current disorders in the West in order to give the federal government an excuse for declaring a state of emergency in both Regions at once. But, according to this theory, the coup supervened and for some reason Boro went ahead regardless. He was sentenced to death but later reprieved under the Gowon regime. In September 1967 he was sent back to Yenagoa province, now in the Rivers State, to agitate against the Ojukwu regime on behalf of the Federal government.

After the second coup of July 1966 returned federal power to Northern hands, the 'Rivers' problem in the East moved right to the centre of the political stage. After the massacres of Easterners in the North, the East made preparations to secede from the Federation. The opponents of this plan, especially the Federal government, were quick to encourage latent separatist tendencies among the non-Ibo minorities. They relied on the fact that the minorities had been reluctant enough citizens of an Ibo-dominated Region within the Federation and would be even more reluctant to form part of an independent Ibo state. However, the success of this plan was hampered by the fact that non-Ibo Easterners had also been among the victims of the massacres. This enhanced regional solidarity. To strengthen it further, the East's military government declared its willingness to re-open the question of self-determination of minorities after the emergency was over. It also reformed the Region's provincial system, giving more autonomy to the non-Ibo groups. The stated aim of the reform was 'to eliminate the fear of domination . . . and to promote even development' throughout the Region.[14] Each of twenty new provinces was to be given legislative as well as executive powers—with jurisdiction over primary and secondary education, local government and agriculture. Each province was to have a provincial council, a provincial executive and a provincial administrator and was to draw revenue from its own resources as well as from regional funds. It was intended that, after the military regime ended, these authorities would be elected.

In the meantime, the old-established political leaders of the minority groups were in Lagos, protected and encouraged by the Federal government. They stated that, if the East were to become an independent state, they wanted no part of it; if, on the other hand, Nigeria were to remain as a federal unit, they would demand their own Region or Regions within it. The Ijaw leader was Prince Harold Dappa Byrie, leader of the NDC. He had represented Rivers interests at the pre-independence constitutional conference of 1957 and had planned to do so again at the constitutional review planned by the Balewa government for 1965. Spokesman for the Ibibio was Effiong Eyo, a veteran politician from Calabar. He had been a leader of the NCNC and had been chief whip, Deputy Speaker and chairman of the Region's Development Board. But, like Professor Eyo Ita and other non-Ibo politicians in the NCNC, he had quarrelled with Azikiwe when he was Premier of the East. He had crossed to the Action Group, which supported the COR State Movement. It was debatable how representative of Rivers interests these politicians now were. Apart from disunity between the various minorities, there were cleavages within each of them. The Ogoja, in particular, had long been divided. It seemed clear that a single Rivers State would be very difficult to create: there would have to be at least an Ibibio state and an Ijaw state. Oil revenues might have made both potentially viable, but in the short run it was difficult to see how they could exist other than as heavily subsidised members of a strong federation.

THE DYNAMIC PARTY

The minority areas were not the only source of opposition during the NCNC regime in the East. Another challenge came from the Dynamic Party of Dr Chike Obi, a brilliant, eccentric mathematician from Onitsha. Like NEPU in the North, the Dynamic Party did not challenge the government on ideological grounds. Its main offering was the personality of its leader—and the promise, not so much of different policies, as of the same policies translated into effective and honest action. 'When we come to power we shall proceed to carry out the complete liberation of Africans in the following manner', the Dynamic Party's "23 Protocols"[15] promised. 'We shall go to the people in the cities, towns, villages and the farms; in their houses and huts and canoes. We shall go to them and teach them how to read and write and win them to the point of view that the interests of each of them can only best be guaranteed by the interests of the individuals of the State taken collectively.' The other twenty-two 'protocols' continue in the same vein. The 'programme' appears to plead its cause in a vacuum; it has no reference to the policies, achievements or failures of the government of the day.

Obi has argued the need for a 'regimental' state for Nigeria.[16] The essence of his doctrine, however, appears to be the need to get Dr Obi into power, 'after which I will be able to take the right decisions'.[17] His party won five seats in the 1961 regional elections, relying partly on local Onitsha feeling against the Okpara regime. In the federal election of 1965 it failed to win a single seat, having lost much of its popularity by allying itself with the Northern-based Alliance.

CATHOLICS AND PROTESTANTS

Something over half the Eastern Region is Christian and the rest is pagan. The Roman Catholics are relatively much stronger here than they are in the West, controlling 42 per cent of the Region's primary schools, while Protestant missions have 38 per cent and the government and local authorities 20 per cent. There has been some tension between the Protestants and the Roman Catholics over education—although it has not always been easily distinguishable from the universal argument between advocates of secular and religious education. In 1965, the regional Minister of Education, a Protestant, with the apparent support of the Governor of the Region, also a Protestant, announced that the government intended to set up local education authorities that would take over all mission schools. A public controversy ensued in which most of the things were said that Roman Catholics and Protestants—and secularists and non-secularists in education—say about each other anywhere in the world. 'What they (the Roman Catholics) are really after is more girls' schools. Of course, every Catholic girl means a future Catholic family', said a senior spokesman of the government side.[18] The Roman Catholic authorities in turn complained of discrimination by the government in withdrawing recognition from schools unfairly classed as 'unviable'. When the Roman Catholics were accused of lateness in paying their teachers, they retorted that it was the government grants that were late and that they had to pay their teachers out of bank overdrafts as a result. In the end the government recognised that there was little it could do to challenge the Roman Catholics. Apart from their strength in the cabinet and Parliament and in the electorate, they controlled and paid for too high a proportion of education—the most precious commodity in the land. In the long run, as government resources grow, education will inevitably become secularised.

The Okpara Regime

Okpara's regime in the East (1959–66) had the reputation in Nigeria and abroad of being the most efficient and energetic, if also perhaps the most corrupt, of the regional governments. The point is disputable. Certainly, the regime had had an enterprising look. Okpara, the son of a labourer, had won a scholarship to a

Lagos College and qualified as a doctor at the Nigerian School of Medicine. He was in medical practice in his native Umuahia region when the 1949 colliery shootings (see chapter 4, p. 83) drew him into politics. He remained faithful to Azikiwe, the NCNC leader, when others rebelled and, when Azikiwe decided to concentrate on the federal end of politics in 1959, Okpara became his successor as regional leader and Premier. An immensely energetic and volatile politician, Okpara devoted much thought to the economic problems of his Region. He was very much less successful as a politician on the national level. He shared with Awolowo a basic inability to understand the North and his tactless electioneering there, as well as his provocative stance during a series of crises, contributed to the breakdown of the federal system during the Balewa regime. His major political error appears to have been the decision to boycott the 1964 federal election (see chapter 7, pp. 164–78).

Okpara seemed to learn the lesson earlier than most of his contemporaries in politics that while industrialisation could provide prestige in the short term and economic growth in the long term, what really yielded results was agriculture. This calculation had a sound political basis. As Premier of the East, Okpara faced more urgently than any of the other premiers the insidious drift of young men from the villages to the towns—a process which had ominous political overtones. His early thinking on agriculture owed much to the example of Israel. After visiting Israel and Malaya at the head of an economic mission in 1961, he concluded that his Region had 'a growing population of primary school leavers, unskilled in trade but yet unwilling to embrace agriculture as a life-long occupation. These young men do not live in villages and are sources of irritation in the townships. Because agriculture is still primitive in the villages, they cannot easily be persuaded to return to the villages to work in the farms. They, like the Israeli refugee, require some sort of resettlement as the only effective means of attracting them and keeping them out on the land.'[19] This was the theory behind the Farm Settlement scheme, aimed at training farmers in modern methods, increasing productivity and bringing uncultivated land into use. Six settlements were established within three years. However, the results were disappointing. The cost, which was brought down to £1,500 per settler after drastic economies, proved prohibitive; land acquisition was time-wasting and expensive, and the new villagers often became disheartened while waiting for their first crops to mature. Of a target of 50,000 acres of oil-palm, citrus, rice and food crops for the period of the 1962–63 Development Plan, less than a tenth had been planted by the end of 1965.

Administrative inexperience was often the chief obstacle. At Igbariam settlement* near Onitsha, most of the 1963 oil-palm plantings were eaten by rats. The following year only citrus was planted and oil-palm plantings, presumably rat-proof, were resumed in 1965. The 400 settlers would therefore not get anything from their oil-palms before 1969, while their citrus would hardly yield before 1968. Meanwhile each settler was given fifty pullets to give him table eggs and a small income from the sale of the surplus eggs. Some of the settlers complained that their chickens had died and that it was difficult for them and their families to manage on the three shillings a day subsistence allowance. The government was unwilling to increase this allowance as this would only increase the settlers' indebtedness still further. The plan is for settlers to repay their debts over twenty-five to thirty years.

A bigger impact on production was to have been made by government-sponsored plantation projects in oil palm, rubber, cocoa and cashew nuts. However, because of 'lack of skilled staff at all levels, lack of planting materials and lack of suitable soils for cocoa',[20] little over half the planned targets had been achieved by the end of 1965. High hopes were also placed on plantations owned by foreign firms, especially Dunlop's 20,000 acres of rubber at Calabar and the United Africa Company's oil-palm plantations. The targets of both government-sponsored and privately-owned plantations had to be reduced during the Plan period because of lack of funds.

*Visited by the author August 1965.

In its later years Okpara's government took a fresh look at some of the underlying problems of development. There was a new understanding that the welter of local differences, vested interests, complexities of land-holding and sheer inertia made 'development planning' on the old lines an anachronism. A new approach, emerging in 1965, was to reverse the direction of planning and make it come from village level to the top instead of the other way round. The new thinking owed much to the British economist Arthur Gaitskell, architect of the Gezira cotton scheme in the Sudan, who visited the Region in 1962. A Ford Foundation unit, aided by United States Peace Corps volunteers, began work in twenty 'operational areas', seeking to establish the right agricultural unit and the right rotational pattern for each community. The idea was to assess the individual potential of each community without being prejudiced by overall plans. 'We have told our DOS that from now on they are Development Officers and their chances of promotion depend on success in this capacity', explained Chief Udoji, the Premier's secretary.[21]

One approach, tried in an experiment at Abia, was for a group of farmers to demarcate and clear an acre each of uncultivated land and plant it with seedlings from a common nursery. Another approach was the formation of a limited liability company, with share capital raised not only by village subscription but also by 'sons abroad'. This approach seems especially suited to the Ibo.

In industry, the Easterners have shown remarkable energy in creating new establishments though the economic results were often disappointing. In the space of three weeks in 1965 Okpara officially opened a ceramics factory, a cement works, a shoe factory, a textile mill, an enamelware factory, a new Rest House and a luxury hotel. Other new industries included a tyre factory, an aluminium products factory, a glass factory, an asbestos products factory and a brewery. In 1966 a gigantic textile mill opened at Onitsha. Most of the government-owned factories had disappointing results (see chapter 12, pp. 290–2). The greatest success story was that of Nigercem, the cement works near Enugu in which the

Federal and Eastern Regional governments together owned a majority of the shares. Its original capacity of 100,000 tons was raised in three years to almost 500,000. A bonus share issue and dividends, which in 1965 were 12½ per cent, were paid out to the shareholders, who included private Nigerian companies as well as individuals. It owed its success to the fact that the government made no attempt to run the industry: it was managed under contract by Tunnel Portland Cement. Also, virtually all raw materials were available locally (in contrast to the experience of most other industries in the Region) and the cement was heavily protected by tariffs.

An Eastern success story of a different kind was that of the small industries. A report made in 1963[22] found that firms employing less than ten persons provided employment for 36,000, three times the number of workers in large industries. Investment in these small industries was £3 million or about £100 per worker, about thirty times less than investment in the large industries. The small entrepreneurs have received loans through government and Commonwealth Development Corporation agencies. At the Industrial Development Centre at Owerri, shoemakers, carpenters, motor mechanics and metal workers are trained. They are entrepreneurs already established and successful in their field who need upgrading, not only in the technical field but in such things as marketing and book-keeping. One Onitsha shoemaker was making a hundred pairs of shoes a month when he started his course. At the end he was producing 6,000 pairs a month and putting up new buildings which would enable him to produce 500,000 a month. Small industries are an especially attractive proposition for this overcrowded and job-hungry Region—the more so since the influx of refugees in 1966–67 turned many of the villages into small towns.

How viable is the East on its own? Its secession from Nigeria in 1967, as the self-proclaimed Republic of Biafra, raised political problems so dramatic that the economic prospects were obscured. Politics apart, and in spite of all its refugees, Biafra is potentially viable. The East was a net earner of revenue before secession, in that income from its ports and mines exceeded the £22·5 million it received from federal sources. Oil rents and royalties—£13 million in 1966 for the whole of Nigeria—will increase sharply, and oil profits tax will also accumulate. In Port Harcourt the East had Nigeria's second port. Natural gas in large quantities solved the problem of power. The biggest economic question mark for an independent or autonomous Biafra is essentially a political one: can the Ibo again venture forth as traders into neighbouring territories? Oil wealth is not likely to alter the fact that the Ibo themselves are their main economic asset.

11. Yoruba and Mid-Westerners

I found the Yorubas much the most difficult to understand among the people of Nigeria. The Northerners have the predominant characteristics of Moslem dignity, courtesy and courage. The Ibos in the East are quick to learn, volatile, uninhibited, gay. The Yorubas are much more complex. They have a long-established system of administration, a complicated set of rules governing the conduct of their governments and their lives—a strange combination of what seem to us barbaric customs and personal dignity and political finesse.
—Sir Hugh Foot, Chief Secretary, Nigeria, 1947–51.[1]

There are tensions within the Mid-West as well as between the Mid-Westerners and the Yorubas.—Sir Henry Willink, 1958.[2]

THE WEST, the land of the Yoruba, is the centre of Nigeria. Lagos, the Federal capital, is a Yoruba town and its Yoruba hinterland experienced the earliest colonisation in Nigeria—the first churches, schools and factories. This early lead in prosperity and sophistication was further enhanced when cocoa became Nigeria's most lucrative crop, making the Yoruba an elite among farmers. In 1955 the Western Region government was the first in Africa to introduce universal free primary education.

However, none of these advantages has brought the Yoruba much happiness. Their central position has helped to make them the cockpit of Nigerian politics, where Northerners and Easterners have fought for control of the Federation. Their plight was aggravated by the perennial internal dissensions of the Yoruba themselves. These divisions, exacerbated from outside, finally brought down the Balewa regime in 1966. But the West's role continued unchanged. Throughout 1966 and beyond it was still the Yoruba, sitting shrewdly on the sidelines of the continuing struggle between the Hausa and the Ibo, who held the balance; and, as usual, they were divided among themselves.

On the face of it the Yoruba have little excuse for being internally divided. Each of the original three Regions had its serious minority problems, but the West alone had its minorities neatly excised when the Mid-West Region was carved out of it in 1963. Since then theirs has been by far the most homogeneous of the Regions, consisting almost exclusively of Yoruba; thereafter, dissensions were not between tribes but between clans, social classes, ideologies and personalities. Ceaseless in-fighting has largely robbed the Yoruba of their natural advantages. Before the British arrived on the scene, they had for centuries participated in the running of their own affairs, they already lived in large towns—and they were almost perpetually at war. When an Alafin of Oyo displeased his subjects they presented him with a gift of parrots' eggs, politely signifying that he was expected to commit suicide. He lost no time in doing so. On such subtle institutions the British attempted to graft modern local government. But the virulence of Yoruba politics was too much for this tender new plant. By the time the civilian regime came to an end in 1966, every one of the elected local councils had been dissolved by order of the government. It was the breakdown of effective government—even of law and order—in the West which precipitated the coup of January 1966. The troubles of the Yoruba and those of Nigeria had interacted, exacerbating each other until the breaking point had been reached.

A distinctive aspect of Yoruba life is the habit of living in towns. A decade ago more than half the Yoruba were already living in townships of more than five thousand people: the six major Yoruba towns had more than 100,000 and Ibadan, the regional capital, had nearly a million. Today Ibadan, the largest city in Black Africa, has an official population of 1·3 million.[3] The habit of living in towns has been historically attributed to the need to seek shelter during long periods of internecine warfare (see chapter 3, pp. 78–9). Today the Yoruba towns—Ibadan, Ife, Oshogbo, Abeokuta, Ilesha, Oyo and Ondo—are very much more than mere receptacles of refugees from the countryside. They do have their full quota of men out of work, but they are as 'traditional' as the villages around them. The Yoruba have a talent for remaining themselves, whether they live in a village or in a town: a suburb and a village are in fact often two halves of a single unit, with constant movement between the two. It has been observed of Abeokuta that it is in some respects 'a large-sized village, and it lacks some of the departures from tradition which we usually associate with urbanisation. Abeokuta is not secular, for example, but rather is the heart of religious activities of all kinds.'[4] Family 'compounds' in the town have the same name as corresponding units in the village; many people live alternately in the town and in 'the bush', while children whose parents are in the village often stay with their relatives in the town to be educated.

While the Ibo tend to predominate in the armed services, the civil service and in industry, the Yoruba excel in the professions and trade. Many of their leading politicians—Awolowo, Akintola, Benson, Fani-Kayede, Akinjide, Rosiji—are lawyers. Most Nigerian doctors, musicians and academicians are Yoruba.

In appearance as well as in its people, the West was the most homogeneous Region. Most of its 30,000 square miles is dense tropical rain-forest. The villages are usually well hidden in forest that is attractively unspoiled except for the aluminium roofs on the mud-walled huts. A Yoruba village is remarkable for its liveliness. The niceties of social intercourse—elaborate greetings, endless gossip, dancing, drumming and formalities—take up much of the day. The women, splendid in their indigo-dyed home-woven robes and superb headgear, do most of the trading and some of the work in the fields. For the men, hard work is generally limited to the rainy season but the Yoruba are not renowned for hard work in any season. The very richness of their social life makes it relatively inaccessible to foreigners: for them the *oyinbo* (white man) is an object of mild curiosity, sometimes amusement, rarely respect. There is enormous respect, on the other hand, for age, rank and power.

PERENNIAL QUARRELS

Yorubaland has always been troubled. Towards the end of the eighteenth century it consisted of four states: Oyo, Egba, Ketu and Jebu. After the Fulani had conquered and unified the North and pushed southwards as far as Ilorin, four new states appeared—the warlike city-states of Ibadan, Ilesha and Ife, and the state of Ekiti Parapo. The nineteenth century Alafin of Oyo had a bigger kingdom than any Northern emir except those of Kano and Sokoto. But even this degree of unity was short-lived. When the British arrived on the scene they found Yorubaland in flux, torn by feuds and wars—and they themselves contributed further to its unrest. Today the Yoruba are divided into seven sub-tribes—the Egba (with their headquarters at Abeokuta), the Oyo, the Ife-Ilesha, the Ibadan, the Ijebu, the Ekiti and the Ondo. However, cultural and spiritual loyalties transcend the sub-tribes. All Yoruba ascribe their ancestry to Oduduwa. Ile-Ife, the cradle of the Yoruba, was supposed to be the birthplace of humanity—the equivalent of the Garden of Eden. There is free intermarriage between the sub-tribes and traditional deities are held in common. The Oni of Ife still holds a position of spiritual preeminence among all Yoruba chiefs, as the Sultan of Sokoto does among the Moslem Hausa/Fulani.

The perennial quarrels of the West go deep; they form an intricate pattern. One strand is the rivalry of clans of sub-tribes; another is the clash of personalities, notably between Chief Awolowo and Chief Akintola, his Action Group lieutenant until 1962. There is also a clash of ideology between radicals and conservatives. The whole is perpetually exacerbated by the local effects of the struggle for federal power in Lagos.

Awolowo belongs to the Ijebu, a clan traditionally noted for its enterprise and ubiquity. Like the Ibo, some of whose characteristics they share, the Ijebu's clannish enterprise and sense of superiority have marked them off from other Yoruba clans among whom they settled and whom they came to dominate. This situation was most marked in Ibadan, where the Ijebu had settled in large numbers as

272

petty traders and artisans. The natural opponents of the Ijebu, the Ibadan indigenes, were supported by a conservative section of the obas and by some of the businessmen.

The intrusion of federal politics was also most marked in Ibadan itself. The NCNC had long been out to control the West as part of its strategy to capture the whole South as a counterbalance to the North. From the earliest days of self-government in 1956, the battle raged most fiercely in Ibadan where, as we have seen, there was natural opposition to Awolowo. In the 1950s this opposition came to be led by Chief Adelabu, a brilliant Ibadan politician who became first national vice-president of the NCNC. Under Adelabu, the NCNC almost captured the West from the Action Group in the 1956 regional election. Two years later Adelabu was killed in a motor accident—a major setback to his party's hopes in the West.

An even more potent source of opposition was in the non-Yoruba areas that, until the creation of the Mid-West Region in 1963, were part of the West. Here too, the NCNC provided a natural champion for the Edo, the Efik, the Ijaw, the Bini, the Itsekiri and the Western Ibo against the Yoruba who ruled through the Action Group. The feud between government and opposition was violent. The Action Group made full use—indeed, in some respects pioneered—the weapons of intimidation, jobbery and electoral malpractice which later, when in opposition themselves, they were loud in condemning. However, after the creation of the Mid-West had left the West a purely Yoruba Region, the divisions continued.

Apart from Ibadan, another natural focus of clannish opposition within Yorubaland was in the north of the Region, the Oshun division, home of Chief Akintola. The dramatic Akintola-Awolowo split of 1962 has still not been healed today, though Akintola is no longer alive. The crisis of 1962 has already been recounted, in chapter 6. Its causes were profound. When Awolowo had built the Action Group he set out to unify the Yoruba clans, to reconcile the traditional obas with the modernising 'elite' and to marry the radica and conservative wings of the Yoruba nationalist movement. Initially the party was united in its analysis. It saw the NCNC, the only effective opposition within the Region, as the main enemy. At the federal level the enemy was the NPC, the instrument of Northern domination. To become dominant at the centre the party had to engage the NPC on its home ground, and here the most promising fields were the non-Hausa minority areas of the Middle Belt and the Yoruba provinces of Ilorin and Kabba.

So long as Awolowo was Premier of the West he could assert his dominance over the regional government and over the party. But when he went to the Federal Parliament as leader of the opposition in 1959, Akintola, who became regional Premier, challenged his leadership. While at the centre, out of the mainstream of Yoruba politics, Awolowo became increasingly radical—and increasingly estranged from conservative elements espoused by Akintola. These rivalries changed the whole picture of federal politics. It gave the NPC its first chance to challenge the Action Group on its home ground—by allying itself to one faction of the party against the other. This design proved so successful that it brought about a dramatic reversal of alliances in 1964: the Action Group and the NCNC joined against the common enemy, the NPC.

This new situation brought to the surface long dormant arguments. The Action Group had begun its life as a protest against what it saw as the excessive Ibo domination of the nationalist movement under Azikiwe. It now found itself in alliance with the predominantly Ibo NCNC against the NPC. But there was another Yoruba view—a view which did not come into prominence until the Awolowo-Akintola split of 1962. The Akintola faction saw the Ibo as a more dangerous threat than the Northerners. According to this view, the backward North could not in any case effectively rule Nigeria without the alliance of one or other of the Southern nations and the obvious interest of the Yoruba was to be that ally. A threat from the North, moreover, was merely political, while that from the Ibo was economic and therefore more insidious. There was a hint of aristocratic, even reactionary, protest in the Akintola mentality: a protest of the 'true' Yoruba against the 'upstarts' —both Ibo and Ijebu.

These deep differences of attitude made the dissensions among the Yoruba much more intractable than those in other Regions. In the critical months of 1966, when civil war seemed possible, both North and East 'closed ranks' dramatically, former opponents appearing on the same platform; but the West remained divided along very much the old lines. Although Akintola was dead and the Action Group officially outlawed, the issues were the same. Awolowo was now out of prison and officially the chief spokesman of all the Yoruba, but behind the scenes all the bitterness of 1962, and of the 'rigged' election of 1965, still remained. General Ironsi's Military Governor in the West, Colonel Fajuyi, ran what was in effect an Action Group regime. The division of Nigeria into 12 new states in May 1967 left the old Western Region virtually intact: it lost only parts of Ikeja, near Lagos. But the old NNDP lobby survived—and quickly raised the standard of revolt against the prospect of a single Western State dominated by the Awolowo group. The ex-NNDP supporters demanded a separate state based on Ogbomosho, while another group agitated for a state based on Abeokuta. However, the Federal Military government, needing Chief Awolowo's support for prosecuting the war against Biafra, kept these separatist movements in check, playing one Yoruba group against the other.

The Action Group's Record

Political feuds largely robbed the West of the enjoyment of its natural economic and social advantages. Accumulated wealth from cocoa had brought the Region to a peak of prosperity in 1960. The Regional Marketing Board had accumulated some £18 million. Old Ibadan was provided with splendid parliament and municipal buildings, dignified approach roads, a prestige office block of twenty-seven storeys, a mammoth race track and stadium. The office block, known as 'Cocoa House' became a symbol of the West's crisis. When the 1962 crisis occurred it was still a shell. Building was stopped, and for two years the shell was a reminder, dominating the Ibadan skyline, of the frustration and disappointment of the Region's early hopes. In 1965 the Akintola government found the money to finish the job.

A fall in the world price of cocoa, which made its most drastic impact in the early 'sixties, combined with the crescendo of political strife to bring the West to the verge of ruin. Chief Akintola managed to hold out until after the crucial election of 1965 before lowering the producer price of cocoa from £120 to £65 a ton. By that time, the violent aftermath of the election was already crippling commerce, halting foreign investment and paralysing agriculture.

Awolowo's pre-independence administration was possibly the most enlightened and the most popular administration West Africa had ever seen. It was also extremely corrupt (see the Coker Commission findings, chapter 6, pp. 137–8). Its most celebrated achievement was the introduction of universal free primary education in 1955. Within five years the primary school population of the Region had risen from half a million to 1·1 million and the secondary school population from 7,000 to 25,000. But the experiment was not a success. Resources were over-strained in terms of money, materials and staff, and standards fell sharply. In this and other fields of government activity, widespread corruption vitiated government efforts.

The post-independence development plan of the West, like that of other Regions, concentrated on the expansion of natural resources in food production and on diversifying agriculture to make the economy less dependent on cocoa, which had become an unreliable source of revenue. The results were disappointing. Because of what was officially called 'shortage of materials, inadequate funds and equipment and administrative and technical problems',[5] almost all targets were grossly under-fulfilled in the years up to 1964. The breakdown of law and order in 1965 and the uncertainties of the military regime in 1966–67 looked like making subsequent results even worse. The Region's cocoa area, about a million acres in 1962 (including the Mid-West), was to have been increased by 122,000 acres in farm settlements and 6,500 acres in agricultural extension work by the end of 1964. In fact, only 7,000 acres were planted in the

276

settlements and none at all under the extension programme.[6] The farm settlement programme established only eight farms instead of the twenty envisaged in the plan. Similar shortfalls were reported in the planting of oil palm and citrus. In the same years there was no progress at all in the establishment of light or heavy industries. However, a cocoa-processing factory, making cocoa butter for export, was established in 1966, as was a rope and fibre factory. Under the headings of health, town and country planning and information, progress was recorded as 'nil' in the plan's first two years. However, two advanced teacher training colleges had been set up and the University of Ife was established on the same comprehensive and ambitious scale as the other regional universities.

THE MID-WEST

The Mid-West, Nigeria's smallest and newest Region, was created in 1963 in less than auspicious circumstances. All Nigeria's minority problems—the Tiv in the North, the Rivers people in the East and the non-Yoruba people in the West—had been thoroughly examined by the Minorities Commission which reported in 1958. The Commission recommended against creating a separate state in any of the Regions. It did, however, envisage their creation later, and provisions to this effect were incorporated in the constitution. What made the Mid-West win its case rather than the others was the political situation resulting from the decline of the Action Group in 1962. The Action Group had long advocated a Mid-West Region, but only as part of a general move creating more Regions in all the existing ones. Now the Action Group's opponents were able to take advantage of the party's weakened position to create the Mid-West alone.

The birth of the state was, however, the culmination of a long campaign. Its powerful spokesmen included the Federal Finance Minister, Chief Festus Okotie-Eboh, one of the most prominent Mid-Westerners. Another was the powerful Oba of Benin who emerged from his huge, mud-walled palace to campaign, just like a politician, for the Region. He complained in a speech of the 'political slavery of the Black man's rule, which has been imposed virtually on the Mid-West since the country became free from the white man's rule over two years ago'. The Mid-Westerners had, indeed, been victims of political neglect and, in some areas, of oppression. Their general feeling (sometimes exaggerated) was that the government in Ibadan favoured only the Yoruba parts of the Region, plus perhaps those that voted for the Action Group. Urging voters in the referendum to reject the black box (for the 'No' votes) the NCNC-oriented *West African Pilot* said: 'The black box should be discarded for it represents the carnage, the pillage, the plague of poverty and want, of ignorance and disease; it represents the evils of tyranny and oppression, suppression, psychological depression, under which Mid-Westerners have been groaning.'

The NCNC, which had long been paramount in the Mid-West, organised the referendum as if it were an election. They felt confident that they would control the new Region's government and thus become the first party in Nigeria to control two Regions. It turned out as predicted. The referendum was overwhelmingly in favour; it was held in a euphoric atmosphere of liberation. Sure enough, in the ensuing elections the NCNC won by a large margin. The whole apparatus of a new Region was now set up in Benin, the somewhat seedy city that had once been the centre of a mighty empire (see chapter 3, pp. 66–8). Two and a half million Mid-Westerners were now to have their own marketing board, development board, radio station (even a television station was planned), House of Assembly, House of Chiefs and High Court. The huge establishment of some sixty-four MPs, fifty-eight House of Chiefs members and forty-two ministers was based exactly on that of the larger and wealthier (and grossly over-staffed) Western Region.

Life for the Region began badly. The Western administration, as if in pique, promptly sent back to their Region of origin all the Mid-Western civil servants in its employ—from permanent secretaries of ministries down to their office messengers. These trooped back, hopeful of employment in a Region with an as yet non-existent administration. However, rapid progress was made, thanks largely to the energy and flair for leadership of Chief Dennis Osadebay, a former teacher from Asaba who was appointed Administrator and, later, Premier of the new Region.

The Minorities Commission had not had a very high opinion of the prospects for viability of the proposed state.

> In the estimates of the fiscal and economic position of such a state which we have seen we believe that the estimates of revenue are optimistic, because it has been assumed that the revenue of the present Western Region should be divided on a basis proportionate to the population, while not only the cocoa farmers but the big urban concentrations are in the Yoruba area. At the same time estimates of the cost of setting up a headquarters and a separate administration have, we think, been put too low.[7]

However, Chief Festus knew better. Although in its early years it depended on Federal government subsidies, the Region is in fact potentially wealthy. It has most of Nigeria's rubber and a large slice of its timber, oil palm and cocoa. It also has some 40 per cent of the oil reserves. Oil exports started in 1965 and exploration, both on-shore and off-shore, is still in progress.

Far more serious than the economic worries of the Mid-West have been its tribal dissensions. Having thrown off the yoke of the Yoruba, the Mid-Westerners found that they were themselves a mixed bag. The Commission had found that the Region enjoyed unity of language 'only in the central congeries of Edo-speaking peoples, who include the Benin Division, the Ishan Division, a group of tribes to the North of Benin in Afenmai, and the Urhobos. The last are sometimes spoken of as a separate tribe and their form of Edo is said to be unintelligible in Ishan, but they are closely linked in sentiment with Benin.'[8] Outside this area, there are the 400,000 Western Ibo in the Asaba and Aboh divisions, and the 70,000 Ijaws, most of whom live along the coastal creeks. 'In general', the Commission concluded, 'the further he is from Benin

City, the more likely is an enquirer to find that it was with appre-
hension of raids rather than in the hope of support or defence that
the centre of the Kingdom was regarded.'[9] The Ijaw of the Niger
Delta are sometimes held to be the original inhabitants of Nigeria,
pushed to the inhospitable coastal creeks and swamps by successive
invaders from the north. Further west are the Itsekiri, numbering
some 33,000, who speak a dialect similar to Yoruba but have
customs closer to those of Benin.

With such a salad of tribes, it was no wonder that trouble brewed.
In the days before the Region was carved out of the West, politics
was dominated by the Action Group—a largely Yoruba (and thus
alien) party. Opposition groups naturally gravitated to the NCNC and
this party duly won the elections after the creation of the Region in
1963. But the NCNC, the party in power in the Eastern Region, was
primarily an Ibo party. Chief Osadebay, the new Mid-West Premier,
was a Western Ibo: that is, an Ibo from the west bank of the Niger.
The non-Ibo groups, especially the Edo people of the Benin area,
now began to wonder whether they had not thrown off the yoke of
the Yoruba only to come under the domination of the Ibo. In fact
the Edo, being the original inhabitants of Benin, the natural centre
of the Region, might have expected to become the dominant group.
Unfortunately their numbers were too small for this.

In the pre-state days, the NCNC had harboured both sections of
protest against Action Group rule. The Edo faction was known as
Otu Edo, the Edo 'lodge', while the Osadebay faction, depending
directly on Enugu, became known as 'NCNC pure'. Trouble began
early in 1965, when Osadebay announced that he had learned of a
plot by the *Owegbe* secret cult to kill him, adding that he could not
rely on the local police to protect him as most of them were members
of the cult. Chief Festus had to issue an official denial, saying that he
was not 'a party to any plan to assassinate anyone'. The Federal
government then appointed Mr Justice Alexander, a Lagos judge of
West Indian origin, to conduct a Commission of Inquiry into the
cult. The central figure in the inquiry was Chief Omo-Osagie, the
Region's seventy-year-old Minister of Local Government, who was

described by the Commission's counsel as 'the commander-in-chief of the *Owegbe*'.[10] Various witnesses named as many as eight regional ministers as members and in the regional Parliament the Minister Without Portfolio, the Onogie of Ewohimi, claimed that 50 per cent of Mid-Westerners were members, adding that there was 'an *Owegbe* shrine in every village'.[11]

Chief Omo-Osagie, who sat impassively through the hearings, in rich chiefly attire and with a ministerial despatch case at his side, had hired one of Nigeria's foremost lawyers, Chief Rotimi Williams, to represent him. This formidable advocate cross-examined the Minister's accusers and suggested to most of them that they had been bribed by his client's political enemies to come and tell a pack of lies. Chief Omo-Osagie admitted that there was an *Owegbe* society, but claimed it was a militant youth wing of the party of which he was the regional head. He denied it had anything to do with any secret cult. However, there obviously was a cult. 'I swear by the God of Iron that the evidence I shall give shall be the truth, the whole truth and nothing but the truth', said an old woman in a red dress ornately covered with gold patterns, putting an iron effigy back on the table beside the Bible and the Koran. She claimed she had been forcibly intiated into the *Owegbe* cult, sang its songs for the judge and described some of its mildly macabre initiation ceremonies. It emerged that *Owegbe* (the word means 'strength') had begun in the 1950s as a protest against the Action Group regime. The Action Group had itself used a quasi-masonic group known as the Reformed Ogboni Fraternity to instill loyalty among its senior supporters and fear among its opponents. Now, under the new regime, it seemed that *Owegbe* had merely switched its targets. After the inquiry little more was heard of it. But the Benin people and their allies clearly had a powerful weapon in reserve, to be summoned against domination, real or supposed, from whatever quarter.

THE WEST'S RESOURCES

If the Federation were to break up, the West would probably claim Lagos as its own. In that event, the area would probably face fewer problems than the other former Regions, while the Mid-West would have a much more uncertain future. Even without Lagos, the West has the bulk of Nigeria's industries and it is the focus of the Federation's transport system. Moreover, it seems as if the downward trend of cocoa prices in the early 1960s has been reversed and a new cocoa boom would renew prosperity in the villages. However, the deep political feud would no doubt continue to plague the Yoruba.

The Mid-West, on the other hand, is the only former Region without a dominant tribe. This would make it difficult to emerge into independent statehood. Particularly difficult would be the position of the Western Ibo—separated by the Niger from the main body of Ibo in the East. The rest of the Mid-Westerners would be unlikely to continue to accept their leadership in conditions of independence. The plight of the Ijaw and the Efik would be similar. The economic worries would be for the short term only. At present, the Region derives more than 80 per cent of its revenue from federal sources, but in the long run, as we have seen, its oil, rubber and timber could make it rich.

12. Economics versus Politics

No solution to the current political and constitutional crisis can be satisfactory to future generations of Nigerians if the oneness of the Nigerian economy is not preserved. . . . Nigeria is on the threshold of an industrial revolution, if only we could get the political and administrative leadership we deserve.
—A. Ayida, Permanent Secretary, Ministry of Economic Development, 1966[1]

The main objectives of the next Plan will be a high overall rate of economic growth with a view to achieving 'self-sustained growth' before the end of the twenty-year Perspective Plan; the rapid industrialisation of the economy; increased production of food for domestic consumption without relaxing efforts in the export sector; and a drastic reduction in the magnitude of the present unemployment problem. . . . It is, of course, fully realised that all these objectives may not be entirely consistent.
—*Guideposts for the Second National Development Plan*, 1966

If it can remain a single entity, Nigeria's economy has an impressive potential. Even at the conservatively realistic figure of 48·6 million estimated in chapter 7, the population of the area provides a powerful magnet for investment and aid. True, only a small proportion of Nigerians as yet buy very much in the way of manufactures other than cloth, but their needs and their buying power are growing at a reasonable rate. Even if the Federation split into two or more parts, it would remain to a large degree an economic unit. In any case, each of the Regions had a respectable population by the standards of modern independent states: the North had some 25·4 million, the East 12·6, the West 7·5, the Mid-West 2·5 and Lagos 0·6. At the same time, while it is bigger and richer in resources

283

than almost all other African countries, Nigeria is also free from the alarming population explosion of the Egyptian or Indian pattern. Furthermore, the deeply ingrained liberalism in Nigeria's economic attitudes has provided the maximum encouragement for foreign investment.

In the wealth and variety of its resources, Nigeria is second only to the Congo in Africa. Crude oil exports, which only began in 1958, had reached 19 million tons in 1966 and promise to reach 50 million tons by 1970. Although still far behind such producers as Kuwait (114 million tons) or Iran (105 million) and unable to produce a significant proportion of the world's output of 1,500 million tons, Nigeria is already the second producer in the Commonwealth after Canada, whose oil lies less accessibly inland. The refinery in Port Harcourt, built and operated by BP and Shell, already meets Nigeria's petrol needs. Natural gas, of which reserves are enormous, already operates several power stations and a handful of factories in the Eastern Region. This natural gas, together with coal, iron ore, cotton, rubber and unlimited hydro-electric power, give Nigeria the natural basic raw materials for industrialisation.

Nigeria is the world's biggest producer of groundnuts (averaging 700,000 tons a year), the second producer of cocoa (200,000 tons) after Ghana, the fourth producer of tin (13,000 tons), the biggest producer of columbite. Oil palms, growing wild as well as, increasingly, in plantations in the Eastern and Western Regions, account for half the world's exports of palm kernels (400,000 tons) and 70 per cent of the world's exports of palm oil (150,000). Nigerian forests cover some 120,000 square miles and produce about 40 million cubic feet of timber a year, in twenty-four species, for export as logs, sawn timber or plywood sheets. Rubber, grown by peasant farmers in the Mid-West Region and, increasingly, in plantations in the Eastern Region, is partially processed in local factories. The Northern Region's ancient livestock industry still supplies the whole country. About a million cattle are slaughtered annually; the trade is now being modernised, with increasing use of refrigerated transport, and it has a considerable industrial potential in canned meat. Another by-product of the Northern livestock industry is an old and valuable trade in hides and skins, of which the best-known species is inaccurately known as 'morocco leather'.

Nigeria's human resources are another powerful economic asset —though shortage of skilled manpower is a long-term problem shared with all developing countries. An important asset is the high degree of competence and discipline in the civil service—which is effectively 'Nigerianised' in the federal and all the regional services (except the North, where the process is not yet complete). Nigerians of all tribes were well versed in commerce long before the arrival of the British. The Hausa traders, in particular, were known throughout Africa. Unlike the French, the British did not export a class of small shopkeepers and entrepreneurs to their West African colonies and, as a result, the liveliness and sophistication of African economic life in Nigeria contrasts markedly with that in the ex-French countries. Lagos is an international money centre, with a stock exchange in which Nigerians buy and sell shares in their own industries, a variety of commercial banks (both foreign and indigenous), hire-purchase companies and insurance firms (again both foreign and local). Commercial bank loans approached £100 millions in 1965. Credit is available from sources ranging from the big British and American banks and the Nigerian Industrial Development Bank to the United Bank for Africa's mobile bank units for market women.

ECONOMIC LIBERALISM

Nigerian firms are prominent in contracting, transport and other services as well as manufacturing. A 1963 survey found 30,000 workers employed in small indigenous industries in Eastern Nigeria alone.[2] A deeply liberal attitude to business and the absence of a strongly entrenched left-wing element in politics have also been a help to the authorities in attracting foreign investments. The Federal Finance Minister, the late Chief Festus Okotie-Eboh, said categorically in his 1965 Budget speech: 'Nigeria's need today is not for doctrinaire theorists importing foreign dogmas that have little relevance for Nigeria, but for men of initiative, men with new ideals, planners and thinkers, the kind of men whose pioneering vision, allied to faith and plain hard work, built the United States, the Great Britain and the Canada that we know today.'[3] He was challenged in Parliament for making this statement. He was, after all, a member of the NCNC which was Socialist in name if not in practice. In reply to his critics Chief Festus explained blandly, and amid general satisfaction, that he had rejected only the 'foreign imported brand', and not the 'African indigenous brand' which, he stressed, was 'evolutionary and not revolutionary'.[4]

This official liberalism has been expressed in practical terms in the shape of generous incentives for foreign investors; these include liberal income tax and import duty relief, accelerated depreciation allowances and the imposition of protective duties and import quotas. The basic machinery for exchange control is on the statute books as a precaution but is not applied; neither in the remission of profits nor in the repatriation of private salaries are there irksome restrictions.* Naturally, the large expatriate trading firms are encouraged to reinvest their profits in the country and this they have been willing to do. The companies which dominated foreign trade at the moment of independence have all withdrawn from the retail and produce-buying sides of their business, and reinvested the capital in new industry. The giant United Africa Company, a subsidiary of Unilever, is now associated with a dozen industrial ventures, including brewing, plywood, vehicle assembly and textiles.

Nigeria's basic resources have been subject to some four decades of somewhat fitful development. The economic infrastructure, moderately good at independence, has made satisfactory progress since then though it still has far to go. Out of 50,000 miles of motor roads, some 10,000 are tarred and there are over 2,000 miles of railway track.[5] All major world airlines serve the two international

* Controls were, however, imposed after the outbreak of civil war in 1967.

airports at Lagos and Kano, while six regional airports are effectively linked by Nigeria Airways. There are half a dozen minor ports along the creeks in addition to the main ports at Lagos/Apapa and Port Harcourt.

All these assets combined to enable Nigeria to begin life in 1960 with a degree of real economic independence rare in new countries. This was further enhanced by the liberal (some would say ingenuous) policy of the British. Unlike the French, who carefully tied the economies of their ex-colonies to their own in an exclusive, high-priced and highly subsidised relationship, the British did little to enhance or perpetuate their natural advantages as the colonial power. While Nigerian goods enjoyed Commonwealth preference in the United Kingdom (admittedly marginal in the case of primary produce), Nigeria was not required in return to give preference to British or Commonwealth goods. The effects of this freedom to buy in all markets were obvious to the most casual visitor even before independence. Especially striking was the ubiquity of French and German cars, Japanese textiles and radios and Dutch beer. The trend away from British imports continued after independence. In 1960 Britain bought 48 per cent of Nigeria's produce and accounted for 42 per cent of imports. Five years later Britain bought only 38 per cent of produce and accounted for 40 per cent of imports. The biggest corresponding advance in the volume of trade was made by Western Europe. The Common Market countries, which in 1960 accounted for 31 per cent of Nigeria's exports and 19 per cent of its imports, had reached 37 per cent of exports and 26 per cent of imports by 1965. These were natural trends and owed little to deliberate Nigerian policy. The major post-independence change in exporting arrangements was the closing down of the London and New York offices of the Nigerian Produce Marketing Company, thus compelling firms to establish offices in Lagos. This was intended to diversify trade but in practice made little difference. The real factors were the growth of the European economies and the relatively lackadaisical salesmanship of the British, who suffered from over-confidence in what had been their market.

FOREIGN INVESTMENT

At the moment of independence, Nigeria's entire import trade and much of its export trade and retailing were in the hands of eight foreign companies. Of these only three were British: the United Africa Company, John Holt's and Patterson Zochonis. Of the rest, two were French: Société Commercial de l'Ouest Africain and Compagnie Française de l'Afrique Occidentale; one was Swiss: Union Trading Company; one was Indian: K. Chellaram; and one was Anglo-Cypriot: A. G. Leventis. After independence the British share, as we have seen, diminished further. The process seemed taken to its logical conclusion in 1966, when Nigeria signed a Convention of Association with the European Common Market which obliged Nigeria, in return for free entry into Europe for most of its produce, to give preference to imports from the Common Market, thus actually discriminating against the British. The object of the agreement had been to safeguard Nigeria's exports in face of the Common Market's progressive external tariff. Nigeria had declined an earlier offer of 'association' in common with eighteen ex-French and ex-Belgian colonies on the grounds that this relationship was too neo-colonialist. The special agreement obliged Nigeria to grant a marginal preference to the products of the six EEC members on twenty-six selected items. In practice the preference is minute; it amounts to only 2 per cent of the duty and was not expected to have a significant effect on the direction of trade.

The pattern of foreign investment is broadly the same as that of trade. Out of some £150 million of fixed foreign investment in Nigeria in 1962, perhaps £100 million—or roughly two-thirds— was British. Today, fixed investments are probably in excess of £300 million and the British proportion is unlikely to exceed 50 per cent.

The British investments are spread over the entire range of industry and services. The Shell-BP oil exploration company and the Port Harcourt refinery in which Shell and BP jointly hold half the shares, are prominent British investments; the British also dominate the tin mining industry which includes one of the world's biggest mines, Amalgamated Tin Mines of Nigeria. British industries include several textile plants, a Guinness brewery, a Dunlop tyre factory and a Portland cement works.

Among non-British sources of investment, the Dutch predominate. Fixed investments of the Netherlands rose sharply from £15 million in 1962 to £44 million, out of a total for Western Europe of £64 million, in 1964. Apart from their half-share in the Shell company and their participation in Unilever, the parent company of the United Africa Company, the Dutch have invested in three breweries (in which Heineken participate), Phillips electrical assembly plants and a variety of concerns including metal containers, wax-block printing, textile printing, leather manufacture, boatyards, timber and trading. A fast-growing share of foreign investment is that of the Americans, whose fixed investments of £15 million in 1962 had more than doubled (£33 million) by 1964.[6] Much of this investment, some £20 million, is in five American oil companies: American Overseas Petroleum, Nigerian Gulf, Mobil Exploration, Phillips Petroleum and Tennessee. Other American ventures are in textiles, plywood and flour and there are currently plans for a large-scale shrimp industry.

The volume and variety of aid, though it fell short of the Six Year Plan's requirements in its first two years, was nevertheless impressive and contributed to Nigeria's comparative freedom of economic manoeuvre. Indeed, if one includes in the total aid figures short-term suppliers' credits and contractor financing, the level of indebtedness is becoming alarming. It rose from £44 million in 1960 to £223 million in 1965, of which some £55 million was short-term contractor-finance. Firm offers of aid received in the Plan's first two years (1962 and 1963) actually totalled £217 million, as against £340 million envisaged as the Plan's foreign aid component. Loans included £57 million from the World Bank and its affiliates, £45 million from the United States, £25 million from the United Kingdom, £15 million from Poland and £8 million from West Germany. Outright grants included £35 million from the United

States and £5 million each from the United Kingdom and the United Nations Special Fund.

INDUSTRIAL GROWTH

The growth of industry has been remarkable in its speed and range and all Regions, as well as the Federal capital, shared in the growth. Added value of manufacturing output more than doubled between 1957 and 1962 (when it reached £45 million) and increased by a further 27 and 25 per cent respectively in 1963 and 1964. Mining, the fastest-growing sector, accounted for 40 per cent of investment in 1964, reaching £128 million. In all, the Six Year Development Plan envisaged a contribution from private investment of £390 million, or £65 million a year during the plan period, representing a third of total fixed investment. The whole non-agricultural sector of the economy, still only 35 per cent of the Gross Domestic Product in 1962–63, was growing at the rate of 8 per cent per annum after that, almost twice the growth rate of the agricultural sector. Employment in manufacturing (excluding small firms), shown at 53,000 in 1962,[7] is today something like three times that figure.

However, the political pressure for factories at all costs has produced many which are non-viable. Where these are managed as well as owned by governments, as were the Eastern Region's glass factory, bottling plant, brewery and ceramics factory, over-staffing and nepotism killed what chances of success there may have been. Many government ventures were 'turn-key projects', financed by suppliers' credits or 'contractor finance'. Under these arrangements the foreign 'investor' made his profit by selling the machinery, irrespective of the viability of the industry. If he has a stake in it at all, his holding is generally so small that any loss is far outweighed by the profit on the machine selling. German, British, Israeli, French and Swiss firms have excelled in this type of business, in Ghana as well as in Nigeria. Early in 1965 outstanding Nigerian debts under this heading totalled £55·3 million. A senior Nigerian civil servant with experience in this field has complained about:

guaranteed riskless investments which involve government guarantees in foreign exchange and in which the government has to undertake to meet all obligations falling due if the investment is not viable. In such projects the foreign investor generally contributes five per cent of the equity capital; the rest comes from the government. The foreign partner supplies the equipment under suppliers' credit terms. There are known cases where the foreign investor is the consultant who prepared the feasibility study for the project, the financial adviser and the banker who finalised the credit arrangements, the manufacturer who supplied the equipment, the technical partner and management agent who runs the factory under a management agency agreement, with fees and commissions. The economic 'Mikado' then gets a government guarantee that if the project fails, the government would from its budgetary resources service the loan for the equipment.[8]

Some purely economic factors militate against the profitability of industry in West Africa. Among these are the need for relatively small production units, the need to import most raw materials as well as many building materials and spare parts for machinery, the expense of installation, the lack of skilled labour, the high cost of services such as electricity and of building materials such as cement, and the unpredictability of labour relations. The Michelin tyre factory at Port Harcourt, for example, is only a fiftieth of the size of that company's main plant in France. Less than half the content of the tyres is Nigerian rubber; the rest—synthetic rubber and the various chemicals—are imported. The glass bottle factory in Port Harcourt imports its limestone, soda ash and dolomite—in fact, everything except the sand. The Turners asbestos plant at Enugu imports its asbestos fibre.

Added to the economic obstacles, most factory managers complain of human ones. Customs officials give rise to much frustration. Materials officially exempt from duty because they are raw materials are charged on entry and there is often a delay of years before the drawback is paid. The Michelin factory was compelled to abandon the export of tyres because of two-year delays in getting the due drawback on imported materials. A senior regional official in Enugu complained to the writer that customs delays were so serious that, he felt, the Federal government must wish for political reasons to frustrate the East's development plans. Frustrations caused by officialdom were no less severe in the case of government-owned industries and these faced other difficulties as well. Political pressures sometimes caused them to be sited in the wrong place. Most were grossly overstaffed, though the oft-told story about the Umuahia ceramics factory—that it employed a storekeeper and an assistant storekeeper for every size of screw—is apocryphal.

REGIONALISM V. PLANNING

Nigeria's economic assets are offset by some serious liabilities, chiefly of a political nature. The federal structure itself has militated against rational, nationwide planning. While the constitution reserved to the Federal government the right to raise long-term loans abroad, short-term credits could be raised by the Regions. The Six-Year Plan was drawn up separately in each Region and then formally integrated. A National Economic Council officially presided over a unified economy, but in practice the Regions were economic rivals. Each government, and, indeed, each minister within it, faced constant pressure for industries to be sited in the home territory, a pressure which increased in proportion to the ever-rising rate of unemployment. Possibly the most flagrant example of this rivalry was the decision reached by the National Economic Council in May 1964 that the proposed iron and steel industry, for which the Plan had set aside £30 million, should be split into two, with half of it sited in the North at Idah and the other half in the East at Onitsha. Indeed it was only after intense negotiations that a claim by the Western Region to have a share as well was rejected—and then only because at the time the West was the weakest of the Regions in terms of federal politics. However, the iron and steel industry is still in the talking stage and the 1964 decision can be reversed.

Too much economic independence in the Regions has presented some new industries with the paradoxical threat of over-production. Among the first to feel it was the soft drinks and brewing industry. In 1949, when Heinekens and the United Africa Company joined in the first 'Star' beer and soft drinks venture, the import of soft drinks totalled around 2,000 gallons a year. In 1964 there were twelve full-scale plants in operation, with a capacity of 12 million gallons but actually producing only 4·5 million gallons. Instead of working two or three shifts, most were working three or four days a week and heavy losses were incurred.[9] Of another soft drinks venture by the Western Region government, the Coker Commission reported a loss of £200,000 on an outlay of £670,000 (see chapter 4, pp. 134–8). The same problem arose in textiles. By 1966, eight plants had been built since independence and present planned capacity was 165,000 spindles and 4,600 looms—more than five times the pre-independence figure. Production capability will be about 170 million square yards by 1968—about 60 million more than the combined import and local production figure in 1964. Production of cement, in five major plants, also threatens to exceed demand.

THE HUMAN FACTOR

The shortage of skilled manpower, contrasting markedly with the ever-growing surplus of unskilled labour, is a problem Nigeria shares with the rest of the developing world. What is lacking is not so much the quantity of education as orientation to provide enough of the required skills. A commission on post-primary education at the time of independence made what it described as 'massive, expensive and unconventional' proposals for expansion.[10] Far from being cut down, these proposals were actually expanded by the Federal government and the targets exceeded. Intake into secondary schools, which the commission recommended at 30,000 by 1970, was increased to 45,000, and the commission's target of 2,500 technicians qualifying annually was doubled. While the commission had recommended four universities by 1980, there are already five; the student population of 10,000 envisaged for the 1970s was already achieved in the 1960s.

However, the education system, built up largely by missionaries on classical lines, had produced a 'white collar' bias in lower echelons, and an 'arts' bias in the universities. While arts courses in universities were overcrowded, there were vacancies in engineering, agriculture and business schools. By 1963, four universities had opened a law school, although there were already over 1,200 practising lawyers, many of them underemployed. In that year, a combined total of some 6,000 students in trade centres, technical institutes and courses run by employers constituted less than one per cent of the 650,000 male persons employed in industry. The first comprehensive manpower survey, made in 1963,[11] lays particular stress on shortages in the intermediate category, that is, people with between one and two years' specialised training after the West African School Certificate or its equivalent. Technical institutes and colleges were turning out less than 700 in this category in 1963, compared with the estimated national requirements of 8,400 per annum.

Nigeria's economy has been as much the victim of politicians as of politics. The educational level and, in many cases, moral qualities of politicians contrasted poorly with that of the civil servants. Chief Festus Okotie-Eboh, who was Federal Finance Minister throughout the Balewa regime, was a shrewd and substantial businessman: he worked hard and his geniality of spirit made him an effective loan raiser for Nigeria. But this did not detract from the fact that he was a living legend of corruption on a grand scale—a reputation which steadily grew until, on the night of the January coup, he was singled out for killing among the Prime Minister's cabinet colleagues. Some ministers were obviously more corrupt than others, but it is generally felt that the honest ones were in the minority, while the traditional '10 per cent'—the ministerial rakeoff on contracts passing through a government department—came to be regarded as normal. Just as Sir Abubakar Tafawa Balewa had been too weak to control political factions, so he lacked decision and power to control corruption (see chapter 2, pp. 39–43).

Corruption has been defended as a 'lubricant' in a poor society. It undoubtedly had this effect in Nigeria, particularly in the employment it indirectly provided out of the proceeds, but on the other hand it clearly acted as a brake on foreign investment. Many a potential investor came away disappointed, if not actually because of the bribes he was expected to pay, then at any rate because of the inordinate delays involved in the corruption process. Nepotism also had its effect in that many of the officials the investor had to deal with were inefficient.

After the military takeover of January 1966 it looked as if a new order had begun. Corruption and nepotism were known to be one of the fundamental public grievances which had caused the coup and the soldiers who came to power seemed innocent of the grosser excesses of the politicians. For a time a new spirit seemed to reign. The absence of the politicians enabled permanent secretaries to make quick and rational decisions. A healthy fear was in the air. It was said that traffic policemen seen taking bribes were being lined up by the roadside and shot. Unfortunately the new spirit did not last long. Minor officials were soon at their old ways again, but what was much worse was that the political failures of the new regime all but wrecked the economy.

MILITARY RULE

Right from the start of the new regime, investors held back prudently from uncommitted expenditure in Nigeria. As the troubles of the new regime increased, culminating in the July counter-coup and its bloody aftermath of massacres, their caution must have seemed to them only too justified. After the October 1966 riots in the North and East, the resultant mass emigration of Ibo from the North and Hausa and Yoruba from the East, and finally the civil war, official and commercial activity was seriously disrupted.

Behind these dislocations lay the ultimate threat of a break-up of the Federation into its component parts. The worst effect of this would be the violence which would inevitably accompany it. Almost equally serious might be the mass movements of population. It is already apparent that, for some years at least, the North will be handicapped without its Ibo clerks, technicians, contractors and entrepreneurs. Conversely, in their native Eastern Region, the return of one or perhaps two million Ibo could create serious problems of unemployment in the already overcrowded Region. Next to such consequences, the loss of a single market would be only a minor disaster. The Nigerian market for manufactures is already to a considerable extent regionalised. Much of the beer, cement and textiles being produced is already being consumed in its Region of origin. Nor would inter-state trade be necessarily halted by a political break-up.

The Development Plan

If its economy can stay in one piece, Nigeria can continue a process of economic development which has made good progress so far. The Six Year Development Plan, 1962 to 1968, aimed at increasing the growth rate of the economy from 3·9 per cent to at least 4 per cent per year.[12] This aim, rather modest compared to, say, Ghana's target of 7 per cent, was to be achieved by investing 15 per cent of the Gross Domestic Product. At the same time, the per capita consumption was to be raised by about one per cent per year. The Plan's long-term objective was to achieve 'self-sustained growth not later than by the end of the third or fourth National Plan'.[13] The rate of domestic savings would have to be raised from about 9·5 per cent of the Gross Domestic Product in 1960–61 to at least 15 per cent by 1975. More broadly, its aims were to increase opportunities, expand manpower training in all fields and at all levels, create more jobs in non-agricultural occupations, modernise agriculture and foster Nigerian business.

Installed electric generating capacity was to be tripled (643 MW by 1968); other objectives included the provision of a further 293 miles of rail track, seven new docks in Lagos Harbour and Port Harcourt, the completion of the bridge over the Niger and the building of a second bridge between Lagos and the mainland, and the expansion of cement capacity to at least 980,000 tons a year. All this was to be achieved by a total capital expenditure of £678 million by all governments. It was calculated that half of this sum could be raised from foreign grants and loans.

The biggest single project, described in the Plan as its 'cornerstone', is the £70 million Niger dam at Kainji in the Northern Region. Although less famous than Ghana's Volta or Zambia's Kariba, the Niger dam, whose first stage was half built in 1966, ranks among the world's biggest. Its commissioning cost of £70 million compares with the Volta's £65 million and Kariba's £80 million and its second-stage generating capacity of 980 MW, due for completion by 1982, compares with the Volta's 768 MW and Kariba's 1,200. The main dam at Kainji, a remote and sparsely populated site, will have four 80 MW generators; this output is calculated to meet Nigeria's needs until 1982, when the commissioning of a second dam at Jebba will raise the installed capacity to 980 MW. A third dam at Shiroro Gorge, will eventually raise the total capacity to 1,730 MW—a far cry from the 200 MW which was Nigeria's total capacity in 1962. Like similar dams elsewhere, the Niger dam will do more than generate power. A 500-mile artificial lake will provide a new fishing industry. An elaborate system of locks at the Kainji dam will make the Niger navigable, for the first time, throughout its length in Nigeria, opening up an important new North-South highway. Flood control, made possible by the dam, will provide all-year-round irrigation over thousands of riverain acres. Although the idea of the dam is open to argument (in view of the vast reserves of natural gas in Nigeria), international banking for it has been impressive. Apart from the Federal government's own £30 million, the World Bank has committed £29 million, Italy (from where the dam contractors, Impregilo, come) has loaned £9 million, the United Kingdom and the United States £5 million each and the Netherlands £1 million.

The rest of the Plan has not fared quite as well as the Niger dam.

Foreign loans were slow to materialise. Even where large sums had been committed, actual disbursements lagged behind, partly because the Nigerians themselves were slow in detailed project preparation. In the first three years of the Plan, only £172 million in foreign loans and £45 million in grants were committed—a total of £217 million, compared with £321 million envisaged for the whole Plan period. Loans included a possible loan element of £45 million out of the total United States' commitment of £80 million, a £10 million Commonwealth Assistance loan from Britain, and £29 million from the World Bank for the Niger dam. The grants included the balance of £35 million from the United States' commitment, and £5 million from the United Kingdom. In the Plan's first two years the actual proportion of expenditure represented by foreign aid was only 12·3 per cent, against the 50 per cent envisaged by the Plan target. However, this percentage was to rise appreciably as project preparation got under way. The total cost of the Plan had to be reassessed at £800 million, plus £23 million in projects for the newly-created Mid-West Region. The 1964 Progress Report reveals serious imbalance between expenditure on the development and on the administrative sectors. In the Plan's first two years the cost of administration accounted for nearly 15 per cent of total capital expenditure, more than twice the percentage allowed in the Plan. On the other hand the economic sector accounted for 61 per cent, against nearly 68 per cent envisaged by the Plan.

The Six Year Plan is no longer in operation. It was formally suspended by the Ironsi regime in March 1966 when the first preparations for a new plan were made. However, the 1962–68 Plan set Nigeria along the road it is likely to follow. But there will be modifications. The Plan had not been without its critics; most of these found that it was not ambitious enough, and that it did not go far enough towards really national planning. In particular, the economist Dr Samuel Aluko, of the University of Nigeria, Nsukka, criticised the excessive economic power of the Regions and the resultant indiscipline and duplication of effort and investment.[14] He found, also, that the Plan had inadequate machinery for measuring progress: there were no sectoral targets and no annual targets. Aluko would have liked to see an investment of 19 per cent of the national product instead of 15 per cent, and has criticised the apparently excessive dependence on foreign sources—50 per cent, compared with only 25 per cent in Ghana. A study published by the Nigerian Institute of Social and Economic Studies echoed some of these points, criticising the low rate of national investment and the paucity of high-yielding projects in real growth terms.[15]

These criticisms have been justified by events. The excessive dependence on foreign sources was apparent in the disappointing response in the first two years.[16] Excessive investment in capital-intensive instead of labour-intensive industry has been reflected in the inexorable growth of unemployment. Fiscal policies have been ineffective in many ways: protective duties levied on imports such as cement, tyres and beer have tended to be used to swell profits rather than bring down prices. Indeed, in many cases the cost of the locally-manufactured article was as high as the cost of the imported article, despite the duty. Possibly the biggest economic failing of the regime which ended in January 1966 was the rate at which reserves of the produce marketing boards were used up. In both the Western and Northern Regions, particularly, substantial reserves in the years before independence, which could have played a key part in investment for the Plan, were turned into deficits. Part of the blame goes to the fall in world commodity prices; also, some of the money was properly invested. But the Coker Commission of 1962 and the Northern Region Marketing Board Inquiry of 1966 showed in detail that a shocking amount was wasted.

These points have not been lost on the civil servants. Soon after the military takeover of January 1966 they published, this time without the aid of foreign advisors, *Guideposts for the Second National Development Plan*. There was to be a five year plan, which itself was to be part of a 'perspective plan of 20 years duration'; by the end of this period, Nigeria would have achieved self-sustained growth. Far more emphasis than in the first plan was to be placed on employment. The planned growth rate, 4 per cent under the first plan, was to be

raised to 6 per cent. Assuming a considerably more modest population increase than that shown in the swollen 1963 census, this would
increase the per capita income from the present £25 to £35. Investment was to be raised to 18 per cent of the Gross Domestic Product.
Given Nigeria's natural and human resources, the new targets are
eminently feasible. Whether politics would permit their achievement was another matter. Early in 1967 it looked as if the political
upheavals of recent months had set Nigeria back several years.

Assuming that Nigeria remains as an effective economic unit, and
that the damage to the economy caused by the 1967–68 civil
war can be mended, the big question mark of the economy
centres on the race between the growth of oil revenues and the
growth of unemployment. Only if the former can keep abreast of, if
not ahead of, the latter can political stability be assured. Oil has only
recently started transforming the economy, although exploration
began as long ago as 1937. By 1966 Shell-BP had spent £200 million
in exploration and other development costs. Three companies were
producing oil in 1966: Shell-BP (Anglo-Dutch) in the Eastern and
Mid-West Regions, on-shore; Gulf (American) in the Mid-West,
off-shore; and SAFRAP (French) in the East. Five other companies
were exploring: Tennessee (American) in the Mid-West, on-shore;
Amoseas (offshoot of Caltex, American), Mobil (American), AGIP
(Italian) and Phillips (American) in the East. Investment in
Nigerian mining, including oil, was 41 per cent (£81 million) of investment in fixed assets in 1962, and 50 per cent (£128 million) in
1964. Because of the high rate of depreciation and investment allowances, Nigeria is only just beginning to benefit significantly from oil.
The income it now derives, some £30 million a year, is mostly in
rentals, royalties and excise. The important real income in the
future will be from profits tax, at the rate of ten shillings in the
pound. Federal law provides that half of all oil revenue is returned
by the Federal government directly to the Region of origin; 15 per
cent is kept for the Federal government's own use and the remaining
35 per cent goes to a distributable pool for distribution among the
Regions on the basis of population. By 1970 Nigeria may be pro-

ducing 50 million tons of oil, compared to the 1966 figure of 20 million. By that time, allowances against profits will be on the decline and very substantial income will accrue. However, the schools and technical colleges and universities are disgorging thousands more 'applicants' a year on to an economy which so far has made extremely small progress in providing openings for them. This is the crucial economic challenge.

Appendix

BASIC FIGURES

		1963 *Census*	*1968* *Author's* *Estimate**
Population: (millions)	North	29·8	25·4
	East	12·4	12·6
	West	10·3	7·5
	Mid-West	2·5	2·5
	Lagos	0·7	0·6
	Nigeria:	55·7	48·6

	1962–63	*1964–65*
Gross Domestic Product (1957 prices, £m):	1,455	1,538

Breakdown of GDP
(per cent):

	1962–63	*1964–65*
Gross Investment	13·3	14·9
Gross Domestic Savings	10·5	11·7
Balance of Payments Deficit	3·0	4·4
Government Revenue	9·8	11·4

External Reserves, 1965: £71 million

1962–68 Development Plan:	Total capital cost: (revised):	£833 million
	Target annual growth rate:	4 per cent
	Actual growth rate 1962–64	6 per cent

Education enrolment:

	1959	*1963*
Primary	2,780,000	2,900,000
Secondary	116,000	212,000
Technical and vocational	4,100	7,400
Teacher training	26,500	32,000
University	1,958	5,148

* See chapter 7 above.

DIRECTION OF EXPORTS

	1960		1963		1965	
	£m	%	£m	%	£m	%
UK	79·9	48·1	74·0	40·0	101·5	38·5
EEC	51·3	30·9	69·1	37·3	96·3	36·6
USA	15·9	9·7	17·4	9·4	26·2	9·9
Japan	2·5	1·5	2·4	1·3	3·2	1·2
Others	16·2	9·8	22·0	12·0	36·1	13·8
Total	165·8	100·0	184·9	100·0	263·3	100·0

ORIGIN OF IMPORTS

	1960		1963		1965	
	£m	%	£m	%	£m	%
UK	91·4	42·3	70·8	34·1	85·0	30·9
USA	11·6	5·4	17·9	8·6	33·1	12·2
West Germany	15·2	7·0	15·4	7·4	29·5	10·6
Japan	27·8	12·8	26·9	12·6	25·6	9·6
Netherlands	11·6	5·4	13·4	6·5	14·8	5·4
France	4·9	2·3	7·5	3·6	12·1	4·3
Others	53·4	24·8	55·7	27·2	75·2	27·0
Total	215·9	100·0	207·6	100·0	275·3	100·0

PRINCIPAL EXPORTS

	1960		1965	
	Tons (ooos)	£m	Tons (ooos)	£m
Oil	0·8	—	13,000·0	68·1
Cocoa	154·0	36·8	255·3	42·7
Groundnuts	332·0	22·9	512·0	37·8
Palm kernels	418·0	26·1	415·5	26·5
Tin	10·7*	6·0	10·6*	14·9
Palm oil	183·0	14·0	150·0	13·6
Rubber	57·2	14·2	67·9	11·0
Groundnut oil	47·0	5·3	90·7	10·0
Timber (logs and sawn)	24·3	7·0	19·2	6·4
Groundnut cake	—	—	112·7	5·3
Hides and skins	8·6	4·5	8·6	4·6
Raw cotton	27·0	6·2	13·5	3·3

* Exported as ore in 1960 and as metal in 1965.

PRINCIPAL IMPORTS (1965)

	Tons *(ooos)*	*£m*
Mining equipment and road construction parts	—	27·0
Cotton piece goods	209·8	21·4
Medical and chemicals	—	20·2
Electrical machinery and apparatus	—	19·5
Construction steel	260·0	18·9
Petrol and oil	322·3	16·3
Cars and kitcars	17·7	9·7
Lorries and chassis	6·6	7·9
Paper and board	—	6·7
Stockfish	26·6	6·7
Rayon piece goods	26·1	4·1

ORIGIN OF INVESTMENT (£m)

	Paid-up Capital, *including Reserves and* *other Liabilities*		*Investment in* *Fixed Assets*	
	1962	*1964*	*1962*	*1964*
UK	135·6	181·4	104·8	162·2
USA	19·4	39·0	15·0	32·7
Netherlands	23·4	37·9	15·3	44·1
France	7·8	9·5	3·0	4·2
Italy	4·1	9·1	0·5	3·2
West Germany	1·4	2·2	0·2	1·5
Others	29·2	42·1	17·9	32·3
Total	220·9	321·2	156·7	280·2

Bibliography

Achebe, Chinua, *Things Fall Apart*, Heinemann, London 1958; McDowell, New York 1959; *No Longer At Ease*, Heinemann, London 1960; Ivan Oblensky, New York 1961; *A Man Of The People*, Heinemann, London 1966; John Day, New York 1966

A White Paper on the Government's Policy for the Rehabilitation of the Tiv Native Authority, Kaduna 1965

A White Paper on the New Provincial System, Enugu, December 1966

Ajayi, J. F. A., *Milestones in Modern Nigerian History*, Ibadan University Press, Ibadan 1962; *Christian Missionaries in Nigeria 1841–1891*, Longmans, London 1965; Northwestern University Press, Evanston 1965

Ajayi, J. F. A., and Smith, R., *Yoruba Warfare in the 19th Century*, Cambridge University Press, London and New York 1964

Anene, J. C., *Southern Nigeria in Transition 1885–1906*, Cambridge University Press, London and New York 1965

Annual Abstract of Statistics, 1964, Federal Office of Statistics, Lagos 1964

Arikpo, Okoi, *Development of Modern Nigeria*, Penguin Africa Library, Harmondsworth and Baltimore 1967

Awolowo, Chief Obafemi, *Awo*, Cambridge University Press, London and New York 1960; *Path to Nigerian Freedom*, Faber, London 1966; *Thoughts on the Nigerian Constitution*, Oxford University Press, London and New York 1966

Ayandele, E. A., *The Missionary Impact on Modern Nigeria, 1842–1914*, Longmans, London 1966; Humanities Press, New York 1967

Ayida, A., "Contractor Finance and Suppliers' Credit in Economic Growth", in Dag Hammarskjold Foundation Seminar on International Finance and National Development, University of Uppsala, Uppsala 1964 (mimeographed)

Azikiwe, Nnamdi, *The Development of Political Parties in Nigeria*, Office of the Commissioner in the UK for the Eastern Regions of Nigeria, London 1957; *Zik: A Selection from the Speeches of Dr Nnamdi Azikiwe*, Cambridge University Press, London and New York 1961

Bello, Sir Ahmadu, the Sardauna of Sokoto, *My Life*, Cambridge University Press, London and New York 1962

Blitz, L. Franklin (ed.), *Politics and Administration of Nigerian Government*, Sweet and Maxwell, London 1965; Praeger, New York 1965

Bower, P. A., et al., *Mining, Commerce and Finance in Nigeria*, Faber, London 1948

Brett, Sir Lionel, *Constitutional Problems of Federation in Nigeria*, Sweet and Maxwell, London 1961

Bretton, H. L., *Power and Stability in Nigeria*, Praeger, New York and London 1962

Brown, Charles V., *Nigerian Banking System*, Allen and Unwin, London 1966; Northwestern University Press, Evanston 1966

Buchanan, K. M., and Pugh, J. C., *Land and People of Nigeria*, University of London Press, London 1955

Burns, Sir Alan, *History of Nigeria*, 6th edn., Allen and Unwin, London 1963; Barnes and Noble, New York 1963

Cmd. 486, *Report on the Amalgamation of Northern and Southern Nigeria*, HMSO, London 1919

Cmd. 51, *Report of the Foster-Sutton Tribunal*, HMSO, London 1957

Cmd. 569, *Report of the Resumed Constitutional Conference*, HMSO, London 1958

Coker, G. B. A., *Family Property Among the Yoruba*, Sweet and Maxwell, London 1966; African Universities Press, Lagos 1966

Coleman, James S., *Nigeria, Background to Nationalism*, University of California Press, Berkeley 1963

Colonial Office Handbook, Crown Agents, London 1953

Colonial Office, *Nigeria: Report of the Commission Appointed to Inquire Into the Fears of Minorities*, HMSO, London 1958

Cook, Arthur N., *British Enterprise in Nigeria*, Frank Cass, London 1963; Barnes and Noble, New York 1965

Crowder, Michael, *The Story of Nigeria*, rev. ed., Faber, London 1966; published as *A Short History of Nigeria*, Praeger, New York 1966

Davies, H. O., *Nigeria: The Prospects for Democracy*, Weidenfeld and Nicolson, London 1961

Dike, Kenneth, *Trade and Politics in the Niger Delta*, Oxford University Press, London and New York 1956; *100 Years of British Rule in Nigeria, 1851–1951*, Federal Ministry of Information, Lagos 1960

Development of Small Industries in Eastern Nigeria (The Kilby Report), USAID, Eastern Ministry of Information, Enugu 1963

Ekwensi, Cyprian, *People of the City*, Heinemann, London 1963; *Jaguar Nana*, Panther, London 1963; Northwestern University Press, Evanston 1963

Egharevba, Jacob, *A Short History of Benin*, Benin 1953

Enahoro, Chief Anthony, *Fugitive Offender*, Cassell, London 1965; Humanities Press, New York 1965

Ezera, Kalu, *Constitutional Developments in Nigeria*, 2nd edn., Cambridge University Press, London and New York 1964

Fagg, Bernard, "The Nok Culture in Pre-history", *Journal of the Historical Society of Nigeria*, Vol. 1, No. 4, December 1959

Foot, Sir Hugh, *A Start in Freedom*, Hodder and Stoughton, London 1964; Harper and Row, New York 1964

308

Forde, Daryll, and Scott, R., *Native Economy of Nigeria*, Faber, London 1946

Geary, William, *Nigeria under British Rule*, Barnes and Noble, New York 1965; Frank Cass, London 1966

Green, M. M., *Igbo Village Affairs*, 2nd edn., Frank Cass, London 1964; Praeger, New York 1964

Guideposts for the Second Development Plan, Federal Ministry of Economic Development, Lagos, June 1966

Hodgkin, Thomas, *Nigerian Perspectives*, Oxford University Press, London and New York 1960

Investment in Education, Federal Ministry of Information, Lagos 1960

Jakande, L. K., *The Trial of Obafemi Awolowo*, Secker and Warburg, London 1966; John West Publications, Lagos 1966

January 15th—Before and After: 1966 Nigerian Crisis, Government Printer, Enugu 1966

Johnson, Samuel, *History of the Yorubas*, CMS Bookshop, Lagos 1937

Johnston, H. A. S., *The Fulani Empire of Sokoto*, Oxford University Press, London and New York 1967

Jones, G. I., *Trading States of the Oil Rivers*, International African Institute, London 1964

Jones-Quartey, K. A. B., *A Life of Azikiwe*, Penguin, Harmondsworth and Baltimore 1965

Karmon, Y., *A Geography of Settlement in Eastern Nigeria*, Oxford University Press, London and New York 1966

Keay, E. A., and Thomas, H., *West African Government for Nigerian Students*, Hutchinson, London 1965

Kirk-Greene, A. H. M., *Principles of Native Administration in Nigeria*, Oxford University Press, London and New York 1965

Legum, Colin, "Great Benin, the Elusive City", *Nigeria Magazine*, Lagos, October 1960

Leighton, A. H., et al., *Psychiatric Disorders Among the Yoruba*, Cornell University Press, Ithaca 1963

Lugard, F. D., *Dual Mandate in Tropical Africa*, Frank Cass, London 1965; Archon Books, Hamden, Conn., 1965; *Annual Reports, Northern Nigeria, 1900–1911*, Colonial Office, London

Mackintosh, J. P., et al., *Nigerian Government and Politics*, Allen and Unwin, London 1966; Northwestern University Press, Evanston 1966

Mba, M. K., *The First Three Years: A Report on the Eastern Nigerian Six-Year Development Plan*, Government Printer, Enugu 1965

Moore, Gerald, and Beier, Ulli, *Modern Poetry from Africa*, Penguin, Harmondsworth and Baltimore 1963

Mr Prime Minister, Federal Ministry of Information, Lagos 1964

National Development Plan: Progress Report 1964, Federal Ministry of Information, Lagos 1964

Niger Delta Development Board Annual Report 1963–4, Port Harcourt 1964

309

Nigeria's Six Year Development Plan, Government Printer, Lagos 1962
Nigeria Trade Journal, Lagos, January, April, July, 1966
Nigeria, 1966, Federal Ministry of Information, Lagos, January 1967
Nigerian Crisis, Vol. IV: The Ad-Hoc Conference, Government Printer, Enugu 1966
Niven, C. R., *Short History of Nigeria*, Longmans, London 1937; *How Nigeria is Governed*, Longmans, London 1962
Nwankwo, Nkem, *Danda*, Andre Deutsch, London 1964
Obi, Chike, *Our Struggle*, Yaba-Lagos 1955
Odumosu, O., *The Nigerian Constitution: History and Development*, Sweet and Maxwell, London 1963
Ojo, G. J. A., *Yoruba Culture*, University of London Press, London 1965
Okigbo, P. N., *Nigerian Public Finance*, Northwestern University Press, Evanston 1965; Longmans, London 1966
Okonjo, C., "A Preliminary Medium Estimate of the 1962 Population", paper presented to the Centre for Population Studies, University of Ibadan, Ibadan 1965
Okoro, N., *Customary Laws of Succession in Eastern Nigeria*, Sweet and Maxwell, London 1966; African Universities Press, Lagos 1966
Onyemelukwe, C. C., *Problems of Industrial Planning and Management in Nigeria*, Longmans, London 1966; Columbia University Press, New York 1967
Orr, C. W. J., *The Making of Northern Nigeria*, Macmillan, London 1911
Perham, Margery, *Native Administration in Nigeria*, Oxford University Press, London and New York 1937
Phillips, Claude S., Jr., *The Development of Nigerian Foreign Policy*, Northwestern University Press, Evanston 1964
Pogrom—1966 Nigeria Crisis, Ministry of Information, Enugu 1966
Post, K. W. J., *The Nigerian Federal Elections of 1959*, Oxford University Press, London and New York 1963
Progress Report 1964, Federal Ministry of Economic Development, Lagos 1964
Proceedings of the Commission of Inquiry into the Owegbe Cult, Midwestern Nigeria, Benin 1965
Report of the Coker Commission of Inquiry 1962, Federal Ministry of Information, Lagos 1962
Report of the Commission on the Review of Wages, Salary and Conditions of Service of the Junior Employees of the Governments of the Federation and in Private Establishments (The Morgan Commission), Federal Ministry of Information, Lagos 1964
Report of the Economic Mission of 1961, Eastern Ministry of Information, Enugu 1962
Report of Inquiry Into the Northern Region Marketing Board, Kaduna, November 1966

Schatz, S. P., "Nigeria's First National Plan", *Nigerian Journal of Economic Studies*, July 1963; *Development of Bank Lending in Nigeria*, Oxford University Press, London and New York 1965

Smith, M. G., *Government in Zazzau, 1880–1950*, Oxford University Press, London and New York 1965

Smith, M., *Baba of Karo*, Faber, London 1964; Praeger, New York 1964

Sixteen Days of Political Crisis—The State House Diary, Federal Ministry of Information, Lagos 1965

Sklar, Richard, *Nigerian Political Parties*, Princeton University Press, Princeton 1963

Solarin, Tai, *Thinking With You*, Longmans, London 1965

Soyinka, Wole, "The Lion and The Jewel", "The Trials of Brother Jero", "The Road" in *Five Plays*, Oxford University Press, London and New York 1964; *Kongi's Harvest*, Oxford University Press, London and New York 1967

Tamuno, Takeno N., *Nigeria and Elective Representation, 1923–1947*, Heinemann, London 1966; Humanities Press, New York 1966

The Nigerian Situation—Facts and Background, Gaskiya Corporation, Zaria 1966

Tilman, Robert O., and Cole, Taylor, (eds.), *The Nigerian Political Scene*, Duke University Press, Durham, NC, 1962

Verbatim Report of Proceedings of Supreme Military Council at Aburi, Ghana, January 4–5, 1967, ENIS Corporation, Enugu 1967

Wheare, Joan, *Nigerian Legislative Council*, Faber, London 1950

White, Stanhope, *Dan Bana*, Cassell, London 1966; James Heineman, New York 1966

Wraith, Ronald, *Local Government in West Africa*, Allen and Unwin, London 1964; Praeger, New York 1964

Wraith, Ronald, and Simpkins, Edgar, *Corruption in Developing Countries*, Allen and Unwin, London 1963; Norton, New York 1964

References

1. TRIBES AND A NATION

1. Chief Obafemi Awolowo, *Thoughts on the Nigerian Constitution*, pp. 100–5
2. K. M. Buchanan and J. C. Pugh, *Land and People in Nigeria*, p. 80
3. Sir Richard Burton, *Wanderings in West Africa*, London 1863, quoted in Thomas Hodgkin, *Nigerian Perspectives*, p. 279
4. Ibid., p. 280
5. 1963 census figure, quoted in the *Nigeria Trade Journal*, April 1966
6. See Hodgkin, op. cit., pp. 258–63
7. Colin Legum, "Great Benin—the Elusive City", *Nigeria Magazine*, October 1960, p. 104
8. 1963 census figures, quoted in the *Nigeria Trade Journal*, January and July 1966
9. 1963 census figure, quoted in the *Nigeria Trade Journal*, January 1966
10. Chief Obafemi Awolowo, *Path to Nigerian Freedom*, pp. 47–8
11. In a private interview with the author, October 1965
12. Press statement by Major-General J. T. U. Aguyi-Ironsi, issued by the Federal Information Service, Lagos, February 21, 1966
13. James S. Coleman, *Nigeria: Background to Nationalism*, p. 156
14. Colonel Ojukwu, in a television interview, April 1967
15. A. H. Leighton, et al., *Psychiatric Disorders among the Yoruba*, pp. 273–8

2. BEHIND THE ELITE

1. Colonial Office, *Nigeria: Report of the Commission Appointed to Enquire into the Fears of Minorities*, p. 11 (hereafter called *Minorities Commission Report*)
2. Awolowo, *Path to Nigerian Freedom*, p. 31
3. See *Sunday Times*, London, October 30, 1966
4. In interviews with the author in 1965
5. *Report of the Commission on the Review of Wages, Salary and Conditions of Service of the Junior Employees of the Governments of the Federation and in Private Establishments (The Morgan Commission)*, p. 20
6. Calculations by Dr S. A. Aluko, unpublished
7. Ibid.
8. See "Portrait" in *West Africa*, November 16, 1963
9. National Manpower Board, *Nigeria's High-Level Manpower, 1963–70*, tables 6 and 8
10. 'Mickey Mouse' in the *Daily Express*, Lagos, February 20, 1965

11. *Daily Times*, Lagos, February 25, 1965
12. "Peter Pan" in the *Daily Times*, Lagos, December 23, 1965
13. *Sunday Times*, Lagos, June 20, 1966
14. Cmd. 51, *Report of the Foster-Sutton Tribunal*, p. 42
15. *Report of the Coker Commission of Inquiry, 1962*, Vol. 1, p. 3
16. Quoted in Ronald Wraith and Edgar Simpkins, *Corruption in Developing Countries*, p. 23
17. Ibid., p. 22
18. Ibid.
19. Ibid., p. 58
20. Ibid., p. 35
21. *Daily Times*, Lagos, June 27, 1965
22. *Parliamentary Debates, Eastern House of Assembly*, April 23, 1965, p. 844
23. Ibid., p. 845
24. Ebenezer Williams in the *Morning Post*, Lagos, February 6, 1965
25. *Daily Times*, Lagos, July 28, 1965
26. *West Africa*, July 9, 1966
27. Tai Solarin, *Thinking With You*
28. *Report of the Coker Commission of Inquiry, 1962*, Vol. 1, p. *iii*
29. Ebenezer Williams in the *Morning Post*, Lagos, February 6, 1965
30. Ernest Ikoli, "The Nigerian Press", *West African Review*, June 1950, p. 616
31. Wole Soyinka, "The Trials of Brother Jero", *Five Plays*, p. 201
32. Gerald Moore and Ulli Beier (eds), *Modern Poetry from Africa*, pp. 111–12

3. How Many Histories?

1. In an article attributed to Flora Shaw, afterwards Lady Lugard, *The Times*, London, January 8, 1897
2. Bernard Fagg, "The Nok Culture in Pre-History", *Journal of the Historical Society of Nigeria*, Vol. 1, No. 4, December 1959
3. Hodgkin, op. cit., p. 21
4. Quoted in ibid., p. 67
5. Ibid., p. 20
6. Samuel Johnson, *History of the Yorubas*, p. 3
7. Quoted in Hodgkin, op. cit., p. 71
8. Quoted in ibid., p. 89
9. Quoted in ibid., p. 92
10. Johnson, op. cit., p. 149
11. Captain John Adams, *Remarks on the Country from Cape Palmas to the Congo River*, London 1823, quoted in Hodgkin, op. cit., p. 171
12. Jacob Egharevba, *A Short History of Benin*, pp. 5–9
13. Ibid., p. 15
14. Quoted in Hodgkin, op. cit., p. 119

15. Dapper, *Description of Africa*, Amsterdam 1686, quoted in ibid., p. 121
16. Ibid.
17. De Barros, *De Asia*, 1553, quoted in ibid., p. 88
18. Richard Jackson, *Journal of a Voyage to Bonny River*, quoted in ibid., p. 234
19. Foreign Office 2/1, No. 1, 1837, quoted in Dike, op. cit., p. 71
20. Ibid., p. 128
21. Ibid., p. 183
22. Letter, Hewitt to Jaja, January 8, 1884, quoted in Michael Crowder, *The Story of Nigeria*, p. 177
23. Mungo Park, *Travels in the Interior Districts of Africa*, London 1798, quoted in Sir Alan Burns, *History of Nigeria*, p. 81
24. Quoted in Hodgkin, op. cit., p. 194
25. Ibid.
26. Quoted in ibid., p. 213
27. Quoted in ibid., p. 198
28. Quoted in Crowder, op. cit., p. 151
29. Burton, op. cit., quoted in Hodgkin, op. cit., p. 281
30. Quoted in Dike, op. cit., p. 208
31. Quoted in ibid., p. 210
32. Ibid.
33. Letter from M. Perham, quoted in Crowder, op. cit., p. 192
34. Ibid., p. 51
35. Quoted in Crowder, op. cit., p. 196
36. Quoted in ibid., p. 199

4. FROM COLONY TO NATION

1. *Mr Prime Minister*, p. 47
2. Chief Obafemi Awolowo, *Awo*, p. 294
3. Ibid., p. 299
4. Coleman, op. cit., pp. 456–7
5. Chief Anthony Enahoro, *Fugitive Offender*, p. 74
6. *West African Pilot*, February 10, 1949
7. Coleman, op. cit., p. 156
8. Ibid.
9. Quoted in C. W. J. Orr, *The Making of Northern Nigeria*, p. 263
10. Coleman, op. cit., p. 275
11. Kalu Ezera, *Constitutional Developments in Nigeria*, 2nd edn., p. 131
12. Awolowo, *Awo*, p. 175
13. K. A. B. Jones-Quartey, *A Life of Azikiwe*, p. 201
14. Awolowo, *Path to Nigerian Freedom*, p. 48
15. Awolowo, *Awo*, p. 163
16. Ezera, op. cit., p. 151
17. Ibid., p. 151

Nigeria

18. Ibid., pp. 197–9
19. *West African Pilot*, November 19, 1954
20. Ezera, op. cit., p. 250
21. I. Nicolson in J. P. Mackintosh, et al., *Nigerian Government and Politics*, pp. 151–5
22. Ibid., p. 146
23. Cmd. 486, *Report on the Amalgamation of Northern and Southern Nigeria*
24. F. D. Lugard, *Annual Reports, Northern Nigeria, 1900–1911*, p. 646
25. Joan Wheare, *The Nigerian Legislative Council*, p. 30
26. R. Sklar, *Nigerian Political Parties*, p. 47
27. Jones-Quartey, op. cit., p. 142
28. Awolowo, *Awo*, p. 135
29. Awolowo, *Path to Nigerian Freedom*, p. 125
30. Awolowo, *Awo*, p. 172
31. Ibid., p. 168
32. Ezera, op. cit., p. 116
33. Sklar, op. cit., p. 94
34. Sardauna of Sokoto, *My Life*, p. 29
35. Ibid., p. 227
36. Quoted in Ezera, op. cit., p. 165
37. Ibid.
38. Ibid., p. 188
39. Ibid., p. 239
40. Ibid., p. 254
41. Ibid., p. 253
42. K. W. J. Post, *The Nigerian Federal Election of 1959*, p. 439
43. Ibid.
44. From a transcript, made available privately to the author
45. Ibid.

5. BIRTH AND WEANING

1. Azikiwe, in his inaugural address as Governor-General, November 1960; quoted in Jones-Quartey, op. cit., p. 21
2. *West Africa*, October 22, 1960
3. *West Africa*, October 8, 1960
4. *Mr Prime Minister*, p. 49
5. Jones-Quartey, op. cit.
6. Letter to *The Times*, London, August 11, 1962
7. Awolowo, *Awo*, p. 309
8. Post, op.cit., p. 311
9. *House of Representatives Debates* (Lagos), November 1960, p. 61
10. Sessional Paper No.4 of 1960, quoted in Claude S. Phillips, Jr, *Development of Nigerian Foreign Policy*, p. 146

316

11. *House of Representatives Debates* (Lagos), November 1960, p. 61
12. Ibid., p. 68
13. *West African Review*, July 1960, p. 6
14. *West Africa*, January 27, 1962
15. *West Africa*, November 12, 1960
16. *West Africa*, January 14, 1961
17. *House of Representatives Debates* (Lagos), January 1960, pp. 89–91
18. *Daily Express*, Lagos, July 24, 1963
19. Mackintosh, op. cit., p. 38
20. K. Ezera, op. cit., p. 285
21. *West Africa*, August 3, 1963
22. *West African Pilot*, September 15, 1964
23. Mackintosh, op. cit., pp. 48–9

6. HAZARDS OF OPPOSITION

1. Nnamdi Azikiwe, *Zik: A Selection from the Speeches of Dr Nnamdi Azikiwe*, pp. 97–8
2. *West Africa*, January 22, 1966; Balewa was interviewed by Bridget Bloom on January 14, the last day of his life
3. *West Africa*, June 6, 1962
4. *West Africa*, February 17, 1962
5. *West Africa*, June 2, 1962
6. Mackintosh, op. cit., p. 449
7. *West Africa*, June 2, 1962
8. *House of Representatives Debates*, Lagos, May 29, 1962
9. Federation of Nigeria Official Gazette, Supplement to No. 38, Vol. 49, May 29, 1962
10. *West Africa*, June 6, 1962
11. *West Africa*, November 17, 1962
12. *Report of the Coker Commission of Inquiry, 1962*
13. Ibid., Vol. I, 73
14. Ibid., Vol. I, p. 70
15. Ibid., Vol. I, p. 69
16. Ibid.
17. Ibid., Vol. II, p. 7
18. Ibid.
19. Ibid., Vol. II, p.36
20. Ibid., Vol. IV, p. 1
21. Ibid., Vol. I, p. 3
22. Balewa, in an interview with the author, April 1965
23. This, and all subsequent quotations from the trial are taken from a private transcript. See also L. K. Jakande, *The Trial of Obafemi Awolowo*
24. Jakande, op. cit., pp. 309–27

317

25. Enahoro, op. cit., p. 246
26. *Mr Prime Minister*, p. 151
27. Ibid., p. 181

7. TOWARDS THE COUP

1. Awolowo, in his own defence in the treason trial, from a private transcript. See also Jakande, op. cit., pp. 172–3
2. Sardauna of Sokoto, op. cit., p. 229
3. *Nigerian Outlook*, May 1, 1962
4. *West Africa*, November 2, 1963
5. Mackintosh, op. cit., p. 552
6. Chukuka Okonjo, "A Preliminary Medium Estimate of the 1962 Population", paper presented to the Centre for Population Studies, University of Ibadan, Ibadan 1965
7. Ibid.
8. Ibid.
9. *Guideposts for the Second National Development Plan*, p. 3
10. *Sunday Express*, Lagos, January 3, 1965
11. *Sixteen Days of Political Crisis—The State House Diary*, p. 3
12. *Sunday Express*, Lagos, January 3, 1965
13. See *Nigeria 1966*
14. *Daily Express*, Lagos, January 5, 1965
15. Ibid.
16. Balewa, in an interview with the author, March 1965
17. Ibid.
18. An interview with the author, March 1965
19. Ibid.
20. *Sixteen Days of Political Crisis—the State House Diary*, p. 1
21. In an interview with the author
22. *West Africa*, January 1966

8. THREE COUPS

1. Nzeogwu, in an interview with Dennis D. Ejindu, *Africa and the World*, May 1967, p. 15
2. *Verbatim Report of Proceedings of Supreme Military Council at Aburi, Ghana, January 4–5, 1967*, p. 43
3. Ibid., p. 27
4. *January 15th—Before and After: 1966 Nigeria Crisis*, Vol. 7, pp. 13–14
5. Mackintosh, op. cit., pp. 590–2
6. *January 15th—Before and After*, op. cit., p. 19
7. Ibid., p. 20
8. Ibid.
9. *West Africa*, January 29, 1966

References

10. Press Release, Federal Ministry of Information, Lagos, January 17, 1966
11. *West Africa*, January 29, 1966
12. *West Africa*, February 12, 1966
13. Press Release No. F.188, Federal Ministry of Information, Lagos, February 21, 1966
14. Press Release No. F.348, Federal Ministry of Information, Lagos, March 31, 1966
15. *Morning Post*, Lagos
16. *Daily Times*, Lagos, April 15, 1966
17. Ibid.
18. Press Release No. F.610, Federal Ministry of Information, Lagos, May 24, 1966
19. *Official Gazette (Extraordinary)*, No. 5, Federal Ministry of Information, Lagos, May 24, 1966
20. *West Africa*, June 4, 1966
21. Press Release No. 723, Ministry of Information, Kaduna, June 2, 1966
22. Press Release No. F.686, Federal Ministry of Information, Lagos, June 8, 1966
23. *West Africa*, June 25, 1966
24. *Nigeria 1966*, p. 9
25. *January 15th—Before and After*, op. cit., p. 44
26. Ibid., p. 46
27. Ibid.
28. *Verbatim Report*, op. cit., p. 19
29. Ibid., p. 22
30. *West Africa*, August 6, 1966
31. *Nigeria 1966*, op. cit., p. 33
32. *January 15th—Before and After*, op. cit., p. 44
33. Ibid., p. 56
34. Ibid., p. 50
35. *Nigerian Crisis*, Vol. IV: *The Ad Hoc Conference*, p. *i*
36. *January 15th—Before and After*, op. cit., p. 49
37. *West Africa*, October 15, 1966
38. *Nigerian Crisis*, Vol. IV, op. cit. p. *ii*
39. Ibid., p. *iv*
40. *Verbatim Report*, op. cit., p. 30
41. *Nigeria 1966*, op. cit., p. 8
42. Ibid., p. 10
43. *The Nigerian Situation—Facts and Background*
44. *Pogrom—1966 Nigeria Crisis*, Vol. III, p. 6
45. Ibid., p. 7
46. Colin Legum in the *Observer*, London, October 16, 1966
47. *Pogrom*, op. cit.

48. *The Nigerian Situation*, op. cit., p. 11
49. *West Africa*, December 3, 1966
50. *West Africa*, December 24, 1966
51. *West Africa*, December 3, 1966
52. *Verbatim Report*, op. cit., p. 9
53. Ibid., p. 17
54. Ibid., p. 18
55. Ibid., p. 21
56. Ibid., p. 27
57. Ibid., pp. 31–3
58. Ibid., p. 42
59. Ibid., p. 47
60. *West Africa*, March 18, 1967
61. *West Africa*, May 6, 1967
62. Ibid.
63. *Address of HE the Military Governor*, Government Printer, Enugu, May 26, 1967

9. The New North

1. Ministry of Information handout, Kaduna, June 1, 1966
2. The Sardauna of Sokoto, in an interview with the author, March 1965
3. Denham, Clapperton and Oudney, *Narrative of Travels and Discoveries in Northern and Central Africa*, London 1826, quoted in Hodgkin, *Nigerian Perspectives*, p. 213
4. Ibid., p. 214
5. The Emir of Kano, in an interview with the author, December 1965
6. The Grand Kadi, in an interview with the author, December 1965
7. The Sardauna of Sokoto, in an interview with the author, March 1965
8. Ibid.
9. Ibid.
10. *A White Paper on the Government's Policy for the Rehabilitation of the Tiv Native Authority*, Kaduna 1965

10. Ibo and Other Easterners

1. Nnamdi Azikiwe, presidential address, Ibo State Conference; published in *West African Pilot*, July 6, 1949
2. *West Africa*, November 13, 1965
3. Balewa, in an interview with the author, March 1965
4. M. M. Green, *Igbo Village Affairs*, p. 255
5. Azikiwe, presidential address, Ibo State Conference, op. cit.
6. Obi, in an interview with the author, October 1965
7. Y. Karmon, *A Geography of Settlement in Eastern Nigeria*

8. Dike, op. cit., p. 44
9. *Minorities Commission Report*, op. cit., p. 34
10. Ibid., p. 34
11. Sklar, op. cit., p. 123
12. *Minorities Commission Report*, op. cit., p. 37
13. *Niger Delta Development Board, Annual Report, 1963–64*
14. *A White Paper on the New Provincial System*
15. Published in 1959 by the Dynamic Party's Department of Propaganda and Spiritual Education
16. Chike Obi, *Our Struggle*, pp. 26–8
17. Obi, in an interview with the author, June 1965
18. In an interview with the author, 1965
19. *Report of the Economic Mission of 1961*
20. M. K. Mba, *The First Three Years: A Report on the Eastern Nigerian Six Year Development Plan*, p. 10
21. Chief Udoji, in an interview with the author, August 1965
22. *Development of Small Industries in Eastern Nigeria (The Kilby Report)*

11. YORUBA AND MID-WESTERNERS

1. Sir Hugh Foot, *A Start in Freedom*, p. 108
2. *Minorities Commission Report*, op. cit., p. 8
3. *Nigeria Trade Journal*, April-June 1966, p. 79
4. A. H. Leighton, *Psychiatric Disorders Among the Yoruba*, p. 43
5. *National Development Plan: Progress Report, 1964*, pp. 173–80
6. Ibid., p. 173
7. *Minorities Commission Report*, op. cit., p. 32
8. Ibid., p. 8
9. Ibid.
10. *Proceedings of the Commission of Inquiry into the Owegbe Cult, Mid-Western Nigeria*, Day 2, p. 18
11. *Parliamentary Debates, House of Chiefs, Mid-Western Nigeria*, April 14, 1965, p. 13, col. 81

12. ECONOMICS VERSUS POLITICS

1. Ayida, in a speech at the opening of the Lagos Computer Centre, November 3, 1966
2. *The Kilby Report*, op. cit.
3. *The Rededication Budget*, Federal Ministry of Information, Lagos, April 1965
4. *Nigerian Morning Post*, April 15, 1965
5. *Annual Abstract of Statistics*, 1964
6. Central Bank of Nigeria, *Economic and Financial Review*, June 1965
7. Article by R. Ward in *West Africa*, December 12, 1964

Nigeria

8. A. Ayida, "Contractor Finance and Suppliers Credit in Economic Growth", in Dag Hammarskjold Foundation Seminar on International Finance and National Development, University of Uppsala
9. "Too Much Beer?", *West Africa*, February 8, 1964
10. *Investment in Education*
11. National Manpower Board, *Nigeria's High-Level Manpower*
12. *Nigeria's Six Year Development Plan*, p. 23
13. Ibid., p. 23
14. Dr Samuel Aluko, unpublished thesis on economic planning
15. S. P. Schatz, "Nigeria's First National Plan", *Nigerian Journal of Economic Studies*, July 1963
16. *Progress Report, 1964*, Federal Ministry of Development, Lagos, pp. 27–30

Index